Praise for *Uniquely Human*

"Uplifting . . .This positive volume should reassure parents and caregivers of kids with autism and any other disability that their kids are not broken, but, indeed, special."

—*Booklist*, starred review

"A long-awaited tour-de-force that parts the ever-expanding sea of books on the topic of autism. A must-read for anyone who lives with and loves a person with autism, this book should also be required for anyone who is striving to be a competent and humanistic professional."

—Pamela Wolfberg, PhD, Professor of Autism Spectrum Studies, San Francisco State University; Founding Director, Autism Institute on Peer Socialization and Play; and author of *Play and Imagination in Children with Autism*

"Prizant distils decades of working with autistic children and adults, and their teams, into practical advice for lowering stress, leveraging strengths and interests, building resilience, and importantly, embracing and celebrating difference. . . . Prizant's is a message of empathy, support and empowerment."

—*Nature*

"The reverence that Dr. Prizant brings to his work with individuals with autism and their families leaps out from every page of this remarkable book, enabling him to tell the story of autism in a deeply personal way that is at once inspirational and informative. The engaging, real-life examples interspersed throughout the book serve both to illuminate the experience of autism from the inside out and to expose the folly of viewing behavior separate and apart from the motivation that fuels it. That is epochal!"

—Diane Twachtman-Cullen, PhD, CCC-SLP, Editor in Chief, *Autism Spectrum Quarterly*

"Prizant is a respected voice in the autism community, and the methods demonstrated here are backed by case study and experience. Parents, especially parents of the newly diagnosed, may find a ray of hope in the often bleak landscape of early diagnosis and the endless search for answers and information that inevitably results."

—*Library Journal*

"Elegant in its simplicity, *Uniquely Human* tackles extremely complex topics and how they impact school, home, and community. Compassion, learning, and supportive strategies—the three essentials for working with folks with ASD—are an integral part of this must-read book."

—Michelle Garcia Winner, speech-language pathologist and founder of Social Thinking®

"*Uniquely Human* . . . details stories that will resonate with parents or loved ones when a child is first diagnosed with autism. Families may find Prizant's approach . . . positive and uplifting."

—*Providence Journal*

"*Uniquely Human* is not just the perfect title for Barry Prizant's book, it's also an appropriate summation of Dr. Prizant's career. Though a clinical scholar, he is a humanist first, and always has been—a professional who is fascinated by unexamined lives that could be lived happily, yet aren't. With every brilliant, illuminating example in his book, he steers us away from the traditional fix-it mentality and toward the beatific, personally rewarding detective work that the entire spectrum world would be well served to adopt."

—Michael John Carley, parent-professional with ASD; founder of GRASP; and author of *Asperger's from the Inside-Out*

"A masterful treatise advocating for necessary changes in the way we see, understand, and provide services to persons with autism. This is a book for all parents and persons providing professional services to individuals with significant disabilities, not just those with autism. My hope is that this exceptional book will bring about the change in thinking and practice it is intended to do."

—David E. Yoder, PhD, Chair and Professor Emeritus, Department of Allied Health Sciences, University of North Carolina School of Medicine, Chapel Hill

"An excellent book that conveys what autism is like and how individuals with autism may be helped to build on their strengths and gain a greater social understanding. The approach involves much practical guidance for families and teachers, but it is refreshingly flexible and nondogmatic."

—Professor Sir Michael Rutter, child psychiatrist, FRCP FRCPsych FMedSci, Institute of Psychiatry, Psychology, and Neuroscience, King's College, London

"From the master clinician and scholar who taught us how to channel different learning styles into successful lives of learning and adaptation, *Uniquely Human* shines a light onto the vast possibilities of people with autism, showing that their lives represent opportunities, not disabilities; promise, not doom. Heed his detailed guidance because therein lies not only the secret for the fulfillment of every child's promise, but also the fulfillment of the promise of our entire society."

—Ami Klin, PhD, Director, Marcus Autism Center, Professor and Chief, Division of Autism and Related Disorders, Department of Pediatrics, Emory University School of Medicine

UNIQUELY HUMAN

A DIFFERENT WAY OF SEEING AUTISM

BARRY M. PRIZANT, PhD

WITH TOM FIELDS-MEYER

SIMON & SCHUSTER PAPERBACKS

New York London Toronto Sydney New Delhi

Simon & Schuster Paperbacks
An Imprint of Simon & Schuster, Inc.
1230 Avenue of the Americas
New York, NY 10020

First Simon & Schuster trade paperback edition July 2016

SIMON & SCHUSTER PAPERBACKS and colophon are registered trademarks of Simon & Schuster, Inc.

For information about special discounts for bulk purchases, please contact Simon & Schuster Special Sales at 1-866-506-1949 or business@simonandschuster.com.

The Simon & Schuster Speakers Bureau can bring authors to your live event. For more information or to book an event, contact the Simon & Schuster Speakers Bureau at 1-866-248-3049 or visit our website at www.simonspeakers.com.

Interior design by Ellen R. Sasahara

Manufactured in the United States of America

5 7 9 10 8 6 4

The Library of Congress has cataloged the
hardcover edition as follows:

Prizant, Barry M.
Uniquely human : a different way of seeing autism / Barry Prizant, Ph.D.; with Tom Fields-Meyer.
pages cm
"Simon & Schuster nonfiction original hardcover."
1. Autism. 2. Autism in children. I. Fields-Meyer, Thomas.
II. Title.
RJ506.A9P77 2015
618.92'85882—dc23
2014035241

ISBN 978-1-4767-7623-1
ISBN 978-1-4767-7624-8 (pbk)
ISBN 978-1-4767-7625-5 (ebook)

To all individuals with autism and their families,
in the hope that this book will help them gain what they
so deserve: understanding and respect.

CONTENTS

AUTHOR'S NOTE

In this book I have chosen to employ what is known as person-first language. Instead of referring to "an autistic person" or "an autistic"—which makes autism a person's defining quality—I generally use phrases such as "person with autism," "child who has autism," or "adult on the autism spectrum." I occasionally also use the term "on the spectrum," which is widely accepted in the autism community. While these are my preferences, they aren't ideal from all perspectives. This choice of language can sometimes make for awkward and cumbersome prose, so allow me to apologize in advance for that.

I am also aware that others, in particular some adults with autism, prefer the label "autistic," feeling that autism is indeed a defining characteristic and is essential to their identity and that person-first language implies that autism is inherently bad. (In the same way, you wouldn't call someone "a person with maleness" but rather "male" or "a male.") While I fully understand and respect that opinion, I have chosen otherwise for this book.

I occasionally make reference to Asperger's syndrome, which for many years was a diagnostic subcategory of Autism Spectrum Disorders in the "bible" of diagnosis, the *Diagnostic and Statistical Manual of Mental Disorders* (*DSM*) of the American Psychiatric Association. Although Asperger's syndrome was dropped as a formal diagnosis in its most recent edition (known as the *DSM-5*), the term continues to be used commonly to describe people with average or higher cognitive and language ability paired with challenges in the social realm as well as other challenges common in autism.

In referring to individuals who do not (or do not yet) communicate by speaking, I use the term "nonspeaking" and similar language. Others commonly refer to such people as "nonverbal," but many such people use words and other symbolic means to communicate through sign language, iPads, and other alternative means.

In most cases, when the text refers in general terms to "children" or "kids" with autism, the observations are also relevant to teenagers and adults. I use the terms "typical," "typically developing," and "neurotypical" to refer to people who do not have autism.

The English language poses challenges for all writers since it has no gender-neutral pronouns. I have tried to be sensitive to gender by alternating between male and female. Of course nearly all of the material in this book applies equally to males and females. Readers will note that the majority of people I mention in examples are male. This reflects both the real world and my professional experience. Approximately four out of five people with autism are male. This also helps explain why all four of the subjects in chapter 10, which describes trajectories over many years, are young men. While I have met and worked with many girls and young women with autism, all of the individuals with whom I have maintained contact over two decades or more are male.

The underlying philosophy, values, and practices I share in this book are consistent with and in some cases derived from the SCERTS® Model (2006), an educational and treatment framework developed with my colleagues. The SCERTS Model prioritizes social communication, emotional regulation, and transactional support as the most important domains to focus on with individuals with autism. Schools and school districts across the United States and in more than a dozen countries have implemented SCERTS. A more detailed description of the SCERTS Model appears at the end of this book.

INTRODUCTION

A Different Way of Seeing Autism

Not long ago I was meeting with a group of educators at an elementary school when things suddenly got personal. I was there in my role as a school district consultant for programs serving children with special needs, and as the meeting was breaking up, the principal asked to see me privately. I figured that he wanted to discuss a staff issue, but the principal—an intense, serious man—closed the door, pulled his chair close to mine, looked me in the eye, and began telling me about his nine-year-old son.

He described a shy, quirky, and solitary youngster who had grown increasingly remote and isolated, spending much of his time playing video games by himself and rarely mingling with other children his age. Then he got to the point: a psychologist had recently diagnosed the boy with Autism Spectrum Disorder. The principal leaned forward, putting his face within inches of mine.

"Barry," he asked, "should I be scared to death?"

It is the sort of question that has become all too familiar to me. Almost every week I meet parents who are intelligent, capable individuals, often confident and accomplished in other realms. But when these mothers and fathers encounter autism, they become disoriented. They lose faith in their own instincts. Facing this unexpected and unfamiliar territory, they feel bewildered, frightened, and lost.

A few years earlier, the person asking was a world-renowned musician. He and his wife had invited me to observe their four-year-old daughter. The girl had not been responding well to intensive autism therapy that required sitting for long periods and responding to directions and commands. Her parents wanted a second opinion about the best approach to helping and supporting her. On my first visit to the family's sprawling home, the father gestured for me to follow him into another room.

"Can I show you something?" he asked. He reached behind an upholstered chair and grabbed a paper shopping bag, then stuck his hand inside and pulled out a toy. It was a Bumble Ball, a battery-powered, textured rubber toy with a motor inside to make it vibrate when it was switched on. I could see that it had never been removed from its original packaging.

"I bought this for my daughter last Christmas," he said apprehensively. "Was that a bad thing? I thought she would like it."

I shrugged. "I can't see how it could be bad," I replied.

"Well," he said, "her therapist told me it would make her more autistic."

It made no sense: a brilliantly talented celebrity so paralyzed by the words of a thirty-year-old therapist that he was scared to give his own daughter a toy.

For more than four decades it has been my job to help parents like these, people from all walks of life who are struggling with the realization and reality that their children have autism—and to support the educators and various professionals who work with these children. More and more often I meet parents who have been thrown off balance—who suddenly feel perplexed, sad, and anxious about their children, not knowing what an autism diagnosis means for the future of their child and their family.

Their distress and confusion stem partly from information overload. Autism Spectrum Disorder is now among the most commonly diagnosed developmental disabilities; the U.S. Centers for Disease Control estimates that it affects as many as one in fifty school-age children. A flood of professionals and programs has emerged to serve these children: physicians, therapists, schools, afterschool programs. There are karate classes and theater programs for children with autism, sports camps and religious schools and yoga classes. At the same time, charlatans and opportunists with minimal or no experience—and even some with professional credentials—advertise their approaches as "breakthroughs." Unfortunately autism treatment is a largely unregulated enterprise.

All of this has made life even more challenging for parents. Which professional to trust? Who can explain your child? Which treatment will succeed? Which diet? Which therapy? Which medication? Which school? Which tutor?

Like any parents, these mothers and fathers want what's best for their children. But, struggling with a developmental disability they don't understand, they don't know where to turn.

My job for four decades has been to help them transform their desperation into hope, to replace anxiety with knowledge, to turn self-doubt into confidence and comfort, and to help them see as possible what they thought was impossible. I have worked with thousands of families touched by autism, helping them to reframe their experience of the condition, and in turn build healthier, fuller lives. That's what I hope this book will help you to do, whether you are a parent, a relative, a friend, or a professional working to support these children and their families.

It starts with shifting the way we understand autism. Again and again I have witnessed the same phenomenon: parents come to perceive their child as so radically different from others that the child's behavior seems beyond comprehension. They have come to believe that the tools and instincts they would bring to raising any other child just won't work with a child who has autism. Influenced by some professionals, they see certain behaviors as "autistic" and undesirable and perceive their goal as eliminating these behaviors and somehow fixing the child.

I have come to believe that this is a flawed understanding—and the wrong approach. Here is my central message: The behavior of people with autism isn't random, deviant, or bizarre, as many professionals have called it for decades. These children don't come from Mars. The things they say aren't—as many professionals still maintain—meaningless or "nonfunctional."

Autism isn't an illness. It's a different way of being human. Children with autism aren't sick; they are progressing through developmental stages as we all do.* To help them, we don't need to change them or fix them. We need to work to understand them, and then change what *we* do.

In other words, the best way to help a person with autism change for the better is to change ourselves—our attitudes, our behavior, and the types of support we provide.

How to do that? First, by listening. I have worked at the highest levels of academia and served on the faculty of an Ivy League medical school. I have published my work in dozens of scholarly journals and books. I have addressed conferences and presented workshops in nearly every state and across the globe, from China to Israel, from New Zealand to Spain. Yet my most valuable lessons about autism have come not from lectures or journals. They have come from children, their parents, and a handful of extremely articulate adults with the rare ability to explain their own experience of having autism.

One of those is Ros Blackburn, a British woman who speaks more insightfully than practically anyone I know about what it feels like to go through life with autism. Ros often repeats this mantra: "If I do something you don't understand, you've got to keep asking, 'Why, why, *why*?' "

---

*While many children with autism experience co-occurring medical issues—including gastrointestinal and sleep disorders, allergies, and ear infections—most are free of these challenges, which are not definitive of autism.

This book is about what I have learned in forty years of asking why—what I have come to understand by asking what it feels like to have autism.

Concerned parents share the same kinds of questions: Why does he rock his body? Why won't he stop talking about trains? Why does she repeat lines from movies over and over? Why does he obsessively adjust the miniblinds? Why is he terrified of butterflies? Why does she stare at the ceiling fan?

Some professionals simply categorize these as "autistic behaviors." Too often the ultimate goal of professionals and parents is to reduce or eliminate these behaviors—to stop the spinning, stop the arm flapping, stop the repeating—without asking, "Why?"

Here is what I have learned from my years in the field and from Ros Blackburn and others: There is no such thing as autistic behavior. These are all *human* behaviors and *human* responses based on a person's experience.

When I present workshops and seminars about autism, I often tell the audience that I have never seen a person with autism do something that I haven't seen a so-called normal person do. Of course, many people find this difficult to believe. So I make it a challenge. I ask the listeners—usually parents, teachers, and professionals—to name a behavior that is central to autism, and I predict that I have witnessed it in a typical person. Immediately people in the audience raise their hands.

"How about repeating the same phrase over and over one thousand times?"

Plenty of kids do that when they're asking for an ice cream cone or how much longer the drive will be.

"Talking to yourself when nobody's around?"

I do that in my car every day.

"Banging her head on the ground when she's frustrated?"

My neighbor's "typical" son did that when he was a toddler.

Rocking, talking to yourself, jumping up and down, flapping your arms? We all do these things. The difference, of course, is that you might not have seen it as persistently or as intensely (or at an older age) in a typical person. And if we do engage in such behavior, we generally make sure we're not doing so in public.

Ros Blackburn says people stare when she jumps up and down and flaps her arms. They're simply not accustomed to seeing an adult act with such abandon. She points out that it's common to see people on TV doing just what she does, after they've won the lottery or a game show. "The difference," she says, "is that I get excited more easily than you do."

We're all human, and these are human behaviors.

That's the paradigm shift this book will bring: instead of classifying legitimate, functional behavior as a sign of pathology, we'll examine it as part of a range of strategies to cope, to adapt, to communicate and deal with a world that feels overwhelming and frightening. Some of the most popular autism therapies make it their sole aim to reduce or *eliminate* behaviors. I'll show how it's better to enhance abilities, teach skills, build coping strategies, and offer supports that will help to prevent behavioral patterns of concern and naturally lead to more desirable behavior.

It's not helpful to dismiss what children do as "autistic behavior" or "aberrant behavior" or "noncompliant behavior" (a phrase used by many therapists). Instead of dismissing it, it's better to ask: What is motivating it? What purpose does it serve? Does it actually help the person, even though it looks different?

I don't have simple answers, but I can offer ways that will lead to a better understanding of children, teens, and adults with autism. The stories in *Uniquely Human* span my four-decade career in many different settings and roles: my early work in summer camp programs, positions at university and hospital clinics, and seventeen years in private practice. They also describe my experiences consulting for more than one hundred public school districts, for hospitals, private agencies, and families, and from many years of traveling the world leading training workshops and consulting. The weekend parent retreat I have facilitated for two decades has given me the opportunity to learn from parents and develop many deep and enduring friendships. Finally, through many conferences and workshops, I have met and presented with leaders of the autism self-advocacy movement, many of whom have become valued friends.

This book offers a comprehensive approach based on my research and work with colleagues, my experience with families and professionals, and the insights shared by people on the spectrum from whom I have learned much.

It's the book I wish I had been able to read more than four decades ago, when I first lived with and cared for people with autism. Many professionals enter the autism field because of a personal connection—a child or a relative with autism. I happened into it almost by accident. After my first year of college, I landed an unfulfilling summer job in a New York City print shop. My girlfriend was teaching music at a sleep-away camp for children and adults with disabilities. A couple of weeks into the summer, she phoned to tell me there was an opening for a counselor. I applied, got the job, and literally overnight found myself, at just eighteen, responsible for a cabin full of boys with a variety of developmental disabilities.

For a boy from Brooklyn, the isolated rural setting in upstate New York felt like a primitive wilderness. But I was even more unprepared for the people I met. One eight-year-old boy in my cabin seemed remote and disconnected, but he had a knack for repeating phrases or whole sentences he heard. Another camper, a young adult known affectionately as Uncle Eddie, lumbered and spoke as if in slow motion because of his seizure medication. He had the endearing habit of offering compliments without inhibition. "Hi Barry," he'd say. "You look *sooo* handsome todaaay."

I felt like I was entering a different culture with different rules of relating and being, full of people who acted very differently from anyone I had met. Yet I soon became so comfortable and so thoroughly enjoyed my campers that I wanted to understand more. In particular, why did these people struggle so much with communicating their thoughts and feelings, and how could we help them? That initial experience inspired me to study developmental psycholinguistics, and then speech and language pathology and child development, and eventually to go on to earn a doctorate in communication disorders and sciences.

This book might have also helped me understand one of my closest friends from my childhood in Brooklyn in the 1960s. Lenny was a brilliant student—skipping two grades before high school—and a talented self-taught guitarist. He was a musical genius, stealing guitar licks from Eric Clapton and Jimi Hendrix before the rest of us had even heard of them.

He was one of the most interesting people I knew, and also one of the most anxious, unfiltered, direct, and abrasive. Peers were put off by his frequent comments about his own superior intelligence. When Lenny lived in his own apartment as an adult, his shelves were lined with his extensive collection of records and first-edition comic books, all in plastic sleeves, impeccably organized and catalogued. But his kitchen sink was routinely overflowing with dirty dishes, his clothes strewn everywhere. Lenny had perfect SAT scores, eventually earned two master's degrees and a law degree, but had a difficult time keeping a job because he had trouble getting along with people.

Still, if Lenny knew you well and trusted you, and if you had common interests, he was as loyal and caring a friend as I have known. Though I frequently found myself in the position of explaining Lenny's eccentric ways to acquaintances—most people thought him rude and arrogant—it took decades before it dawned on me that he probably had Asperger's syndrome. (Asperger's wasn't a formal diagnosis in the United States until 1994.) When Lenny died in his sixties, it struck me that his life surely would have been easier if those around him had better understood what was causing his unusual habits and often brusque manner.

Finally, this is the book I wish I had been able to share a few decades ago with the parents of Michael, one of the first little boys with autism whose family I came to know well. I was a newly minted

PhD, teaching at a large university in the Midwest, and Michael was the nine-year-old son of an English professor. Like many children with autism, Michael had a habit of fluttering his fingers in front of his eyes and staring at them, apparently delighted and captivated. For long stretches he would sit, mesmerized by the movement of his own hands. His teachers and parents routinely badgered Michael to dissuade him: "Michael, put your hands down. . . . Michael, stop looking at your hands!" But he persisted, eventually learning to enjoy secretively peeking at his hands during routine activities such as playing piano.

Around that time Michael's grandfather died. Michael had developed a very close relationship to his grandfather, spending time with him every weekend, and the death was his first experience of loss. Of course he felt confused and anxious, repeatedly asking his parents when he would be able to see his grandfather again. They explained that Grandpa was in heaven and that some day, in the very distant future, Michael would surely join him there. Michael listened intently, then replied with a single question: "In heaven, are people allowed to look at their hands?"

When Michael considered the idea of eternal bliss, that was what came to mind: not angels and harps and eternal sunshine, but a world where he could watch his own fingers flutter when he wanted to.

His simple question taught me much about Michael and about autism. I have seen hundreds of children with autism who visually fixate on something: their fingers, a toy they carry with them, a fan, garden sprinklers. You could call that "autistic" behavior, or you could watch, listen, pay attention, and ask why they do it. When I have done that I have learned what underlies a fixation like Michael's: he finds it calming and grounding; it provides a sense of predictability; it's within his control. With that understanding and insight, behavior like Michael's isn't so strange—it's a unique way of being human.

This book's scope encompasses the full spectrum of autism, including the most extreme challenges facing individuals of all ages and their families. I am well aware of how debilitating and stressful some patterns of behavior can be. I have cared for individuals who are so overwhelmed by pain or confusion that their behavior becomes dangerous, destructive, and even harmful to themselves and others. I have directly experienced injuries (bites, bruises, scratches, broken fingers) while attempting to support people in extreme states of distress. I have lived with people with autism who also have sleep disorders, and I have experienced the frustration of trying to ensure proper nutrition for individuals with highly restricted food preferences. I have dealt with children who have become lost, have fled, or have unintentionally put themselves and others in danger.

While I don't claim to have experienced the chronic level of stress and concern that a parent might, I know those concerns and fears intimately. From observing and supporting countless families, I have learned this important lesson: Even under extremely challenging circumstances, our attitudes about and perspective on people with autism and their behavior make a critical difference in their lives—and in ours.

That is the message I hope to share in this book—one that can eliminate the fear I sensed from the principal and the musician and replace it with awe and love. It's the heart of what I taught recently at an autism workshop in Nanaimo, a small city in British Columbia. Throughout the two days there a young father in a baseball cap sat in the front row with his wife, taking it all in but not speaking. The moment the workshop ended, he rushed up to me, hugged me, and buried his head in my shoulder.

"You have opened my eyes," he said, "and I will always be grateful."

I hope this book will open your eyes—and your ears and your heart. I hope to capture and share the unique spirit of the many children, adolescents, and adults with autism I have known—their enthusiasm, their sense of wonder, their honesty and innocence. I will also describe the many obstacles I have seen these individuals and their families overcome. In turn, I hope you will be able to learn from what I have learned. Despite the challenges you may experience as a parent, family member, educator, or one of the many people who help individuals on the spectrum, my hope is that understanding what it means to be uniquely human will make your experience with these distinctive people deeper, more awe-inspiring, and more joyful.

PART ONE

Understanding Autism

CHAPTER 1

Ask "Why?"

THE first thing I noticed about Jesse was the fear and anxiety in his eyes.

I was visiting a small New England school district when I heard about an eight-year-old boy who had recently transferred from a nearby district. There he had earned a dubious distinction: administrators called Jesse the worst behavior problem they had ever encountered.

It wasn't difficult to understand why, given his challenges. Jesse, a sturdy boy with straight brown hair and wire-rimmed glasses, struggled with severe social anxiety, extreme sensitivity to touch, and difficulty processing language. He also had a seizure disorder that was detected when he was a toddler, about the time he lost the ability to speak. He communicated with little more than guttural sounds and grunts, pushing away people and objects or physically leading people to what he wanted.

Since it was so difficult for Jesse to make his needs known, he often seemed aggravated and miserable. He sometimes took out his frustration and anxiety on himself, pounding his fists against his thighs and his forehead, covering his body with bruises. When teachers tried to direct him from one activity to the next, he often reacted with flailing limbs or by pushing them away with his arms or legs. Reports from the previous school described kicking, scratching, and biting episodes escalating into fits so severe that almost daily, three or four adults had to pin the boy down to subdue him, then isolate him in a "time-out" room.

The staff had interpreted all of this as willful, uncooperative behavior. But Jesse's mother knew better. She understood that his actions were his way of communicating—a direct reflection of his confusion, agitation, and fear. When she explained to the administrators that her son struggled with sensory challenges that made him unusually sensitive to loud noises and being touched, they had been dismissive. Clearly, they insisted, the boy was displaying noncompliant behavior. In their eyes, Jesse was strong-willed, stubborn, and defiant, and their response was to try to break him—to treat him as a trainer would treat a horse.

What did these educators offer to help Jesse learn to communicate? Practically nothing. The district's policy was to focus first on controlling a child's behavior, and, only after achieving success, to address the area of communication.

They had it all wrong.

I had heard so many awful things about Jesse that I was intrigued to come face-to-face with him. When I finally did, I didn't observe any of what I had heard described—not the defiance, not the aggression, not the willful disobedience. What I saw was a boy who was understandably frightened, anxious, and constantly on guard. And I saw something else: Jesse's extreme vigilance and anxiety were manifestations of the inevitable damage that occurs when people—however well meaning—completely misunderstand the behavior of individuals with autism.

How does this happen? The short answer is that caregivers neglect to ask "Why?" They don't listen carefully or observe closely. Instead of seeking to understand the child's perspective and experience, they simply try to manage the behavior.

Unfortunately this behavioral-assessment approach—that is, using a checklist of deficits—has become the standard way of determining whether a person has autism. We say a child has autism if he displays a combination of traits and behaviors that are deemed to be problematic: difficulty in communicating, trouble developing relationships, and a restricted repertoire of interests and behaviors, including repetitive speech—known as echolalia—and actions, such as rocking, arm flapping, and spinning. Professionals observe these "autistic behaviors" and then assess the people who display them by using a sort of circular reasoning: Why does Rachel flap her hands? Because she has autism. Why has she been diagnosed with autism? Because she flaps.

Following this approach means defining a child as the sum of his deficits. How best to help such a child? By managing those behaviors or attempting to get rid of them: to halt the rocking, to squelch the echoing speech, to reduce the flapping. And what denotes success? The more we can make a child look and act "normal," the better.

This way of understanding and supporting people with autism is sorely lacking. It treats the person as a problem to be solved rather than an individual to be understood. It fails to show respect for the individual and ignores that person's perspective and experience. It neglects the importance of listening, paying close attention to what the person is trying to tell us, whether through speech or patterns of behavior.

On top of that, in my experience it doesn't work—and often makes things worse.

What's more helpful is to dig deeper: to ask what is motivating these behaviors, what is underlying these patterns. It's more appropriate, and more effective, to ask "Why?" Why is she rocking? Why does he line up his toy cars that way, and why only when he arrives home from school? Why does he stare at his hands fluttering in front of his eyes, and always during English class and recess? Why does she repeat certain phrases when she is upset?

The Challenge of Dysregulation

Usually the answer is that the person is experiencing some degree of *emotional dysregulation.* When we are well regulated emotionally, we are most available for learning and engaging with others. We all strive to be alert, focused, and prepared to participate in activities in our daily lives. Our neurological systems help by filtering out excessive stimulation, telling us when we're hungry or tired or when to protect ourselves from danger. People with autism, primarily due to underlying neurology (the way the brain's wiring works), are unusually vulnerable to everyday emotional and physiological challenges. So they experience more feelings of discomfort, anxiety, and confusion than others. They also have more difficulty learning how to cope with these feelings and challenges.

To be clear: Difficulty staying well regulated emotionally and physiologically should be a core, defining feature of autism. Unfortunately professionals have long overlooked this, focusing on the resulting *behaviors* instead of the underlying *causes.*

If you know a person with autism, consider what makes this person *less* able to stay well regulated: problems in communicating, environments that are chaotic, people who are confusing because they talk or move too quickly, unexpected change, excessive worry about things that are uncertain. Then there are associated challenges, such as sensory sensitivities to touch and sound, motor and movement disturbances, sleep deprivation, allergies, and gastrointestinal issues.

Of course people with autism aren't alone in experiencing these challenges. We *all* feel dysregulated from time to time. Speaking in front of a large audience, you might feel sweat collecting on your brow, your hands might quiver, your heart might race. Wearing a scratchy wool sweater might be so irritating that you can't focus. When your normal morning routine—coffee, newspaper, shower—is thrown off by an unexpected intrusion, you might feel out of sorts for the rest of the morning. When these factors accumulate—you miss sleep, you're under a deadline, you skip lunch, and then your computer crashes—it's easy to become extremely agitated.

We all have these challenges, but people with autism are unusually ill equipped to deal with them because of their neurology. That makes them far more vulnerable than others—that is, their threshold can be much lower—and they have fewer innate coping strategies. In many cases, they also have sensory-processing differences: they are either highly sensitive or undersensitive to sound, light, touch, and other sensations and therefore less able to manage. In addition many people with autism are innately unaware of how others might interpret their actions when they are dysregulated.

Feeling emotionally dysregulated affects different people in different ways. Often the reactions are immediate and impulsive. A child's behavior may shift suddenly, with no apparent cause. When a child is exposed to a loud noise, for instance, he might drop to the floor. I often see children refuse to enter a gym class or the school cafeteria. Their teachers might mistakenly believe that this is willful disobedience, a planned attempt to escape an activity the child doesn't enjoy. The reason is typically much deeper than that: the child can't bear the volume or quality of the noise or the chaos of the setting.

When I worked in a preschool autism program based in a hospital, the children ate lunch in the classroom on trays brought up from the hospital cafeteria. Once a teacher and I led the four- and five-year-olds to the cafeteria's kitchen so they could see how the trays were cleaned. At exactly the moment we arrived, the industrial-size dishwasher spewed forth steam and suddenly emitted a high-frequency *SSSHHHH!* Instantly all the children dropped their trays, some covered their ears and screamed, and they ran for the exit. It was as if a monster had suddenly appeared, inches from their faces.

That's dysregulation, sudden and visible.

Sometimes the cause of dysregulation is less obvious. While visiting a preschool where I consulted, I was walking outdoors with Dylan, a four-year-old with autism, when suddenly and without warning, he dropped to the ground and refused to proceed. I gently picked him up and helped him along, but soon he dropped again. As I helped him again, we heard a dog barking. He immediately panicked and tried to run away from the sound. It dawned on me that Dylan, with his hypersensitive hearing, had heard the dog all along, but its bark had been so distant that it hadn't registered with me. What might have appeared as uncooperative, random, or defiant behavior was in fact a very understandable expression of fear.

That too is dysregulation.

Many children with autism flap their arms, either as an expression of their level of excitement or to calm themselves. When Conner felt joyful, and sometimes when he was anxious about a transition between activities, he did what his parents called his "happy dance." He stood on his toes and stepped forward, then back, while flicking his fingers in front of his eyes. An earlier therapist had advised Conner's parents to respond with a firm "Hands down!" And if he didn't comply: "Sit down, sit on hands!" (To their credit, his parents ignored the suggestion, instead helping Conner to label his feelings or easing transitions by telling him what to expect.)

It's easy to dismiss flapping or rocking or dancing as just so much "autistic behavior." But parents raising children with autism, and the professionals who work with them, need to take an extra step. Like detectives, we need to examine and consider all available clues and work to discern what is underlying or triggering a particular reaction. What is making the child dysregulated? Is it internal or external? Is it visible? Is it in the sensory realm? Is it pain, or physical discomfort, or a traumatic memory? In most cases the child can't explain the behavior in words, so it's up to those close to him to sort through the clues.

Coping Strategies and Regulating Behaviors

Here is the important irony: Most of the behaviors commonly labeled "autistic behaviors" aren't actually deficits at all. They're strategies the person uses to feel better regulated emotionally.

In other words, in many cases they're strengths.

When a child with extreme sensory sensitivities enters a noisy room and cups his hands over his ears and rocks his body, this pattern of behavior is simultaneously a sign of dysregulation and a coping strategy. You could call it "autistic behavior." Or you could ask "Why is he doing that?" The answer is twofold: the child is revealing that something is amiss and that he has developed a response to shut out what is causing him anxiety.

Whether or not we realize it, all humans employ these rituals and habits to help us regulate ourselves—soothe ourselves, calm our minds and bodies, and help us cope. Perhaps, like many people, you find public speaking unnerving. To calm yourself, you might take a series of deep breaths or pace back and forth while you speak. That's not exactly the way humans typically breathe or behave in public, but an observer would not judge this as deviant behavior. The person would understand that it's your way to cope with the stress of the situation and to soothe your nerves so that you can do your best.

When I return home from a day of work, I immediately check the mailbox, then sort the mail, placing bills in one pile, magazines in another, and tossing what I don't need in the recycling bin. It would take a significant distraction for me to skip that small but important ritual; then I would feel out of sorts on some level until I took care of it. It's a calming routine; it's how I come home. When my wife has had a bad day or feels worried, she organizes and cleans. If I come home and find our home more immaculate than usual, I know that something is bothering her. Religious services include layers of comforting rituals—chanting and praying, symbolic gestures and body movements—to enable people to let go of the worries and trivialities of everyday life and enter a higher spiritual realm.

For people with autism, comforting rituals and coping mechanisms come in all varieties: moving in particular ways, speaking in various patterns, carrying familiar items, lining up objects to create predictable and unchanging surroundings. Even proximity to certain people can serve as a regulating strategy.

After coming home from a busy school day, Aaron, who was eight, had a habit of placing both palms on a table in front of him and then rhythmically jumping in place. His parents noted that the intensity and duration of his jumping were a good barometer of how stressful his day had been. Just as infants are comforted and soothed by being rocked, and toddlers run in circles to stay awake, we all use movement to modulate our emotional and physiological arousal. If people with autism feel underaroused, they increase their alertness by spinning, bouncing, or swinging. If they're overstimulated, they might calm themselves by pacing, snapping their fingers, or staring at a fan.

Many people call these simply "behaviors." Again and again I have heard parents or educators describe children as having "behaviors." Don't we all? It's only in the field of autism that the word *behavior*—without any modifier—has a negative connotation. "Our new student, Sally, has really got a lot of behaviors," a teacher will say. Or "We're working on getting rid of Scott's behaviors." Others use the term *stim* or *stimming* (for repetitive, self-stimulatory behavior), terms that also have negative connotations. In earlier decades many researchers aimed to rid children of stims, some employing punishment and even shock as a means to eliminate "autistic behaviors."

We should not view these merely as *behaviors*, however. They are most often *strategies* to cope with dysregulation.

When an American psychiatrist named Leo Kanner first introduced the autism diagnosis, in 1943, he noticed a striking trait among the children he described. He called it "insistence on preservation of sameness" (a trait still considered definitive of autism). Indeed many children with autism regulate themselves by trying to control their surroundings—by seeking sameness. That isn't a pathological symptom. It's a coping strategy.

Every time Clayton returned home, he would survey every window in the house, adjusting the blinds so they were all at exactly the same height. Why? He was trying to ground himself by taking control and making his environment predictable and visually symmetrical. Others habitually eat the same foods, close all the cabinet doors in the classroom, watch the same DVD over and over, or insist on sitting in the same chair every day.

Are rituals like Clayton's indications of Obsessive-Compulsive Disorder? Actually their impact is quite different. True OCD behavior is disruptive and rarely serves to make the person feel better. In other words, the need to repeatedly wash one's hands or to touch every chair before leaving a room can interfere with everyday activities. But when a child with autism seeks out the same clothing or music or creates visual order by organizing items, it's because the child has learned that these things help him to emotionally regulate himself so he can function.

A couple once brought their seven-year-old son, Anton, for an initial evaluation at the clinical practice I ran. After a colleague and I interacted with the boy and observed him for a while, it was time to chat with his parents, so we gave Anton some paper and colored markers to entertain himself.

As we conversed, Anton was intently drawing. He carefully took one marker at a time, removed the cap, wrote down a number, replaced the cap, and put the marker back in the can, then repeated the process with different markers dozens of times. When we took a break and looked at what he had drawn, I was amazed. Anton had created an elaborate grid of numbers from 1 to 180, arranged in order, by systematically alternating seven colors. The result was a tidy, precisely ordered sequence of rows of numbers with the diagonal columns creating a rainbow of color. This was a boy who could speak only a single word at a time and echo a few phrases, but he had kept himself calm for some thirty minutes by focusing his attention on creating this ingenious visual display.

"He's never done anything like this before," his mother told me.

The drawing revealed not only that Anton's mind was more nimble and complex than I could have imagined, but also that he had devised his own ways to keep himself regulated. In this new environment, with adults—some unfamiliar—conversing around him, he found a way to remain grounded. Another observer might have concluded that he was stimming. I call it *self-regulation* (and remarkably creative).

Sometimes what helps a child self-regulate is an object. One boy would keep a particular stone—small, black, and polished—with him at all times, the way babies hold security blankets or stuffed animals. It calmed him; it regulated him. When he lost it, his father was anguished. "We've tried all kinds of other black rocks," he told me, "but he knew they weren't *that* rock." Eventually the boy found a replacement, a ring of plastic keys.

Often children with autism mouth, chew, or lick things to regulate themselves, just as many people habitually chew gum or suck on hard candy. Glen would pick up twigs on his kindergarten playground, lick them, and often chew them. He constantly gnawed on pencils in the classroom, and his mother said that he chewed on his sleeves and collars so frequently that the family's clothing bills were rapidly mounting. When I observed Glen in class, it was clear that he would seek things to mouth or chew at the times he felt most dysregulated: during unstructured times (such as recess), transitions, or when noise increased. Working with his occupational therapist, I suggested better ways to provide the sensory input he craved: offering crunchy snacks (carrots, pretzel nuggets) and a rubber toy or tube to chew on. We also provided a variety of supports to decrease his level of anxiety and confusion.

People as Regulating Factors

One of the many harmful myths about children with autism is that they are isolated loners who neither need nor seek relationships. That's not true. In fact, for many the presence and proximity of another human being is the key to emotional regulation. The McCanns had recently relocated to a new town, where their four-year-old with autism, Jason, was enrolled in a public preschool program. His mother asked the school to give the boy scheduled movement breaks—chances to go outside or to the gym once or twice daily—and she requested that his eight-year-old brother join him. Since the boys were adjusting to the new environment, she felt it would be helpful to both. Not only did Jason regulate himself by getting the movement he needed, but he experienced the regulating presence of a familiar and trusted person, his brother.

Sometimes people with autism become dysregulated if a particular person is absent. Seven-year-old Jamal repeatedly asked his teacher, "Mommy at home?" One therapist suggested that the teacher answer affirmatively just once, but then ignore repeated questions. The ignoring only made Jamal more anxious, and his questioning became louder and more urgent. I suggested instead placing on his desk a photo of his mother at home and assuring him, "Mommy's at home. You will see Mommy after school." That reduced his need to question and helped him focus on schoolwork.

A third-grader named Caleb benefited from a different kind of companion: an imaginary friend he called Stephen. In class Caleb would sometimes insist on saving the seat next to him for Stephen. On the playground he would pretend to play with Stephen. His teacher said Caleb tended to invoke Stephen only in difficult moments: transitions between activities or settings or at particularly chaotic times. When I visited as a consultant, his young classmates told me Stephen was Caleb's make-believe friend who helped him because he had autism. They understood! Clearly Caleb was using the imaginary friend as an emotional regulatory strategy, a way to soothe himself in difficult moments.

"Should we discourage this?" the teacher asked. As long as it wasn't making him less present or engaged, I assured her, it seemed a useful strategy. As Caleb made friends and became more comfortable, he mentioned Stephen far less frequently, and then not at all.

Some strategies are verbal. Many people with autism display echolalia, the repetition of spoken language, repeated either immediately or some time later (see chapter 2). This too has often been dismissed as autistic behavior and irrelevant, nonsense talk. But echoing serves many functions for people with autism, including emotional regulation. A boy might ask over and over, "Going swimming this afternoon?" One could label the child an incessant questioner and aim to stop his echoing. Or we could ask "Why does he need to do that? What purpose does it serve?" Perhaps he has a need for things to be predictable. So the questioning is both a sign of feeling ill at ease and a coping strategy he employs to get information so he knows what to expect, reducing his uncertainty and anxiety.

Some people with autism not only repeat themselves but dominate conversations, sharing great amounts of information about a favorite topic (say, geography or trains) without considering the other person's thoughts, feelings, or interests. This too can be a sign of dysregulation. For a person with a poor grasp of social cues who finds the unpredictability of typical conversation stressful, speaking incessantly on a familiar and beloved topic might provide a sense of control.

I often see children go an extra step, trying to control *both* sides of the conversation. Some feed their parents lines: "Ask me, 'Do you want Cheerios or Frosted Flakes?' Ask me!" Many children repeatedly ask questions when they already know the answers: "What's your favorite baseball team?" "What color is your car?" "Where do you live?" If I intentionally and playfully give the wrong answer, they immediately correct me. So why did they ask? Doing so might be yet another effort to exert control, to increase predictability and sameness in the face of the anxiety triggered by social conversation. At the same time, it shows the child's desire to connect and stay engaged socially.

The Importance of Understanding "Behaviors"

Once you understand the role emotional regulation and dysregulation play in autism, it's easy to see why "deficit checklist" approaches to treating autism prove ineffective. They can actually cause *more* anxiety for the person involved, particularly when they aim to decrease strategies that help the person. These methods define certain traits and behaviors as autistic and focus on "extinguishing" them (a term many therapists use). They fail to delve into the true motivations underlying the behaviors, and they often blame the child for being noncompliant or intentionally manipulative rather than recognizing that the child is successfully using appropriate strategies—however unconventional in appearance. If they succeed at eliminating these behaviors, what they're really doing is stripping the person of coping strategies. A better approach is to recognize the value of such behavior and, when necessary, to teach other strategies to stay well regulated.

Seeking to eliminate behavior without fully understanding its purpose is not only unhelpful; it also shows a lack of respect for the individual. Worse, it can make life more difficult for the person with autism.

That was the case for Lucy, an eleven-year-old. Her public school teachers had reported that Lucy, who did not speak, was an extremely aggressive child, prone to unpredictably lunging and clawing at the faces and necks of teachers and therapists. When I spent a morning observing her in my role advising the district, the problem became clear. Much of the work the educators and therapists were doing with Lucy consisted of matching exercises; they repeatedly asked her to match pictures and images on cards or to point to pictures on command.

I quickly deduced why Lucy appeared to be springing at her teachers. In the midst of the activity, the assistant abruptly changed course. She stopped showing pictures and instead wrote Lucy's name on a card, placed it in a row with other cards, and asked the girl to identify it. Almost immediately Lucy dove toward the young woman, trying to pull on her blouse in protest. Why? The therapist had shifted the pattern, changing the rules without warning. When a highly anxious child craves routine to understand the world, it's no wonder a sudden change throws her off.

To test my theory, later that day I watched Lucy stroll with a teacher along a familiar school hallway. Then I suggested that the teacher alter the route from the usual routine. When she did, Lucy, suddenly upset, again lunged and grabbed at the teacher's neck and blouse just as she had before.

It was clear that the grabbing wasn't *aggressive* behavior; it was a plea for support at a moment of extreme confusion. Lucy didn't intend harm. She was confounded during a familiar activity; she had become more anxious and dysregulated, approaching a state of panic.

How Adults Can Cause Dysregulation

Lucy's experience shows how the various adults in a child's life can actually be the cause of dysregulation. When I lead autism workshops for parents and professionals, I often tell the audience, "Raise your hand if you have ever been the primary reason your child or student experienced a full-blown meltdown." After some nervous laughter, virtually every hand goes up. We're not bad people, I point out. We might be acting with the best of intentions—asking a child to stay in a noisy and challenging social activity just five more minutes, for example, or complete two more math problems. But that's all it takes.

Of course we can also play a significant role in helping children to cope. If a child is hypersensitive to sound, a parent can offer noise-dampening headphones. Often a child will repeatedly ask a question—"Going to the park this afternoon? Going to the park this afternoon?"—even after the parent has repeatedly answered. Instead of answering directly, a parent might say, "Let's write down the answer and put it on our daily calendar so we don't forget." That not only acknowledges the child's concern and helps calm and reassure her in the short term; it also provides her with a model, a strategy to keep herself regulated in the future.

Often the most important things we can do to help are to acknowledge and validate the child's feelings of dysregulation, yet teachers and others frequently overlook this basic measure. I paid a classroom visit to eight-year-old James, whose school I advised, when he was having a particularly difficult day. James was a sweet, wiry, and active little boy with saucer-like eyes who sometimes had unpredictable and uncontrollable episodes of dysregulation. One of his favorite parts of the day was gym class, an opportunity to expend energy and relax his body. But on this particular day, the gymnasium was being used for class photos. Children with autism find such changes in schedule challenging and confusing, so it wasn't surprising that James had reacted with dismay. The teachers offered to take him on an extended walk, but that didn't satisfy him.

"But I *need* to go," he told his teacher. "I need to *move in the gym.*"

By the time I was called from another part of the building, James's meltdown had become so severe that the teacher had taken him out of his classroom to a small conference room, where he was hiding under a table, growling and refusing to come out. Previously a therapist had suggested the staff ignore such behavior to avoid reinforcing it with attention. Instead I offered James a beanbag chair he liked and a weighted stuffed animal, a frog, that he liked to hold when he needed to calm himself. I slid them both under the table to where he was curled up in fetal position.

"James," I said calmly, "I think you're upset because you couldn't go to gym today."

"Couldn't go to gym," he echoed. "I need to *move.*"

Slowly I scrunched my body under the table and scooted toward the boy. Sitting beside him, I acknowledged his feelings of confusion and anger and offered some words of encouragement: "Everybody's feeling sad because they know you're upset."

Taking in my words, he slowly calmed down and turned in my direction. "No pictures tomorrow?" he finally said. "Go to gym tomorrow?"

"Yes," I said, "you will go to the gym tomorrow."

James emerged voluntarily, quietly walked out of the room, and asked to take a stroll in the hallway. His teachers said he recovered far more quickly than when they had ignored him.

What James needed wasn't to be ignored, and his reaction clearly told us that. The regulating routine he relied on had been interrupted. The rules had changed without warning. His expectations were not met. He needed someone to acknowledge and validate his feelings.

Near the end of the school day, a school aide flagged me down in the hallway and brought James over to me, holding his stuffed frog. "Dr. Barry, I just want to say goodbye," James said. "And my frog wants to say goodbye too." It was not the first time that a simple gesture from a sweet child brought a tear to my eye.

A parent or teacher can make a difference, positive or negative, merely with tone of voice or energy level or by being predictable—or surprising. If a stranger, or even a relative, tries without warning to offer a hug to a child with autism, the child might react defensively. But the same child might not mind a hug if she does the initiating. Once when my British friend Ros Blackburn visited the United States, I accompanied her to several speaking engagements where I introduced her to acquaintances. When people approached her with great excitement and energy—"Ros! It's *so* great to meet you!"—she would often step back, even recoil, stiffening her body and assuming a protective, guarded posture. But when people stood farther away, moved slowly, and spoke calmly, Ros responded with much greater ease and confidence.

Sometimes offering the best support means suppressing your instinctive reaction. Barbara picked up her four-year-old son, Nick, at preschool every day at 3 p.m. One day, on her way there she got a flat tire and had to wait forty-five minutes for a tow truck. She alerted the school, but her son was so dependent on his fixed routine that she worried in the meantime how Nick would react. Would he panic? Would he have a meltdown?

When she finally arrived, Nick was sitting on a mat in the corner, frenetically rocking, looking disconnected, lost, and distraught. All of the other children had been picked up, and he was the last one waiting. Feeling anxious herself, Barbara felt the urge to dash to reassure Nick. Instead she walked over slowly and calmly sat down next to him. "Nick, honey, Mommy's here," she said in a soft, measured tone. "Everything's okay." Gradually Nick looked up at her, stopped rocking, and echoed, "*Mommy's* here, Mommy's here, Mommy's here." He stood up, took her hand, and silently led her to the door. Barbara understood that to help Nick recover she herself needed to stay well regulated.

Her moment of restraint was emblematic of an important idea: Instead of trying to change how a person with autism reacts to us, we need to pay close attention to how *we* react to the person.

The Power of Listening and Building Trust

I learned that lesson in a larger way from my experience with Jesse, the eight-year-old whose difficult behavior had proven such a problem at his former school. At his new school, where I consulted, we clearly had much work to do to help him. My approach, whenever possible, is to work as a member of a team rather than presuming I have all the answers. In collaboration, parents, teachers, therapists, administrators, and others involved in a child's life can develop and execute the best possible plan. When his new school team first assembled shortly after Jesse arrived, nearly everyone agreed that Jesse wasn't aggressive but rather defensive, scared, and confused.

"We're going to have to build trust," I told the team. Jesse didn't speak, and since the previous school made compliance training—not social communication—its priority, he lacked an effective way of communicating. He didn't have control over how he spent his time, or even an understanding of what to expect, since his teachers didn't utilize visual schedules, which help prepare kids and make things more predictable. While his teachers and therapists had been focused on getting him to behave, he had been fighting to express himself and survive.

He was routinely dysregulated and had no way to share how he felt or what he needed—other than for people to back off.

His new school team immediately focused on giving him tools to communicate, using cards with picture symbols and photos, and always presenting him with choices to ensure that he felt some degree of autonomy and dignity. We gave him a schedule so he could know what to expect. We understood that he had severe sensory challenges, so an occupational therapist created a plan with various sensory strategies to help him regulate his body. As part of his morning routine, for instance, he would sit in a rocking chair in a quiet area in his classroom while an occupational therapist massaged his hands with lotion and then massaged his forehead; he found deep pressure calming. I once joked that they should have called the room Spa Jesse.

Within weeks the team had organized Jesse's photos and picture symbols into a communication book to help him express himself by pointing to what he wanted or wanted to do. (This was before iPads.) The book included activities he found regulating, such as running in the gym, head squeezes, massage, and listening to music. The therapist let him choose the hand or arm he wanted to have massaged and also taught him to massage himself. Now able to communicate, Jesse—previously so anxious and frightened that he swatted away anyone who came near—became comfortable interacting with classmates and teachers for extended periods. He spent part of his days in mainstream classrooms, supported by an aide, and only a few months after his arrival, his teacher reported good news: for the first time in his new school, Jesse had flashed a broad smile. For the first time in his life, Jesse was delighted to head off to school each day.

What was different? At the previous school, the staff had focused on getting Jesse to comply, to follow their plan—not on listening to him, not on communication. Now the focus was fostering social communication and finding ways to support a well-regulated emotional state. His new team gave him a sense of control over his life—not unlimited, open-ended control but choices within a predictable structure. They taught him things he could do independently to feel a sense of control and stay well regulated. They helped him understand that they were there to support him, not to control him.

To be sure, he still had his share of struggles. But over time Jesse opened up and clearly felt more comfortable in his classes, around people, in his own skin. In middle school Jesse continued to progress and took on two different jobs. Working with a classmate, he collected paper from classrooms for recycling. He also delivered mail to classrooms. Though Jesse wasn't a fluent reader, the staff established a color-coded system to help him sort the mail. In the process he had opportunities to interact with adults and peers. With the help of a speech-generating device, Jesse carried on brief conversations with the teachers as he delivered the letters and packages each day.

No tantrums, no hitting, no resistance, and lots of smiles based on lots of trust.

The boy who had appeared to be so frightened, bruised, and alone was now staffing the school store, selling snacks and drinks to classmates and teachers, collecting money and making change. He celebrated completing middle school by attending the end-of-the-year dance with a friend. Later, in high school, this teenager, who had once been so anxious and unpredictable that staff would steer clear of him in the hallways, worked as an assistant to the chemistry teacher. Jesse so excelled at keeping the beakers and test tubes in order on the shelves (with the help of a visual guide) that the teacher said the lab had never been so organized.

I clearly remember a moment at a team meeting when Jesse was ten. Two years earlier his mother had given up on the previous school district, frustrated and angry at the way Jesse was treated as a behavior problem. Now she looked around the table at the therapists, the teachers, and the staffers with tears in her eyes.

"You saved my son's life," she told the group.

If we had, it wasn't through heroic measures or brilliant insights. It was because instead of trying to change Jesse, we listened, we observed, we asked why, and we changed our approach based on what we saw and heard. We recognized what was making him feel dysregulated, and we helped give him the tools to cope and to exert some control over his own life.

If that approach can work for Jesse, it can help almost any child.

CHAPTER 2

Listen

DAVID taught me to listen.

David was an energetic and joyful little four-year-old who seemed to be in constant motion, bouncing like a pinball from place to place. Observing him in his preschool classroom when I was beginning my career, I came to understand that although David was verbal, almost all of his speech came in the form of echoes. Instead of typical, creative speech and language, he had his own kind of communication: either he would mimic what he had just heard someone say, or he would produce a phrase or sentence that could seem completely out of context or even nonsensical. Sometimes he immediately echoed what he heard; sometimes it was hours, days, or months later.

David had a fascination with textures and tactile sensations, and he had a particular affinity for my sweaters. One day I was working to get him to take turns with me putting pieces in a puzzle, but I could tell he was distracted. In the unabashed manner young children have, he began picking tiny wool pills from an arm of my sweater and then the front, examining each ball up close, holding it to his eyes and rolling it between his thumb and index finger. Instead of protesting, I decided to follow his interest.

"See that, David?" I said. "That's a piece of fuzz."

"That's a piece of fuzz, fuzz, *fuzz*," he repeated.

I listened as he delighted in playing with the tiny ball of wool, and then in playing with the word itself, seeming to enjoy the sensation as it crossed his lips: "That's a piece of fuzz, fuzz, fuzz! That's a piece of *fuzz*!"

It was obvious to me how happy this combination of touch and sound made David, so I saw it as a way to draw more of his attention. The next day I brought a bowl of cotton balls. That enchanted him. I placed the balls around the room and devised a game, asking David to follow my directions and hunt down the cotton balls—on a chair, say, or under a stuffed animal. Clearly something about the textures excited him, making him more present and eager to connect with me. Imposing activities on him might have provoked resistance, but by following his interests and his energy I discovered that David would be motivated, even persistent in finding his own ways to communicate.

One day we had the children create an art project with paints, but instead of paint brushes, they used pieces of sponge. Afterward David discovered bits of the cut-up sponge on the floor of the classroom. Just as he had with the fuzz balls, he began picking them up one at a time, closely examining each as he rubbed it between his fingers, savoring the texture.

"That's a piece of sponge," I said.

"That's a piece of sponge," he echoed. "That's a piece of sponge, sponge, *sponge*!"

Again I could see the joy he derived from the combination of the feeling of the material and the sound of the words coming out of his mouth. As he clutched the bits of sponge in his cupped hands and looked at the others on the floor, he began to dance around the room on tiptoes. "That's a piece of sponge, sponge, *sponge!*" he kept saying. "That's a piece of *sponge*!"

The real revelation came the next day. By then the classroom had been cleaned. We had cleared away the art project and someone had straightened up and vacuumed away all the debris. When David arrived in the classroom, though, he returned to exactly the spot in the room where a day earlier he had come upon the sponge bits. I watched as he repeated his dance, shifting his gaze to me and saying, "That's a piece of sponge, sponge, sponge! That's a piece of sponge!"

Consider this: What if a visitor had happened into the classroom that day to observe the children? Imagine such a person watching this little boy coming into the room, full of energy, and then performing a little dance and babbling on about a sponge. The visitor might easily have dismissed the behavior as absurd. Or silly. Or random. The visitor might have questioned David's grip on reality—or at least his understanding of the word *sponge*.

But if you had been in the room the previous day, if you had shared the conversation with David that I did, if you knew about his enthusiasm for new textures, then you would have understood exactly what was going on. This little boy was recounting his experience of the previous day—not only the facts of the experience (the materials used in the art project) but, more important, his own feelings of excitement about it.

He was telling a story.

Reframing Echolalia

Anyone who has spent time with a verbal person with autism is familiar with this tendency to repeat words, phrases, or whole sentences, often ad infinitum. Indeed echolalia is one of autism's defining characteristics. In children who can speak it is often among the first indications to parents that something is amiss in a child, when, instead of responding or initiating with the child's own language, the child echoes words or phrases borrowed from others.

Mother: Honey, you want to go outside?
Daughter: You want to go outside?

Those initial exchanges take many forms: the child repeats snippets from videos she's watched, announcements on the subway, greetings from teachers, or even select phrases from an argument her parents had at home. Anything can become an echo. Utterances children hear at moments of great excitement, pain, anxiety, or joy seem to take on a life of their own, becoming the source of echoes, with the child seeming to relive the moment and the emotion that accompanied it.

A colleague once asked me to visit an elementary school to offer insight about a fifth-grader with autism named Eliza. When I arrived at the classroom to observe her, the teacher gestured for me to come in and take a seat. But when I approached Eliza, the girl suddenly had a worried look on her face and said three words: "Got a splinter!"

I wasn't sure I'd heard right. A splinter? But I proceeded with my friendliest and gentlest demeanor and sat nearby, only to hear Eliza repeat the same words, "Got a splinter! Got a splinter!," as she watched me out of the corner of her eye.

I looked at her hands to see if she might have hurt herself, but the teacher spoke up. "Don't worry," she told the girl. "Barry's a nice man. He's just visiting today."

Eliza repeated verbatim, "Barry's a nice man. He's just visiting today."

That seemed to calm her, but it only made me wonder what feelings Eliza was experiencing and what was going through her mind to make her say "Got a splinter!" What was she talking about? Did it have anything to do with me? Was it just random? And why had the teacher responded in that way?

When I asked the teacher later, she explained that Eliza had suffered a painful splinter on the playground two years earlier. Since then she had used the phrase "Got a splinter!" whenever she felt anxious or scared.

Just as Eliza's teacher knew what she meant, and just as I fully understood and delighted in David's celebration of the sponges, parents and others close to a child often comprehend exactly what the child is saying—and why. "Oh, that's a line from a *SpongeBob* episode he watched last year." Or "He heard his teacher say that when there was a fire drill at school last month." Or "I said that to him when I gave him a bath last month!" Or "That's what the announcer on *The Price Is Right* says."

Yet these same parents grow apprehensive when they hear some "experts" speak of echolalia through the lens of pathology—when they're told that echolalia is just another "autistic behavior," a problematic trait that's considered an obstacle to the child's ability to fit in and appear "normal."

That's a mistake.

Certainly on the surface it looks that way, and many parents worry that this persistent echoing hinders the child's ability to connect with other children, to develop relationships, or to learn in school. It seems to isolate the child, to mark him as quirky, different, or weird.

Some professionals have reinforced those impressions, labeling this kind of communication "silly talk" or "video talk" (since so many of the phrases come from videos and DVDs) and working to arm parents with strategies to stop it. Early in my career it was common for educators and professionals to use harsh and negative techniques to get children to stop these speech patterns. Therapists would respond to a child's "silly talk" with loud, annoying (to the child) noises such as clapping their hands near the child's face, the way you might try to dissuade a dog from barking in the house. In one school I visited, teachers would squirt lemon juice in a child's mouth to punish "undesirable" behavior and remind her to speak in turn or get back on topic. More recently practices have become less harsh and aversive; some involve ignoring the child (known as "planned ignoring"). Some professionals instruct parents to hold up an index finger to the child and issue a firm command: "Be quiet!" or "No talking!" or "No silly talk!" All of these approaches share the same goal: stopping the talk.

I have long felt that this is wrong, that professionals were misunderstanding echolalia and that the responses they were prescribing were not only misguided but maybe even harmful. In their attempts to make children appear more "normal," these "experts" were plainly ignoring what were clearly legitimate attempts at communication, and—worse—they were disrupting the child's process of learning to communicate and connect with the world.

How I Came to Understand Echolalia

Shortly after I earned my master's degree in speech and language pathology, I landed what felt like a dream job. As part of my required clinical fellowship, I was offered a position at the Buffalo Children's Hospital Autism Program. (People are sometimes surprised to hear that such a program existed in 1975, but I can vouch for its existence and excellent quality.) That year I worked as a speech and language specialist in a classroom with five young boys, all of whom had autism. At the same time, I was conducting a pilot study, observing these boys to try to understand what role echolalia played in their communication and language development.

One reason I wanted to study echolalia was that many of the judgments about children with autism had been made by people who were not experts in speech and language or in child development. They were behavior therapists, specialists in developing programs to reduce undesirable behavior and increase desirable behavior. Most shared the belief that echolalia was in the "undesirable" category of behavior without really understanding it. In Ros Blackburn's terms, they hadn't asked "Why?"

I suspected that there was more to this kind of speech than just random or noncompliant behavior. My observations, and my training in psycholinguistics and speech-language pathology, had taught me that echolalia was far more complex than "meaningless parroting," that this kind of speech served a purpose. And I wanted to test this hypothesis.

Up until that time the limited research on echolalia had been conducted in the more artificial, contrived conditions of a laboratory. Mine was a social-pragmatic study; that is, I studied language as the children used it in the context of everyday activities and settings. I watched these little boys in the classroom. I observed them at home. I videotaped them as they interacted with peers and siblings on the playground. In short, I observed them and listened to them as they lived their lives.

It was the first time I had worked with so many children who displayed echolalia, and as I got to know them well, I could see that for none of them was this meaningless speech. These little boys were communicating, and using echolalia for other purposes as well. In talking with their mothers and fathers, I found that the parents had similar perceptions.

I first saw it in David, the same boy who had celebrated over the sponge pieces. Every time one of the teachers or aides would say "No!" to David in a way that indicated displeasure, he would react the same way. He would skip around the room, repeating in a voice with strong negative emotion, "We don't slam doors. We don't pee on the wall."

Those ten words told an entire story. He wasn't saying them as an order to someone else; nor was it random or silly—though, admittedly, the adults in the room found it quite entertaining. David had been scolded before, and this was his way of acknowledging the social import of the moment: "We don't slam doors. We don't pee on the wall." It meant that he comprehended that he was being reprimanded. Whatever he had been doing fit into the same category as door slamming and urinating: things you're not supposed to do in the classroom. He was indicating in his own way, "Understood."

I learned that the echoing could also communicate important information and feelings. One afternoon Jeff, another boy in the class, seemed less energetic than usual, but since he wasn't yet communicating directly, we didn't know why. Then he started approaching the various adults in the classroom, got close to their faces, and made a noise we hadn't heard before: "Doo-aaah! Doo-aaah!" As he said it, he opened his mouth wide and extending his jaw downward with the prolonged "aaah."

He continued that pattern through the entire afternoon, pacing around the classroom but then finding his way back, making eye contact, and repeating those two syllables: "Doo-aaah! Doo-aaah!" My first impression was that he was playing with sounds, seeing how it felt for various noises to emanate from his mouth. Hard as I tried, I could not discern what he was trying to say—though it was clear from his approach, his intent expression, and his persistence that he was trying to communicate something. He was seeking and expecting a response.

When Jeff repeated his "Doo-aaah!" again the following morning the teacher phoned his mother to investigate. She didn't even have to pause to figure it out. "Oh," she said, "we think he might be coming down with a cold."

We waited for more. "And?"

"Well, when I think he's getting sick, I tell him to open his mouth and do 'Aaah.' "

It made perfect sense. Jeff was trying to tell us that he didn't feel well. He had a cold, or maybe a sore throat. At his developmental stage, he was unable to explain that in words, so he was acting out a scene for us, reliving what he had heard his mother say at home: "Do 'Ahh!' "

Out of context it meant nothing; it was a little boy making funny sounds. But we kept asking "Why?" With some careful listening and probing, I understood Jeff perfectly.

I did a lot of listening that year. With a federal grant from the Department of Education's Bureau of Education for the Handicapped, I recorded twenty-five videotapes of the boys in everyday activities: in school during playtime, at lunch, and during individual and group therapy sessions, and at home with their siblings and parents, over the period of a year. I spent months analyzing them, in the process identifying 1,009 distinct echoes and categorizing them (as good academics do) into seven functional categories. I distinguished immediate echolalia (when a child repeats a word or phrase on the spot) from delayed echolalia or "scripting" (when the speech is repeated hours, days, or even months or years later).*

The bottom line was this: These little boys were communicating in all sorts of ways. Sometimes they were affirming what they understood. Sometimes they were taking turns, as one might in conversation. Sometimes they were repeating words as a way of rehearsing something they were going to say later. Sometimes they were repeating certain sounds because the sounds themselves were calming, as chanting a mantra might be. Sometimes they were talking themselves through the steps of a process or reasoning through the situation aloud to reassure themselves.

In other words, they were using language for the same purposes we all do.

We just had to listen, observe, and pay attention.

An Alternative Way of Communicating

The more I have listened over the years, the more I have developed my ability to recognize and make sense of the echoes I hear in children with autism. Does echolalia ever appear to be nonpurposeful, in the sense that we cannot decipher the meaning or purpose? Of course. But most of the time, with careful listening and a bit of detective work, it becomes clear that the child is communicating—in the child's own unique way. My research has proven that, and other researchers have found similar results.†

Aidan, for example, was an adorable three-year-old whose ability

---

* I focused on immediate echolalia for this study, but later studied delayed echolalia with Patrick Rydell, a student of mine, and we reached similar conclusions.

† Inspired by our research, Marge Blanc addresses this issue and the research in her book *Natural Language Acquisition on the Autism Spectrum: The Journey from Echolalia to Self-Generated Language* (Madison, WI: Communication Development Center, 2013).

to speak wasn't developing as expected but who showed a knack for picking up whole chunks of language. Most typically developing children add a word at a time to their vocabulary (*mommy, daddy, baby*), and then build short sentences ("Mommy hug." "Daddy eat cookie."). Instead Aidan would surprise his parents with whole phrases and sentences, sometimes quite sophisticated grammatically. At four he would greet people he met not by saying "Hi" or "Hello" but with a line from his favorite movie. He would cock his head to the side, squint his sparkly eyes, and ask, "Are you a good witch or a bad witch?"

Of course that is how Glinda, the Witch of the North, greets Dorothy in the famous scene from *The Wizard of Oz*. It's a dramatic moment. Dorothy has just landed in Oz when a tiny glowing bubble shows up, gradually growing in size as it nears, then suddenly bursts, and Glinda appears, looking like a fairy princess in a gown and holding a wand. She approaches Dorothy and says those immortal words: "Are you a good witch or a bad witch?"

What more powerful example could there be of one person greeting another? This boy wasn't speaking gibberish; he was capturing the essence of what it means for one human being to encounter another. (Later his teachers and therapist taught him to use the more conventional "Hi, my name is Aidan." As much as his mother appreciated that, she missed her son's more distinctive greeting.)

Sometimes children echo to narrate their way through an experience—sometimes the most mundane experiences. That was true of Bernie. He was a high-energy youngster, and much of his communication consisted of enthusiastically repeating things he had obviously heard from other people, including his mother. He had an uncanny ability to re-create the speaker's accent. When I worked in his preschool decades ago, I would sometimes be in the men's room with him when suddenly I heard his voice emanating from a lavatory stall, sounding exactly like his mother: "You done now, boy! Now wipe yo' butt!"

Often children use echoes to tell us what they're thinking, but rarely in ways that are immediately obvious. The father of Kyle, a young boy with autism, once invited me to join the two of them on a sailboat in Narragansett Bay, Rhode Island. In the middle of a lovely afternoon, we were anchoring in a little cove when the boy began running up and down the deck as he anxiously leaned over to peer into the water.

"No dogs! Dogs bite!" he kept saying with increasing urgency, looking back at his dad. "No dogs! Dogs bite!"

No dogs? We were out on the water, with no other boats nearby—no people, no animals. Just waves and wind. What could he have been talking about? His father knew exactly what he meant. "He's asking if he can go swimming."

I asked the father to explain. He told me that Kyle had a fear of dogs. When he felt anxious about his safety, that was how he expressed it: "No dogs! Dogs bite!" Now he wanted to go swimming in the shallow cove, but he wasn't sure whether this was a safe place, so he was asking. With that phrase he accomplished three things: he expressed his fear, requested permission from his dad, and made sure it was safe. And when his father responded "It's okay, it's safe! No dogs!," Kyle jumped in with great glee.

Every Family Has a Language

As stories like these illustrate, echolalia offers lessons not just about language and communication development but about raising children. Many parents look to doctors or therapists to be the experts, appealing to them to explain their children. Over time I have come to realize that the best approaches to autism are those centered on the family. Parents almost always know their children better than anyone else does. And based on innumerable shared experiences over so many years, every family develops its own language: its own familiar phrases, its own terms, its own shorthand. In other words, every family develops its own culture that allows for mutual communication, understanding, and support.

Each family has its own native culture, and outsiders are most often alien to that culture. So rather than parents relying on outsiders, such as professionals, to make sense of things, the professionals need to rely more on the insiders: parents, their children, and other family members. When parents ask me to explain their child's habit of repeating phrases and words (or any perplexing pattern of behavior), my first response is always to turn the question around: "Well, what do you think?" Usually they can tell me—or at least make an educated guess. In either case they often provide important information about their child that I was not aware of, and in the process their expertise about their child is validated.

For one study I sent parents questionnaires asking about their experiences of echolalia. Nearly all of their children with autism had experienced echolalia, for which the parents had their own explanations: "Sometimes he does it to keep something in mind to help him understand it better." "Sometimes she uses it to request something." "That's how he takes his turn when he doesn't understand." "When he echoes he's saying 'Yes.'" Nearly all of them found meaning in their children's unusual speech.

Echolalia as a Learning Strategy

In fact echolalia serves an even more vital purpose for many children with autism: it's a path to acquiring language. In the simplest terms, it works like this: Children with autism struggle with communication, but they tend to have a very strong memory. So they learn language by hearing it and repeating it back, either immediately or with some delay. As the child continues to grow socially, cognitively, and linguistically, she begins to discern the rules of language, but she does so, in part, through the use of echolalia, breaking down the memorized chunks of speech.

Of course that doesn't mean it's easy to live with. I always tell parents that just because it's functional language—and vital to their child's developing communication—doesn't mean it won't drive them crazy at times! The fiftieth time your daughter repeats the same line from *Toy Story 2*, your head might be ready to burst. The hundredth time your son says, "We don't slam doors. We don't pee on the wall," you might feel like slamming the door yourself. But it's important to take heart in two things: first, the knowledge that this kind of communication serves a purpose for the child, and second, that it represents an ever-evolving developmental process. Over time the echoing will most likely lessen as a child's creative language system develops, though of course progress comes at different rates and at different times in every child.

Parents and others can help a child learn to use more creative language—instead of echoing—through various strategies, including simplifying the language they use with the child, breaking down echolalic chunks into words and smaller phrases, adding gestures, and introducing visual supports and written language. For example, a father might say to his daughter, "Please go over to the refrigerator and get some milk and cookies." The child might fill her "turn" in the conversation by merely echoing the sentence, or part of it, but not really respond. Then the father might simplify the complex sentence by dividing it into segments: "Go to the refrigerator (while pointing). Get milk. Open the cabinet. Get cookies."

Another strategy is to introduce photographs, pictures, or written words instead of exclusively using spoken language. This can help a child understand more readily and rapidly, making it less necessary to use echolalia as a strategy to understand.

For some children it's helpful for the child to write or type what he wants to say. This can improve his ability to formulate language rather than relying on retrieving memorized chunks. Most people with autism are stronger using visual ways to express and understand language than communicating purely by hearing and speaking. While it's crucial to acknowledge and understand the intentions and functions of echolalia, it's equally important to help the child move to more creative language and more conventional ways of communicating.

Many children who use echolalia persistently when they are young use it less and less as they mature, but when faced with challenging circumstances or difficult moments of dysregulation, these children revert to echoing. Elijah, a middle school student, was a passionate fan of Broadway musicals, in particular *The Lion King*. Though Elijah had significant academic challenges, particularly in subjects requiring high-level comprehension of abstract language, he attended mainstream classes in his public middle school so he could benefit from the typical social environment. For the most part he thrived there, except when he felt overwhelmed and anxious about the more challenging academic work. As his anxiety increased, Elijah would stand up in the middle of his history class and start singing "Circle of Life" at the top of his lungs, first in English, then in German (which he'd learned from videos he'd found on the Internet).

The teachers at his school (for which I consulted) wanted to honor Elijah's creative spirit, but it's disruptive to have a student break out in show tunes in history class. So I asked Elijah why he sang during this class. His explanation: The teacher was talking too quickly, and Elijah couldn't keep up. He had a difficult time paying attention, and this was Elijah's way of regulating himself emotionally. The song was just another form of echoing, what some professionals have referred to as "scripting." He wasn't being bizarre or displaying random behavior; he was coping, the same way another person might play a favorite tune in his head when feeling bored or stressed (but without projecting it publicly).

Working with his teacher, parents, and others in the school, I sought a less disruptive way for him to calm himself. In addition to the songs, Elijah also liked drawing the *Lion King* characters. So we suggested that he bring a sketchpad to class, and later a small whiteboard and markers, so that when he felt anxious, he could quietly draw instead of interrupting the class.

Another teen who benefited from that kind of alternative outlet was Justin, a talented artist. When he was eleven, a small local café agreed to host a show of his artwork. His parents welcomed the opportunity to work on his social skills, so he spent time rehearsing how he would greet the friends and strangers who might come to the show. The night of the opening he shook hands and welcomed the first few guests appropriately, but as more and more people arrived, Justin became increasingly anxious and overwhelmed. So in place of a standard greeting, he asked, "Who's your favorite cartoon character?" (Justin loved animation, and many of his pictures were cartoons.) Even when he knew the individuals well, he forgot the greetings he had prepared and instead blurted out his question, showing little interest in the answer. The anxiety in his voice seemed to increase with each repetition. Justin repeating his familiar question was like Elijah singing *Lion King* songs. In each case the echo softened the anxiety.

To replace this unusual greeting with a more conventional one, his parents prepared an index card with reminders of what to say in social situations. It wasn't a script, but it had some key words to remind him to stay engaged in a conversation rather than reverting to his familiar question. Knowing he had that visual and written reminder was enough to help Justin through social situations in which he felt overwhelmed and anxious.

Echolalia also serves a developmental purpose. A child cannot become a creative and fully functional user of language merely by repeating memorized words or phrases, but echolalia is a start. For many of these children, it's the first step in understanding the basic concept that they can use their body as an instrument to produce speech that expresses wants, needs, observations, and feelings. And in that way they can connect with other human beings.

Listening Encourages Communication

That is why it is so important for parents to listen to their children and not be dismissive of this type of communication. One of my early mentors, the late Dr. Warren Fay, a speech and language specialist who worked at what is now Oregon Health & Science University, put it this way: If we don't yet fully understand what echolalia is all about, shouldn't we at least give the children the benefit of the doubt?

Consider the perspective of the child, who is desperately trying to communicate, despite the neurological challenges that come with autism: social anxiety, sensory overload, often language-processing challenges. When that child's early attempts to communicate are met with harsh orders recommended by some professionals to "be quiet!" or "stop the silly talk!" it's not only unhelpful; it's actually discouraging the child's efforts to communicate and work through the challenging process of figuring out what speech, language, and communication are all about. Besides, shutting down these attempts at communication may provoke even greater stress and confusion for the child. It is not surprising that many such children react by avoiding certain people, shutting down, and giving up.

My simple advice: Listen, observe, and ask "Why?"

When parents, teachers, and caring professionals do that—when they pay close attention to words and gestures and context—they often understand intuitively that echolalia is part of the process of learning to communicate. I watched that happen in Namir, a little boy I first met when he was two and a half and captivated by Disney videos.

That's a common theme in the children with whom I have worked. Animated movies of all kinds hold a particular fascination for children on the autism spectrum, capturing their attention like almost nothing else. Why? Many children find the predictability and consistency of animated characters (as well as the music) comforting, a welcome contrast to the unpredictable nature of real people in everyday situations. In *Monsters, Inc.* or *Madagascar*, the characters' vocal, facial, and body language is exaggerated, making emotions easier to decipher for such children. People with autism also find the clear delineation of good and evil characters an appealing alternative to the more nuanced gray areas they encounter in real life. And repetitive viewings engender a reassuring sense of familiarity and mastery.

Many parents express concern that their children are spending too much time focusing on *The Lion King* or *Shrek*, worried that this is harmful to their development. Therapists or other professionals often compound their fears, cautioning that repeated viewing of these movies can serve to exacerbate the behaviors or somehow intensify autism. Parents often ask me if these movies are only serving to provide more fodder for "silly talk," more useless phrases for children to echo.

I learned from Namir and his parents to take a longer perspective, a more nuanced view. As a three-year-old, Namir seemed lost in Disney films. Much of what came out of his mouth consisted of snippets from *Peter Pan*, his favorite. Instead of using language to interact with other people, he would repeat lines from the movie to himself, sometimes seeming oblivious to the real human beings surrounding him.

Others might have tried to dissuade him by reacting with demands to stop using such speech, convinced that this "meaningless parroting" was hindering his progress. Instead Namir's parents listened to him—and joined him. They bought *Peter Pan* action figures and interacted with him as he acted out imaginary scenes with the toys. They honored his interest and supported his engagement, so that Namir felt listened to and respected.

In time his play progressed. He showed increasing understanding of what he was saying. He was still using the phrases he had picked up from *Peter Pan*, but he found ways to use the Disney dialogues in their appropriate social context. Like Aidan, the boy who employed *The Wizard of Oz* line to greet people, Namir began integrating the snippets of speech spinning in his head as a way to connect with other people.

As he learned to use language more creatively, he used the "Disney talk" more selectively, when it was appropriate to the social context and his own intentions. When he wanted someone to leave, for example, he would say, "Tinker Bell, I hereby banish you forever!" By encouraging his unique efforts to communicate, Namir's parents dramatically aided his development. Between preschool and elementary school, he transformed from a boy who seemed lost in a world of random scripting and playing alone to an interactive and social little boy.*

When his fourth-grade teacher assigned the children to do a research project on a famous American, Namir chose Walt Disney. And when he produced a lovely report, his parents took another opportunity to celebrate their son—and the value of having faith in one's own child.

---

* Ron Suskind documented a similar progression in his son's language development in *Life, Animated* (New York: Kingswell, 2014).

CHAPTER 3

Enthusiasms

SOMETIMES a single word can change your perspective forever.

I once invited the late Clara Claiborne Park to speak at an annual autism fundraising conference I help run. Clara, who was an English professor at Williams College, was the mother of Jessy Park, a gifted painter with autism. Clara and her husband, David, were pioneers in the autism world. In the 1960s they were among the founders of the National Society for Autistic Children, the first advocacy organization of its type, and in 1967 she published *The Siege*, the first widely read memoir by a parent about raising a child with autism. I was privileged to get to know Clara and David early in my career and savored every opportunity to spend time with them.

Jessy displays many classic characteristics of autism. She struggles with social interactions, has difficulty expressing herself in speech, and recoils if someone touches her without warning. Over the years Jessy's parents appreciated and supported her deep interests, many of which became themes for her vivid, rainbow-colored paintings: architecture, prime numbers, clouds, odometers, quartz heaters, constellations, streetlamps, ATM machines, and many others.

After her speech at the conference, Clara, then in her late seventies, took questions from the audience. "I'm curious about your daughter's obsessions," someone said. "How have you dealt with them?"

"Obsessions," Clara repeated, contemplating the question for a moment. "Hmm. We've always thought of them as *enthusiasms*."

Clara and David had a particularly constructive attitude toward the many subjects that attracted their daughter's focus, no matter how unusual they were. Clara explained that if something truly gripped Jessy's attention, she and David would seek ways to steer Jessy's interest in a way that would help her.

That wasn't always easy, since her taste was so unpredictable. For a time Jessy focused on quartz space heaters. She admired the design; she categorized the styles and brands; she would carefully examine their parts. That enthusiasm gave way to another: the logos of rock bands. She would pore over album covers and photographs in magazines, closely scrutinizing the letters and graphics. She began integrating quartz heaters and rock band logos into her paintings, many of which have hung in museums and been featured in gallery shows. Rather than directing her daughter away from her interests, Clara treated Jessy with respect, assuming there were reasons for her fascinations—that to Jessy it all made sense.

Children with autism develop all kinds of enthusiasms, talking nonstop about or focusing endlessly on subjects like skyscrapers, animal species, geography, particular kinds of music, sunrise and sunset times, or turnpike exits. Perhaps focusing on one topic gives the child a sense of control, of predictability and security in a world that can be unpredictable and feel scary.

Building on Enthusiasms

Still, some parents and professionals view these interests as yet another undesirable symptom of autism, one that makes it even more difficult for the child to fit in. Often their instinct is to discourage the child, to redirect his attention and suggest interests that are more socially acceptable and conventional. But discouraging an enthusiasm can be just another way of dismantling a strategy that helps a child with autism feel better regulated—or, worse, removing a source of interest and joy. A more helpful approach is to do as Jessy Park's parents did and use the enthusiasm as a way to expand the child's outlook and improve the child's life.

That was the case with Eddie, a fourth-grader who showed little interest in reading the stories his teacher assigned as part of the standard reading curriculum. He didn't seem to have difficulty reading and didn't typically avoid doing schoolwork. Rather he found the subject matter too abstract and the stories irrelevant to his life experience.

When I met with his talented special education teacher, Kate, in my role as consultant for the district, I suggested that we make an effort to find a hook that would draw him in to his academic work. Surely we could discover *something* that would motivate him to read and write. Was there anything that seemed to engage Eddie? Kate had noticed one thing: Eddie liked to spend time closely examining license plates on the cars in the school lot, then later enjoyed matching plate numbers and cars from memory.

A casual observer or a teacher who was less attuned might not have registered that a child's interest in something as mundane as license plates could actually become an opportunity. I suggested that Kate pay attention to that particular interest. Perhaps it might inspire an idea to engage Eddie.

When I returned a month later, she was excited to show me a project Eddie had recently completed. Working from a plan Kate had helped Eddie to create, he had spent time photographing each car and license plate in the school lot. With help from his teacher and the school office, he matched each car with the staffer who owned it. Then he met with each car owner, photographed the person, and conducted an interview to get to know the person: Do you have any hobbies? Are you married? How many children do you have?

Over time he assembled the photographs, documented the interviews, and developed a PowerPoint presentation for his class. Not only did the project serve its purpose, offering Eddie the chance to focus on reading, writing, research, and organizing material, but the experience had also proven transformative. The same child who had seemed disengaged and unmotivated to read went about his project eagerly, engaging with teachers, gathering information and assembling it to share with his class. It also provided an opportunity to work on social and communication skills, as he proudly presented the finished project to his classmates, then fielded their questions.

His parents could not have been more surprised or delighted. At our next team meeting to review Eddie's progress, Kate explained the project and its goals, and Eddie's father's eyes were wide with amazement. "He did *what*? He interviewed *teachers*?" he said. "That's *incredible*!" When Kate showed him photographs of Eddie presenting his project to a roomful of classmates, his father was overwhelmed. Eddie was achieving things his parents couldn't have imagined. He was progressing academically and socially, and his self-esteem was soaring.

Other parents might have disapproved of a teacher who engaged their child in a subject as trivial as license plates. Another teacher might have insisted that Eddie read the same stories his classmates were reading, whether he liked it or not. Another school might not have been open to an alternative, individualized academic approach, instead letting the child struggle (and possibly fail) in the standard curriculum. But Eddie's success didn't require extra money or radical innovation, just a teacher who paid close attention and had the instinct to see an enthusiasm as a strength. Kate did this by focusing on what was most motivating for Eddie, and she used his interest as a powerful inspiration for learning. She saw enthusiasm as a source of potential rather than an impediment or a problem.

What Inspires Enthusiasms?

Why do people with autism develop enthusiasms? To answer that, it's useful to consider how all kinds of people take comfort in hobbies, passions, and collections. If you were to visit my home, you might be surprised to see that I have a glass china cabinet holding more than a hundred pieces of walrus tusk in various shapes and sizes. Years ago, on a visit to Vancouver Island, I first came across Inuit ivory carvings, and something about them appealed to me. (The ivory walrus tusk used is acquired legally by native peoples who hunt walrus for food, clothes, tools, and materials for indigenous crafts.) Perhaps it was the shiny appearance of the ivory or the way its smooth texture felt in my hands. As I expanded my collection, part of the allure was certainly the detail and visual appeal of the carvings—the way the craftsmen carved the raw material into the shapes of walruses, bears, and whales. For whatever combination of reasons, I began collecting these pieces and found emotional satisfaction in the process.

I don't think of myself as obsessive, but, like a lot of people, I have gone through various phases of collecting. When I lived in the Midwest in my thirties, on weekends I drove to used-furniture stores and farm auctions in search of antique furniture. Later it was old quilts, then Navajo rugs; after that antique clocks and piano stools and antique slag glass lamps.

That I maintain these modest collections doesn't make me unusual. And that's the point. Nearly everyone has passions and interests. They fill a need; they give us pleasure; they make us feel good for reasons we may not always understand. They're part of being human.

Why, though, do people with autism display a far greater tendency than others to have these strong passions? Why do their enthusiasms often seem exponentially more powerful than other people's interests? As with any kind of hobby or pastime, it often begins with an emotional response. An experience feeds a basic neurological need to be engaged, to appreciate beauty, and to experience positive emotion. When a person with autism develops an interest, we must assume that the particular subject of the interest is a good match for that person's neurophysiology and serves an important function. An adult with Asperger's syndrome explained to me that because connecting socially is challenging, many people with autism direct their energies into their areas of interest, leading, in some cases, to stronger and more focused passions.

Michael's focus was on music. When he was eight, long before he could engage in conversation comfortably, he demonstrated the gift of perfect pitch. He could hear the horn of a passing car and spontaneously identify its musical note. Suddenly distracted, he would look up and exclaim, "B flat!" Later he would hear a song on the radio, then sit at the piano and re-create it on the first attempt. He also could immediately transpose songs into other keys on request.

As many as 15 percent of those with autism demonstrate these high-level natural talents or gifts, known as savant skills, but most do not. Many others have "splinter skills"—strengths, such as rote memory or artistic talent, that stand out relative to their overall profile. These unusual abilities are rooted in different learning styles, based on differences in how the brain processes and retains information. Some children feel drawn to information, activities, or tasks that jibe with their more rote learning styles. Some like concrete and factual information that can be easily memorized; others enjoy activities that require good visual-spatial judgment, such as fitting things together. An older child might effortlessly memorize countless facts and details about dinosaurs or sports teams. A toddler might easily complete complex puzzles.

Some parents of more challenged children confide that their children show no such surprising skills, talents, or interests. Still, children might demonstrate clear preferences for particular kinds of sensory stimulation. Perhaps they seek visual, auditory, or tactile stimulation by flicking their fingers in front of their eyes, producing particular vocal patterns, or exploring specific textures through touch. Children are often drawn to certain toys because of the sensory input they provide. One toddler I worked with seemed magnetically drawn to electric fans of all kinds. If he knew there was a fan in a room, he would practically fight to get in to see and feel it, and when he encountered a fan, he would inspect it closely from all angles. Something about the sensation—feeling the breeze, seeing the spinning, feeling the vibrations, or the combination of them all—excited him and captured his attention.

The King of Carwashes and Other Remarkable Tales of Passion

Once a child becomes aware of such a preference, what begins as a pleasurable sensory sensation often transforms into a focus of attention, interest, and preoccupation. The child seeks out what brought the positive feelings, and it can occupy his thoughts at all hours of the day.

Carwashes caught Alexander's attention. From an early age, when his father took the family car for its occasional cleaning, Alexander was simultaneously fascinated and frightened—by the sound, the splashing water, the brushes, the sight of the cars making their way through. Alexander couldn't explain why, but he begged his parents to take him back again and again so he could watch and listen. They visited so often that the owner of the local carwash befriended the family, welcoming Alexander to help out at the entrance by waving his arms to direct drivers into the wash.

His parents didn't understand what motivated Alexander's fascination, but they could sense how happy it made him. Other children savored amusement parks or fast cars or ski slopes. Their son delighted in carwashes. Whenever the family traveled, they sought out carwashes and mapped their journeys accordingly, visiting carwashes from Florida to Maine. At each stop on the tour, Alexander excitedly stood outside, surveying the grounds and taking in the operation the way another child might watch an NBA game or an action movie.

When he was ten, his parents contacted the International Carwash Association to request brochures they thought Alexander might enjoy. To their surprise, that led to a dream vacation for Alexander—not a trip to Disneyworld or Hawaii but to Las Vegas, as an honored guest at the association's annual convention. He was so filled with excitement that for three nights he could barely sleep. Alexander's father calls him the King of Carwashes.

Then there was Chad. His passion was garden sprinklers. Everywhere he went as a child and teen, he would search the ground for pop-up sprinklers. At a park crowded for holiday fireworks, Chad would keep his eyes to the ground, searching out the sprinkler heads. When he found one, he would pull it up to identify the maker. At age eight he could tell a Toro from an Orbit from a Rain Bird. When he drew pictures in art class, along with the animals and trees he always included a sprinkler head popping up from the ground and shooting a spray of water into the air.

What inspired his fondness for garden sprinklers? Perhaps it started with a sensory experience: perhaps Chad was intrigued by the sight and sound of sprinklers popping out of the ground, then mysteriously disappearing, or the gentle sensations of water sprinkling the grass. Over time his interest morphed into a preoccupation. In unfamiliar surroundings he found it difficult to focus on anything else until he surveyed the area and found the sprinklers. And while it certainly wasn't what was occupying the attention of other children his age, his parents appreciated that their son had found something that brought him joy. Other dads took their kids to baseball games or fishing. Chad's dad surfed eBay to purchase secondhand sprinkler heads. Chad would give them names and toted them to school in his backpack. His parents drew smiley faces on the sprinkler heads. Sometimes Chad took them to bed with him at night like stuffed animals.

These deep interests can help children stay more engaged and attentive. They can be used to motivate learning and to enable participation in situations that might otherwise be difficult. That was true for Ken, a teenager with autism. From a young age Ken was fascinated with drawing—not so much artistically but simply focusing on drawing lines on paper. Over time he became interested in solving mazes, staring intently at a page while using a pen or pencil to make his way through the labyrinth. The appeal for Ken wasn't just drawing lines; it was solving problems. Each maze offered a sense of logic and order, a beginning and an end.

Wherever the family went, Ken would bring his maze books. Though he communicated very little in speech—he was learning to use a speech-generating device—his parents always brought him to meetings of his educational team, as they knew he could understand more than he could say. Merely sitting and listening to a meeting would have proved challenging, but Ken's stack of maze books helped him to stay in the room. While he did his mazes, he was engaged in the meeting, looking on intently when he was interested in the conversation, turning his attention back to his maze when he wasn't. With this strategy Ken was able to stay focused and well regulated by shifting his attention away from the more demanding task of following the conversation to an activity with which he felt more competent.

Many people with autism find it helpful to bring a toy or other item or an activity related to an enthusiasm to settings that may pose difficulties, such as restaurants, family events, or larger group activities at school. Almost any enthusiasm can help in this manner. Five-year-old Vinny's interest was Oreck vacuum cleaners. When Vinny was feeling overwhelmed at school, he would often ask to go to the bathroom, whether or not he needed to. There he would take refuge in a stall, sometimes refusing to come back to class. His mother devised a unique strategy to use his interest as a way to provide a break when he needed one, especially from larger group activities. She collected Oreck catalogues, cut out pictures of vacuum cleaners, and organized them in a book she titled "Vinny's Happy Book." When he needed a break from large-group classroom activities, he could ask for the Happy Book and sit in a corner on a beanbag chair for a few minutes, examining photos of uprights and canisters, and refueling before he rejoined his classmates.

Some enthusiasms come and go as passing phases, and others last decades. Specific deep interests may have more obvious connections to future hobbies. Matt was passionate about everything related to time. When he was a young child and I visited his classroom as a school consultant, he would rush up to me and grab my arm to see my wristwatch. "Dr. Barry," he would say, without looking at me, "it's nine-fifteen in the morning!"

It was his entrée to a social connection. One December morning when he was just over five years old he was filled with excitement as he told me his latest discovery: "Dr. Barry, do you know what happens after eleven-fifty-nine p.m. on December thirty-first?"

"What?" I asked.

His body tensed as he raised himself up on tiptoe, hands flapping like wings on a bird. "The big ball comes down!" he said, his face lighting up with joy. "And it becomes the *next year*!" That was his enthusiasm, his way of having a conversation, of sharing what he knew and cared about. Years later, as a young adult, Matt remained enthusiastic about clocks and time, even preferring sports with a time element (such as hockey) over those without (such as baseball).

Nine-year-old Danny's enthusiasm was spices used in cooking. As a young boy he often watched his mother working in the kitchen. Without any kind of formal introduction, he took an interest in the seasonings she used. He made a habit of organizing the spices in alphabetical order and later took up watching cooking shows on TV and searching food websites. He became an expert in regional variations of barbecue, reeling off the differences among the styles from Texas, Kentucky, Louisiana, and North Carolina. His parents couldn't identify what first piqued his interest in these topics or why they appealed to him, but clearly he found them fulfilling. His mother imagined it might lead Danny to attend a college for culinary arts and become a chef. Far from wanting to redirect him, his parents took great pride in Danny's expertise and found his enthusiasm infectious.

That's how I felt when I first met Brandon. I was visiting the classroom in a district I advised when one of the therapists introduced me to an adorable and wonderfully articulate four-year-old who immediately told me his family had just relocated to the town.

"What state are you from?" he asked immediately.

I told him I lived in Rhode Island.

"Providence, Rhode Island?" he asked.

Just outside Providence, I told him.

"Providence is kind of a small city," he said. "Do you like big cities?"

I told him I did, that I had grown up in New York City. Brandon's eyes lit up.

"You grew up in New York *City*?" he asked. "My family likes to visit New York City and I *love* New York City. We stay at the Marriott Marquis in Times Square. We always stay on the sixteenth floor because the sixteenth floor has the best views of all the signs in Times Square." He went on to tell me the numbers of the various rooms they had stayed in on recent visits and which ones had the best views.

I asked what he liked to look at from the hotel room windows. As he answered, he got a distant look, as if he were running a video of the scene in his mind. "There was a billboard for Nike with a picture of Kobe Bryant over there," he began, pointing at the classroom wall, then continued to describe the entire panorama in his mind's eye.

Using Interests to Build Connections

When a child fixates on a topic, the way Brandon did on New York, and we join with the child, we can make the enthusiasm the basis for building relationships and trust. One significant reason many children focus on a particular topic is that it gives them a safe place to start a conversation. Even the most obscure, out-of-context, and seemingly irrelevant question ("What's your favorite dog breed?" "What kind of refrigerator do you have?") can be a strategy to connect. Whenever Brandon saw me, he seized the chance to talk to me about New York: "Did you live in Manhattan, or one of the other four boroughs? Brooklyn? Which part?"

That wasn't the end of the conversation, just the beginning. Often an enthusiasm offers the hook to engage a child, the lure to bring him into an activity or a conversation. Once he is engaged, we can gradually change or expand the subject and test his flexibility and willingness. Of course how much is possible greatly depends on the child's level of development. But with creativity, parents and teachers can use the child's passion for a topic to motivate him to become more engaged socially and to solve problems.

Matt, for example, was enrolled in a mainstream kindergarten class, but his teacher questioned whether he belonged there. One issue: he had trouble staying focused in group activities. He would participate in the class's morning meeting solely by chanting the days of the week when asked, but then tuned out the rest of the discussion, apparently lost in his thoughts.

Matt's mother knew what her five-year-old *did* pay attention to: Winnie the Pooh. Matt loved the Disney movie and talked endlessly about its characters. His mother brought the teacher a few packs of stickers with various Pooh characters. "If you can find a way to incorporate these into morning time," she said "maybe Matt will be more engaged."

The teacher introduced the stickers at the morning circle, assigning a character to each day of the week. Monday was Tigger day, Tuesday Roo day, Wednesday Eeyore day. That was enough to engage Matt far more than previously, and the other children in the class were happy to join him in using the character names for the days of the week.

Instead of considering Matt's fixation a detrimental factor that separated him from his peers, the teacher successfully used it as a way to connect him with his classmates and with the material she was teaching (days of the week, months of the year). He became more willing to participate with his peers than ever before and was less distracted because she provided a way to engage Matt so that he could continue to progress.

The same kind of growth and development can occur when families find ways to acknowledge and honor a child's particular interest and integrate it into family routines. I saw this years ago when a father brought me to meet his teenage son, Hakeem, a student at an international school in Kuwait, to offer advice about both his school and home life. Though the boy had many of the challenges common to autism, it was clear from observing him that he had far more flexibility and resilience than many such children. I soon learned that was largely thanks to his parents' very open approach to his enthusiasms.

When I visited their home, the first thing they shared with me was Hakeem's fascination with trains and, in particular, train schedules. They explained that they encouraged him to take an active role in planning the family's annual August vacation to Europe. The parents gave the boy a voice in choosing destinations, then they spent months researching the particulars, assembling maps, guide books, and all of the information necessary for the planning. Once the family had determined the general shape of the trip, it was up to Hakeem to figure out the particulars: which trains they would take, how many days they would stay in a city, when they would move on to the next destination.

They showed me scrapbooks they had assembled for each trip, with photographs and clippings from brochures and maps. Each section of the book started with a train schedule—clearly emblematic of how the family celebrated Hakeem's interests. By acknowledging and honoring their son's focus on train schedules, they had helped him to become more engaged with his family and the world, with a healthy sense of self. Not only did Hakeem have a remarkable breadth of knowledge of European cities and landmarks, but he felt like a valued member of his family.

Enthusiasms Focused on People

Sometimes the child's focus isn't a topic but a person. Like many children, kids with autism often become fascinated with certain movie stars, musicians, or athletes. Sometimes a child becomes focused on a peer, in the way teenagers develop romantic crushes on each other. The difference is that children with autism often don't intuitively understand the boundaries others perceive, so these enthusiasms can become awkward. A child with autism might not understand that kids don't generally announce their strong feelings for another person to that person or to anyone else. Those situations can be troubling, but an intense interest in a peer is also an opportunity for a teacher or parent to teach about friendships and social boundaries.

Tyler was a kindergartner with Asperger's syndrome and ADHD whose fixation was the principal of his elementary school. I had first seen Tyler in his preschool (where I was a consultant), when he was an energetic youngster who would roll on the classroom floor instead of joining his classmates in circle time. Blond and compact, bright and verbal, in preschool Tyler was primarily focused on robots and Lego.

Just a few weeks into kindergarten, he developed his fascination with Ms. Anderson, the principal. Whenever he saw her, he would ask a rapid-fire series of questions: Where do you sit? What do you do? What's your job? Do you have kids? She reciprocated, taking a special interest in Tyler, and invited him to visit her office. Seeing an opportunity to use his fixation as a motivator, she offered him a deal: If he could continue to make appropriate choices for a month, then she would let him join her as principal for a day. For Tyler that meant if he joined circle time rather than crawling under a desk, if he asked for help rather than getting upset, if he could improve in a few other areas, he would earn this special privilege.

That got Tyler's attention, and he immediately fell into line. With his teacher he reviewed his progress daily. He practiced asking for help or a break when needed, a strategy that helped him stay well regulated emotionally. He became more attentive in the classroom; he did his best to participate appropriately. By the end of the month he had earned his special day. The school documented the experience in a photo album: Tyler dressed in a suit and tie, shadowed the principal on her rounds and in meetings, and sat at a small desk in the corner of her office. He was delighted, felt like an important part of the school, and had learned about his own ability to control his behavior in pursuit of something important to him.

When Enthusiasms Cause Trouble

There are times when the object of a child's attention is genuinely problematic. Gabriel's particular interest was in women's ankles. In another person that might have been considered a fetish, but for this teenager it was merely an object of fascination that he wanted to explore—close up. Occasionally in a mall or on the street, when he spotted a woman in high heels with bare ankles, Gabriel, who was over six feet tall, would squat down, trying to touch her ankles. Those who knew him understood he was a sweet, gentle soul, but certainly the women whose ankles got his attention didn't know how to respond. Innocent as his motivation was, his behavior could easily have been interpreted as lewd, threatening, or even dangerous.

In such situations it is important to help the individual understand the rules and expectations for acceptable behavior, but to do so at a level that is appropriate for that person's abilities. For a person with a high level of understanding, it might be helpful to create a list of acceptable or expected behaviors in social situations and discuss how the other person might perceive the situation. For children or those with more limited understanding, it's important to state rules in a more straightforward manner, with an emphasis on what they should do rather than what they shouldn't do. For those at all levels of ability, it's useful to employ visual supports—such as photographs, drawings, or even videos—rather than rely on talking. The long-term goal is to help individuals develop a sense of the appropriate responses in different social situations and to be able to inhibit impulsive behavior, even if it's related to a passion or interest.

Even when the focus of a child's fixation is more acceptable, enthusiasms can pose challenges. The most common complaint I hear from parents is that their child talks excessively about a topic—dinosaurs, trains, cartoons, elevators—and won't stop. Even if parents understand and respect their child's particular interest, they still might feel frustration that the child doesn't seem to understand that it's not appropriate to talk about it nonstop, particularly when peers or adults indicate their displeasure or just stop listening.

We all have preferred topics, but we need to learn when we've shared too much. When I meet another New York Yankees fan, we might spend an hour reliving the highlights of last night's game. But someone else might be bored after a minute or two and wondering why I won't stop. If I'm fluent in reading social cues, I can tell the difference and change my behavior. But if I have trouble understanding those subtle indicators, I might continue with the pitch-by-pitch details of the ninth inning while you're desperately trying to escape.

Teaching "Time and Place"

In helping a child or teen understand this, it's useful to use what I call a "time and place" strategy: sometimes other people might want to hear about his particular interest, but other times they're less interested. A parent might explain to the child that there's nothing wrong with his enthusiasm for train schedules or breakfast cereals, but it's not what he should be talking about during his math lesson or dental appointment. ("We're here eating brunch with our relatives, so everybody wants to hear about how you're doing in school. But at one o'clock, we can hear about the train schedule. Okay?") It's an opportunity to deepen the child's social understanding. Together the parent and child can devise a list of places and times when it's appropriate to focus on an interest, those when it's not, and with whom it's okay to converse about them.

The truth is that doesn't always work. Some children and teens aren't yet developmentally at a place where they can monitor themselves and exert self-control, consider somebody else's perspective, or repress their desire to share information. Parents can feel desperate to find a way to get the child to control the impulse to focus too much on a topic. They worry that it accentuates how different the child appears to peers, and family members might be tired of hearing about the same themes over and over again. Many times I have heard the most patient of parents finally say, "We just need him to stop."

The problem with that response is that it focuses on the *behavior* without asking what is *motivating* it. It's essential to ask questions: Are there times the child focuses on this topic more than other times? Do you see patterns? Could it be when the child feels stress? What might be causing the stress? How can you alleviate the pressure and anxiety? Is the child using this kind of talk to calm himself down? If it works for him, is it really a priority to eliminate this kind of talk? Is the child aware of his own behavior? How can we make him more aware?

In other words, it's not as simple as just stopping the child's behavior. As always, the first step is asking what is underlying the behavior.

It's also important to remember that if a child consistently opens a conversation by talking about his own interest, that's often because it's a comfortable place to start. For a person with autism, social interactions can provoke anxiety and confusion because they have no fixed structure and one can't always predict what another person will say. So a person with autism will try to create predictability by limiting the conversation to an area in which he has mastery.

When a child or teenager needs help developing or refining conversational skills, social skills groups can provide help, offering a safe and supportive space in which to gain awareness of how to negotiate a conversation and show interest in others. Instead of reprimanding a child and damaging her self-esteem, it's preferable to offer more positive options, such as activities or games that provide opportunities to practice conversational skills or role-playing everyday interactions.

Building on Strengths

Though they come with challenges, enthusiasms often represent the greatest potential for people with autism. What begins as a strong interest or passion can become a way to connect with others with similar interests, a lifelong hobby, or, in many cases, a career. Remember Michael, the child who had a passion for music and the uncanny ability to hear a song for the first time and then sit down and pluck it out on the piano? Now in his forties and living semi-independently, he plays organ at his church and sings in a choir.

When Matt Savage was young, he was so hypersensitive to sound that if his mother played piano, he would cover his ears and run away screaming. With therapy he overcame that challenge and began displaying exceptional musical ability. When I met Matt he was only eleven, and already jazz legends such as Dave Brubeck and Chick Corea were hailing his remarkable piano talent. Now in his twenties, Matt has become an internationally known jazz pianist, composer, and recording artist with an infectious personality. He also finds time to teach music to children with autism.

When Justin Canha (see chapter 10) was a toddler, he was not yet speaking but loved watching animated movies and cartoons and showed an early talent for drawing. Now, as a young adult, he displays his work in New York galleries, has become a professional storyboard artist, and teaches art to young children.

One of my favorite enthusiasm stories is of Stanford James, a young man with autism who was raised by a determined single mother in the housing projects of Chicago. From the time he was young, he had a passion for trains and loved to stand at the window of his grandmother's apartment, watching the elevated trains pass by.

"I don't know what the trains did for him," his mother, Dorothy, told a reporter for the *Chicago Tribune*.* "But they sure got him."

Though she was young and poor and knew little about autism, Dorothy fought for her son. She encouraged Stanford's interest and watched him use his remarkable ability to master the routes and schedules of Chicago's extensive transportation system, committing much of it to memory. In his early twenties he landed a job with Chicago's Regional Transit Authority, helping customers find the routes and schedules to match their needs.

Not only was he a natural for the job, but he showed such dedication, focus, and responsibility that the RTA named him Employee of the Year. "He comes to work no matter the weather and he's polite all the time," his supervisor told the newspaper. "He's thorough, and that's what the customers want."

More important, Stanford felt like an important and valued member of his community. When he was young, his mother wondered what would become of him. After he helps a customer, Stanford says, "I congratulate myself in my imagination, saying, 'Stanford, you are the best man who can do everything!' " Stanford is a testament to where following an enthusiasm can lead.

---

* "The Man with the Map in His Head," *Chicago Tribune*, June 11, 2000.

CHAPTER 4

Trust, Fear, and Control

After just a few minutes with Derek, I could tell that something was bothering him, but I wasn't sure precisely what it was.*

For years I had visited Derek a few times annually at his parents' request to offer guidance and advice. I would observe him at school and at home, then meet with his parents and the school team. My fall visit had always been in September, a few weeks into the school year. But the year he turned eight, I arrived a few weeks later on the calendar. In the past Derek had always greeted me enthusiastically—or at least with a low-key smile. This time, though, he seemed anxious and disconnected from the moment I arrived, repeatedly resisting my attempts to engage him. After a while I asked him why. "Is something wrong?" I asked. "You seem a little uncomfortable with me."

He did not hesitate to reply. "Dr. Barry, you always first come in September," he said. "Why are you here in October?"

It was only two weeks later than he typically saw me, but it was

---

*Some of the ideas and insights in this chapter first appeared in "The Primacy of Trust," a two-part article I coauthored with Michael John Carley, in *Autism Spectrum Quarterly* in 2009.

a different month on the calendar, and in his mind that made a big difference. Without discussing it, Derek had internalized the rhythm of my periodic visits. Since nobody realized that, no one had made the effort to explain to him that I would be coming later than in the past. So it was left to Derek to figure out why this violation had occurred in the order of his universe.

Without knowing it, I had breached his trust. Derek had developed an understanding of how things should happen based on how they had always happened, or at least how he remembered them. Now he had reason to wonder whether he could rely on me—or on the world he thought he had understood.

A Disability of Trust

Derek's reaction highlights a central challenge of autism: for the vast majority of people on the spectrum, autism can be best understood as a disability of trust. Because of their neurological challenges, people with autism face tremendous obstacles of three kinds: trusting their body, trusting the world around them, and—most challenging of all—trusting other people.

Daniel Tammet, the author of *Born on a Blue Day*, is known for feats of memory such as recalling more than twenty-two thousand digits of pi and learning a language in a week. Interviewed on *60 Minutes* in 2007, he described how difficult it had been for him as a child to fit in socially. He felt uncomfortable among other children, whose behavior he found difficult to predict. He was baffled by the nuances of social interactions. So he found solace in math. "Numbers were my friends and they never changed," he said. "They were reliable. I could trust them."

My friend Michael John Carley, an adult with Asperger's who is a leader in the self-advocacy movement for people with autism, once put it this way: "The opposite of anxiety isn't calm, it's trust."

That insight helps to explain much of what makes all of us anxious, not just those on the spectrum, and why we react with fear and often seek ways to control our lives, surroundings, and relationships. These tendencies are even more pronounced in people with autism.

Trust in the Body

If a typical person wakes up with a common cold, it's a minor inconvenience. Since you've most likely come down with a cold before, you have the perspective and experience to understand that your cough and runny nose are likely to last just a few days before you begin feeling like yourself again. But when a person with autism experiences those same physical symptoms, she might react with anxiety and fear: What's happening to me? Why can't I breathe normally? Will this last forever?

That response isn't so different from the way most of us react to more severe illness. Some years ago I developed severe carpal tunnel syndrome. Years of splitting wood to heat our home had taken its toll. I had played drums since childhood, but now when I played, my hands went numb and I couldn't grip the drumsticks. When I tried to hold up a newspaper to read, needles of pain shot through my fingers. My arms and wrists didn't feel or act the way I had always relied on them to. Suddenly I *couldn't trust my body*. I felt upset and worried about the future course of my condition. Fortunately successful surgery on both wrists alleviated the symptoms. The tingling was gone; the numbness abated. I could trust my hands and play drums again.

Cancer patients often experience similar challenges. In some ways cancer can be thought of as one's body attacking itself. Much of the stress of the disease comes from the physical changes that occur, the uncertainty of the future course, and that same question: Will I ever be able to trust my body again?

A large proportion of people with autism cope with motor and movement disturbances, often including involuntary movement in various parts of their body. Martin expressed to his mother his bewilderment at the way his jaw would move, his arms would thrust out, and the other unpredictable tics he experienced, particularly when he felt dysregulated. "Am I going crazy?" he asked.

"What makes you think that?" she replied.

Martin's answer: "My body does things I can't control."

Colin, a third-grader with Asperger's, once showed me two elaborately detailed diagrams he had created: a map of his own brain and another he labeled a "normal" brain. The normal brain was a tidy grid, with symmetrical rows and columns drawn across the whole cerebral cortex—an image of orderliness and organization. The map of Colin's brain was a frenetic, chaotic mess, divided into uneven sections of various shapes and sizes. It included a video theater, which he described as the source of the virtual movies that constantly preoccupied him. He labeled his spinal cord the source of "cramps" he suffered. The largest section of the brain he labeled "Crazy Part," the part he blamed when he couldn't control his own thoughts or behavior.

Clearly Colin was trying to express that he couldn't trust his own brain.

Trust in the World

Even if you can trust your own body, it's hard to trust the world surrounding us. I often ask parents of young children with autism, "What does your child find most upsetting?" Often the source of frustration is a mechanical plaything that stops functioning as it once did. The batteries might run out on a toy car, or a DVD player malfunctions, triggering a full-blown meltdown. Parents often find this baffling: the reaction seems far out of proportion to the problem. But take the child's perspective: his sense of order—of how things work—has been violated. He's come up against a world he can't trust.

Children manifest that experience in more subtle ways as well. Sharon noticed that her six-year-old's behavior took a marked turn for the worse in a particular week in the fall, though the change seemed unrelated to anything going on at home or in school. Dmitri would become so upset that he was practically inconsolable, and he wouldn't eat dinner. Then she identified the trigger: The change happened just after the switch from Daylight Savings Time to Standard Time. Dmitri's routine had been undermined. For months the family had eaten dinner when it was still light outside. Now, suddenly, he was expected to eat when it was dark. "It's like he can't trust what a day is," Sharon said, "or when the meal is supposed to be." As he saw it, his parents had changed the rules without any warning. Is it any wonder he was upset? For similar reasons, many parents dread school vacations—the very time other families eagerly anticipate—because the change in routine so upsets their children with autism.

Matthew, fifteen, experienced a different sort of breach of trust in his physical surroundings. When I visited his home, he excitedly told me that the family had recently visited New York City.

"How did you enjoy the trip?" I asked.

"It was fine," he said, "except we got delayed for four minutes near Exit 87 on Route 95, and then we got delayed for three minutes near Exit 54," and on and on, listing every delay and detour the family had encountered, until his mother was able to stop him. What Matthew remembered about the three-day trip was the unexpected, the times things didn't happen the way they were supposed to—the times he discovered that he couldn't trust the world.

When I was a counselor at a summer camp serving children with developmental disabilities, one of my favorite campers was Dennis, a large, energetic twelve-year-old with autism who had curly hair and rosy cheeks. One Monday morning our group set out by bus to an amusement park. Dennis loved roller coasters and Ferris wheels, and he had fixated on talking about this field trip for days. As our bus arrived at the park, though, I was chagrined to see that the parking lot was empty. The driver stepped on the brakes and, without bothering to consult with me, blurted out the bad news: "Sorry kids. The park is closed!"

Dennis's response was explosive. He rushed over to me screaming, "No, no, *no*!" His gaze averted upward and away, he suddenly began pounding on me with his fists. As I tried to fend him off—and at the same time keep us both safe—he ripped my shirt off and in his flailing frenzy he dug his nails into my arms and chest, causing deep scratches. It was heartbreaking and frightening to see this normally delightful child in this out-of-control state.

With help I was able to move Dennis to a seat, where he buried his head in a pillow and rocked, obviously perplexed about what had just happened. When well regulated, he was a happy and sweet boy who brought smiles to everyone around him. But when he experienced heightened anxiety, fear, or confusion, he often went after the people to whom he felt closest. Why? In this instance, it was because the world had breached his trust. It was as if he had been pounded with a sledgehammer. We had made a promise about that day, and we had disappointed him—suddenly and abruptly.

Fortunately I was able to redeem the situation with what seemed like divine intervention. Once Dennis was safe and I had gathered myself, I stood up and explained that the park was closed. Then words mysteriously came to me and I heard myself say, "But we're going to go on a magical mystery tour!" (This was in 1970, just a couple of years after the Beatles album came out.) Dennis immediately looked up, showed interest, then repeated, "Magical mystery tour?," then "Magical mystery tour! Magical mystery tour!"

We counselors scurried to hatch a new plan. I quietly asked the driver if there were any other destinations nearby, and we patched together a morning stop at a small zoo, followed by miniature golf. When we shared the plan with the children, Dennis adjusted, and he ended up enjoying the day—and we promised to reschedule the amusement park trip.

I understood that Dennis's outburst was completely beyond his control, and even his awareness. The unexpected event triggered an extreme reaction in him because of his neurologically based disability. But I never forgot the lessons from that day: that some children with autism can go from zero to sixty without warning; that when severely dysregulated they may take out their frustration and confusion on the people they trust most; and that breaches of trust come in many forms.

Trust in People

The most significant trust-related challenge for people with autism is trusting other people. Most of us are neurologically hardwired with the ability to predict the behavior of others—to read body language intuitively and make subconscious judgments based on how relaxed a person's body is, on how a person looks at other people, or by the social context. But that is often more difficult for people with autism. Ros Blackburn explains that she lives every day trying to understand people's intentions when they approach her. "Because I find it so difficult to predict the behavior of other people," Ros explains, "what they do often comes across as very sudden and threatening to me."

Ros's insight helps explain the defensive reaction I saw in Christopher. A teenager, he communicated mostly with a picture communication system or by echoing phrases he had picked up or by uttering a single word at a time. If a peer or teacher in the high school hallway suddenly said, "Hi, Chris!," he would instinctively recoil, ducking and looking startled, as if the person had jumped out and pulled a knife on him.

Not knowing whom to trust or what a person might do next means living in a constant state of vigilance, like the soldiers who work on bomb-disposal teams. Imagine going through life in that heightened, hypervigilant state of alert, wary of every person, every object. If your neurological system is constantly on heightened alert, how can you pay attention to anything else? It's exhausting. It becomes difficult to function. All of your energy is focused on merely keeping your defenses up.

Some people with autism have almost the opposite challenge. These individuals may move and react more slowly than others and appear less alert. Their feelings are often more difficult to read because their facial expressions do not vary much. Being in a low state of arousal is like walking around in a nonfocused, drowsy condition. Professionals refer to these individuals as having a "low arousal bias." Because they display fewer problem behaviors, they appear to be better regulated and are often thought of as well-behaved. Does that mean they don't experience anxiety? Not necessarily. When they feel dysregulated, these individuals tend to internalize their anxiety rather than directing their behavior outward. The anxious feelings build over time, with few observable, or only very subtle, signs of anxiety or dysregulation, so outbursts or meltdowns can be difficult to predict.

The Role of Fear

We all face situations in which we feel uncertain or threatened. When we sense danger or risk, our natural reaction is to feel fear—and to fight or flee. People with autism have a similar innate response, but the reaction threshold is far lower, especially for those with hyperreactive profiles. The source of anxiety doesn't have to be a lion or a fire or a man with a gun. When trust is broken, when the order a person depends on is breached, that triggers fear.

Temple Grandin is probably the world's best-known person with autism. A professor of animal science, she is an accomplished speaker who conveys self-confidence and poise. But she often describes her emotional life this way: "My primary emotion is, and always has been, fear." Most of her fears are rooted in her sensory sensitivities. While thunder has little effect on her, for instance, the high-pitched alarm of a truck backing up can make her heart race.

That fear is often what I observe in my first encounters with children who have autism; it is in their eyes and in their body language. When they face situations in which they feel insecure, when they're exposed to the sensory overload of a crowded, bustling school cafeteria or a noisy gymnasium, I see fear.

I saw that look in the eyes of Jeremy, a second-grader who one spring began displaying extreme anxiety around recess. When it was time for his class to go out to the play yard, he was deeply resistant, protesting and refusing to go at just the time the other children were excited and happy for the break.

The reason eventually became clear: The shrubbery bordering the playground attracted butterflies, and Jeremy was terrified of them. Why would a child be afraid of butterflies, creatures most children find beautiful and fascinating? They don't bite or sting or even make a sound. What scared Jeremy was that they were out of his control: he couldn't predict what they would do. Maybe he had once had a butterfly land on his arm or face, frightening him, and he hadn't been able to shoo it away. He didn't understand butterflies. They seemed to emerge from nowhere and surprise him. At Jeremy's developmental stage, he wasn't able to reason through and consider that even if a butterfly landed on his nose, it wouldn't hurt him. He had very limited communication skills, so a stranger might conclude that he was irrational and deeply disturbed. But his behavior made sense: on a very primal level, he was trying to stay safe.

To help him, I suggested that his teacher give Jeremy a sense of control by spending time with pretend, paper butterflies, allowing them to "fly" close and then having Jeremy wave them off, saying, "Bye-bye butterflies!" He also spent time looking through books about butterflies to understand that they are harmless. This reframing helped him overcome his anxiety.

Lily had her own unique fear: she was afraid of statues. When she was seven, her class was strolling in a park at lunchtime when she spotted a sculpture of a man on a horse. A look of terror crossed her face. Why would a child be afraid of a bronze figure that doesn't move? Because it defied logic. It *looked* like a person, and it *looked* like a horse, but the rule she knew and understood was that people and animals move. The statue in the park shattered Lily's conception of what people are and what animals are, so she felt unsettled, anxious, and afraid. I have seen similar reactions when children with autism spot street fair performers acting like statues or robots—living things behaving as if they're not.

Helping Kids Overcome Fear

When that kind of fear grips a child with autism, it can be difficult to overcome. Ned, a fifth-grader at a New York City school, grew terrified when his teacher announced an upcoming field trip on the Staten Island Ferry. The idea of it seemed to capture the imagination of his classmates. Filled with excitement, one girl asked about the waves they might encounter out on the water. A boy wanted to know if they might see any whales from the ferry. Ned fixated on something else: a boat accident that he'd heard about on the news. Then he mentioned another disaster: the sinking of the *Titanic*. Those associations meant that, for him, the Staten Island Ferry was out of the question. He stubbornly refused even to consider joining his class on the trip.

As the date of the field trip neared, Ned became increasingly preoccupied with the *Titanic*. He wanted to look at photographs of the disaster and the movie and repeatedly asked his teachers and parents what it would be like to be at the bottom of the ocean, with fish swimming all around. Clearly it would be difficult to get him to participate in the field trip.

When I met with his teachers and parents, who had sought my advice, we discussed the challenge: Ned didn't feel safe. We agreed that the priority should be to reassure him, to provide information to make him confident that he would be safe. Together we explained to him that on the ferry he would be protected by a lifejacket, and lifeboats would be available in case of a problem. He was listening calmly, until he heard the word *problem*. Then he suddenly blurted out, "What kind of *PROBLEM*!?," becoming more anxious and nervous rather than less.

To try to calm him down and encourage him, we focused on two solutions: First, we tried to create positive emotion by describing the excitement of boarding the ferry with his friends, spotting the colorful flags he might see in Battery Park, and some of the other highlights he would experience. Second, I introduced the concept of courage. "Being brave means that you try to do something even though it's scary," I said, "and that you trust the people you are with."

What we didn't do was force him to go. Ned was frightened. His fear was causing his dysregulation. Imposing the field trip on him against his will would only have served to make things worse. It would have also broken the trust he felt in the adults around him. It was essential that Ned feel that going on the trip was his choice. So after consulting with his parents, we told him that he had the option to be brave—to face his fears. But we also gave him the choice to stay home with his mother that day. We gave him until a few days before the trip to decide.

When the day arrived, he made his decision: "I'm going to be brave."

Ned went on the field trip and had a wonderful time with his classmates. When I saw him at our next appointment, a month later, he proudly told me, "Dr. Barry, I went on the ferry. I was a little scared when the boat rocked, but I was brave!" I could sense his pride—and so could his parents. He owned his success. After that, he frequently embraced the idea of being brave to help him face the sorts of challenging situations he would have avoided in the past.

Ned's anxiety is a reminder that what a typical child might consider a treat can instill fear in children with autism. I once helped plan a holiday party for a group of young children with autism. The idea was to create a special experience for children for whom it was impossible, or at least very difficult, to attend a typical holiday party.

We wanted parents to be able to relax and not worry about explaining their children's behavior. The teachers, parents, and volunteers who helped in the planning were careful to create a tranquil atmosphere with low stimulation, in which the children would be comfortable and happy. We brought in toys the children were familiar with, created visual supports to help them choose favorite activities, and integrated familiar rituals from the preschool program to make the children feel comfortable.

Everything was going beautifully—until Santa arrived. The volunteer who had offered to play St. Nick was a colleague of one of the fathers but apparently was not well acquainted with autism. After a sudden, loud knock on the door, he came bounding into the room in his bright red suit, shouting "Ho, ho, ho!" His abrupt appearance so startled the children that they scattered, some screaming or dropping to the floor, others fleeing to the corners of the room, to their parents, or into the coat closet. Santa was a sensory tsunami, and against the background of an event that was already unfamiliar and full of excitement, they couldn't handle it. No matter how much you prepare, there are always surprises. We did our best to manage the situation and help the children recover.

Children with autism have a range of responses when unexpected events trigger fear and anxiety: they flee; they panic; sometimes they become still, like deer in the headlights. Fainting goats are a breed with *myotonia congenita*, a condition that causes their leg muscles to become tense when they feel excited or threatened; they freeze in place and fall to the ground. That's similar to what happens to many children with autism. When they feel overwhelmed, anxious, or frightened, they abruptly stop in place. Sometimes they close their eyes and cover their ears, trying to shut out the world.

Such reactions often make parents and others close to these children wonder about an apparent irony: Why do these children often seem so frightened of ordinary, harmless things like butterflies and statues, when they're *not* afraid of so many other things they *should* be afraid of? Why will a boy who's terrified of statues dart into traffic or climb precariously high on the roof or ride a roller coaster seemingly without fear?

It's important to understand that children who seem fearless in such situations truly are; that is, they don't feel fear. When a six-year-old with autism climbs onto a roof, she's not assessing the situation and then considering what the potential outcome might be. She acts instinctively: *Maybe I'll climb up there because then I can see things that I wouldn't be able to see otherwise.* She's not weighing the risk because she doesn't perceive it. She doesn't feel fear in her body, and putting herself in that position may actually provoke excitement or pleasure. Her brain isn't sending signals that warn that this could be dangerous, and her mind isn't predicting the potential dangerous consequence of her actions. She might feel frightened of a butterfly because she can't control it, but the prospect of falling twenty-five feet to the ground doesn't enter her thoughts. Focused on the sensation of the moment, she doesn't worry about possible harmful outcomes. To address these concerns, many programs for children with autism emphasize issues of safety and help children understand when situations may pose dangers or be harmful.

Control: A Natural Response to Fear and Anxiety

When our sense of trust is challenged and we feel frightened and anxious, our natural response is to try to exert control. Some autism professionals speak of control in negative terms. "Oh, she's being controlling again," they'll say, or "He's trying to control the conversation." But when you understand the underlying motivations, it becomes clear that many of these behaviors represent strategies to cope with anxiety or dysregulation. Some professionals work hard to seize control from children with autism, but when they do, they're not helping; they're causing *increased* dysregulation by interfering with the children's strategy to stay well-regulated.

Talking incessantly about a fixation—trains or dinosaurs or automobiles—is one way of exerting control (see chapter 3). A child might feel uncomfortable and anxious in social situations, unable to predict what another person might say or ask of him. But when he fills the silence with lengthy monologues about his area of interest, he feels that he has some control. Speaking wards off anxiety about the unknown.

While some children react to anxiety with excessive talking, others retreat into the protection of silence. Grace, eleven, had just transferred to a new school. She functioned capably, making her way through the school cafeteria, sitting with classmates, and playing games with a therapist. But she never spoke—and never smiled.

It wasn't that she was incapable of speaking. Grace had spoken at her previous school. But in the context of the new school, she had become silent, instead using gestures to make her needs known. In seven weeks, the staff reported, they had heard her whisper only a single word, on one occasion: "Cheese."

Her mother reported that Grace did talk at home—though much of her speaking was echoing—and could read aloud. In home videos her mother shared, Grace also readily smiled and laughed. The mother urged the staff not to pressure her daughter to speak, fearing that such efforts would increase her anxiety and do more damage than good. Observing as a consultant for the district, I agreed that it was more important to build trusting relationships with Grace, encouraging her active participation in activities and her communication (albeit nonverbal) rather than trying to force the girl to speak against her will.

Some professionals might have labeled Grace's behavior "controlling" or "withholding"—willfully and stubbornly refusing to speak. What I saw, though, was an alert, intelligent, and capable girl who was anxious about her new surroundings and did not yet know whom or what to trust. Not speaking was her way of coping, of exerting control and giving herself a chance to adjust. She was displaying a variation of selective (or elective) mutism, which is also sometimes seen in children without autism. It is not primarily a speech and language problem but rather a reflection of significant anxiety.

Over time the teachers and therapist working with her built trusting relationships with Grace. When she was comfortable and felt ready, she began to read aloud at school and eventually grew more willing to speak and interact playfully with her classmates—and smile and laugh. Trust had been established—and her mother's instinct not to force her proved correct.

How Children Exert Control

Some children try to gain a sense of control in invisible ways, creating rules in their head to make sense of the world, trying to make it behave according to their logic. One was a second-grader named Jose, who was involved in planning his eighth birthday party. But in considering the guest list, Jose decided he would invite only one group: the boys in his class. His parents and teachers suggested that it would be nice to include the girls too, as well as other children from school and other parts of his life. But Jose was insistent: only boys, and only those from his class. It wasn't that he didn't like other children. He showed great interest in a variety of children in his life, but for some reason he had narrowed the birthday list to one category.

During a monthly consult at his elementary school, I met with his mother, teachers, and one of the therapists who worked with him to discuss how best to help him approach the party. Many of the adults wondered aloud why Jose seemed so stuck and stubbornly insistent about who would be included. Was he being insensitive or exclusionary? I didn't think so. I suspected he simply felt overwhelmed. Jose had never planned an event like this, and it surely felt overwhelming to consider the entire universe of people in his life. His way of exerting some control was to create a rule, however random it seemed, that narrowed the overwhelming array of possibilities. That kept things simple and calmed his anxiety.

His parents wanted to encourage Jose to open the party to more children, but I knew we couldn't accomplish that by appealing to his logic with lengthy explanations or by imposing a rule that didn't make sense to him. We knew that Jose loved board games, so we created a game-like grid, with various categories of children he knew: cousins, classmates, baseball teammates, boys, girls, and more. The teacher and a therapist wrote down and told him the rules of the "birthday party game": choose at least one child for each box on the grid, a boy from his class, a girl from his class, a boy cousin, a girl cousin, and so on. Jose was happy to play. After he had chosen at least one child to fill each box, he could select other children to put in boxes as he desired. The categories made sense to him, the process felt logical and predictable, and the structure helped simplify what had been an intimidating set of decisions. In short, Jose felt a sense of control.

The need to feel control also helps to explain one of the more perplexing challenges related to autism: diet. Parents often wonder why their children with autism are such picky eaters. Some choose to eat only foods of a certain color (often beige) or won't eat the broccoli if it has touched the chicken on their plate. In a preschool program for children with autism where I worked, every child expressed a different preference in sandwiches, and most of the children scrutinized the contents of their sandwiches every day at lunchtime so they could be certain that no objectionable ingredients had infiltrated. One boy, Brian, didn't eat cheese, so if he found even the smallest trace his mom had snuck in, he would carefully remove it.

Often these preferences are related to sensory challenges. Children might be bothered by the texture of a particular food or its temperature, smell, or taste. Their choices of foods, how they are served, and the rituals surrounding eating are all ways of asserting control, efforts to make the world feel safer and more dependable.

In fact people with autism who don't speak often communicate loudly through their food preferences. That was true of Ron, a fifteen-year-old I met during my second summer camp job, when I was only nineteen. He was a large, barrel-chested teenager who didn't speak and rarely made a sound except when he was delighted or distressed. He wore black, unlaced army boots, even with shorts on hot August days. Ron maintained many small rituals to keep himself grounded. On the way from the cabin to the dining hall, he always lumbered off the fieldstone path and stopped to rub the bark of a particular maple tree and babble. He also loved to wiggle his fingers to the side of his eyes while enjoying his own happy, high-frequency sounds. I was taken by Ron's quiet dignity and his attention to the details of his daily routine.

On my first day on the job, a counselor who knew Ron instructed me *never, ever* to give Ron anything with mayonnaise. At lunch the next day, I was doing my best in the new routine, trying to distribute lunch quickly, and not thinking. I placed a bowl of potato salad in front of Ron, then turned around. Suddenly I felt something drop on my head. Ron had dumped the potato salad on me! In my haste it hadn't struck me that it contained mayonnaise. It wasn't a violent or aggressive act; he was reminding me of his preference, asserting his sense of control and personhood by refusing what I had given him. It was his way of saying "I'm Ron, and welcome to camp!"

Control in Relationships

That effort to achieve control in the face of a confusing or overwhelming world often extends to relationships as well. Miguel and William were kindergartners, both with autism, who seemed to gravitate toward each other and enjoy each other's company. But then their teacher expressed concern that Miguel had begun displaying disturbing behavior, following William around the classroom and playground so closely that he was practically clinging to him. "Sometimes he orders William to sit down next to him," she told me. "And now William is pushing him away—he doesn't want to be around him."

It's always worth asking "Why?" So when I met with the teacher in my role advising the school, I inquired whether anything had changed recently for Miguel—perhaps something unusual was going on at home. In fact something was: Miguel's father had broken his leg in a ski accident, landing him in the hospital for several days. Miguel faced a sudden interruption in his home routine. His father wasn't around, and his mother needed to leave him in the care of a babysitter when she visited the hospital. As he perceived it, things had changed dramatically, and the people he counted on every day weren't reliable. Was it any wonder that he was trying to exert control where he could, literally clinging to the relationship he thought he could count on?

Building Trust

Jonah's teachers reported that he was having great difficulty since starting middle school and was becoming increasingly disengaged from peers and educators. He had no real friends and often sat in class with his head down on the desk. He was a bright, articulate boy, who had experienced some success in elementary school. When he agreed to speak with me in my role consulting for the school, Jonah told me that he frequently felt sad. He didn't like his teachers, and the classmates who had once seemed to enjoy discussing his interests—dinosaurs, baseball, and video games—no longer did.

"Is there anyone in the school you can trust?" I asked.

"Not a chance!" he said.

I asked him what he thought it would take for him to make a new friend he could trust.

He answered, "A year of knowing someone, and at least four visits at my house and the other person's house."

Like many individuals on the spectrum, Jonah struggled with trust, which made it difficult to forge relationships. In my experience, developing trusting relationships is the key to helping people with autism cope with a world they perceive as confusing, unpredictable, and overwhelming. Many people with autism routinely experience misunderstandings: they misinterpret the actions of others, and their own behavior is regularly misunderstood by peers, educators, strangers, and even those close to them. The more often such misunderstanding occurs, the less the individual trusts people and the more likely he will shut down and disconnect, feeling *Why should I even try?* In times of change, such as moving from elementary to middle school, where schedules involve many changes and relationships become more complex, it's difficult to know what or whom to trust.

That is why it is essential for the other people in their lives—parents, educators, peers, practitioners—to make the extra effort to build trusting relationships. What I have learned from my years of experience, and from valued friends on the spectrum, is that rather than demanding or pressuring the person with autism to change, we must change first. When we change, the person with autism changes too.

Too often, though, the opposite happens: the people around a person with autism serve to increase anxiety and fear instead of alleviating stress.

By persistently giving the message "You must change," we are inadvertently communicating "You're not getting it right. You're screwing up." Thus we quash self-esteem and, ultimately, trust. The child cannot trust other people to offer understanding and support. The child cannot trust that the world is a safe place. As a result, anxiety mounts.

What can we do to help people with autism foster trusting relationships?

- **Acknowledge attempts to communicate.** One of the core elements of a trusting relationship is feeling that another person hears you. Even though people with autism often communicate without speaking or, when they do, use idiosyncratic speech, it's crucial for those around them to strive to listen, acknowledge, and, whenever possible, respond. This often requires great patience. And it can be the foundation for the kind of progress that cannot otherwise occur.

- **Practice shared control to build self-determination.** Think of a marriage: if one partner feels that the other is constantly trying to be the boss, directing the other partner, the victim is trust. Instead of imposing external control, it is essential to offer choices, to give the person with autism a voice in planning schedules, activities, and significant aspects of his life. When he feels respected and feels a sense of power over his own life, he feels more trusting of the people around him.

- **Acknowledge the individual's emotional state.** When people with autism are feeling emotionally dysregulated, they sometimes engage in behavior that appears inappropriate or disruptive. Instead of blaming them, we should pause and ask ourselves, "What must this person be feeling now? And what can I do to lessen the anxiety?" If we respond accordingly, we alleviate rather than exacerbate stress and, in turn, build trust.

- **Be dependable, reliable, and clear.** People with autism can find social situations confusing and can find it difficult to read the nuances of others' behavior in social encounters. We need to take the time and effort to explain social rules and expectations and why they exist. It is not enough merely to state the rules, especially for people who understand language at a high level. If rules don't make sense to an individual with autism, she may feel resentful and resist following them. However, when we take the time to discuss why rules exist and that we are all expected to follow them, we show greater respect. When we're clear about our intentions and we're consistent, we help to instill a sense of trust.

- **Celebrate successes.** Too often those who work with people with autism—as well as some parents—pay excessive attention to what is going wrong, what is challenging and difficult. It's hard to trust a person who consistently responds to you with negative comments and criticism or who is constantly trying to change or fix you. Life is challenging enough without being reminded what you can't do or what you do wrong. When we focus on successes, we build self-esteem and enhance the child's ability to trust us, others, and the world.

CHAPTER 5

Emotional Memory

I ONCE paid a visit to the school in Buffalo where, a dozen years earlier, I had worked as a graduate student with several children with autism. Walking the familiar halls, I thought of the children I had so enjoyed, wondering what had become of them. As I entered one of the classrooms equipped with a small kitchen, some of the teens and young adults were working together to make breakfast. One of the students—around eighteen, over six feet tall, bursting with energy—eyed me from across the room and seemed immediately to recognize me. He smiled, jumping on his toes, then rocking and speaking excitedly, as he looked toward me.

Noticing his reaction, the teacher approached me. "I know you used to work here," she said. "Did you know Bernie?"

In fact I had worked with a boy named Bernie there. At the time he had been just six or seven years old.

The teacher called to the young man across the room. "Bernie, come over here. I want you to meet somebody."

Smiling again, he came bounding toward me, full of excitement. Clearly he recognized me, but his greeting was anything but typical. "It's Barry!" he said, embracing me in a tight hug. "Now let's sit down so we can tie our shoes!"

The memories flooded back: I had worked in Bernie's classroom years earlier. One of my tasks had been to teach him, over many weeks, how to tie his shoelaces.

"Let's sit down so we can tie our shoes," he repeated. As he did, he seemed to be not so much recalling those days as reliving them. A huge grin lit up his face, and I could hear the excitement and joy in his voice as he repeated the sentence. "Now let's sit down so we can tie our shoes!"

Another story: Louis contacted me because he and his wife were baffled by a mysterious habit of their four-year-old son, Julio. Every time they stopped their car at a particular stop sign, the child, who didn't speak, went into a panic, suddenly screaming and then pounding on his own head with his fists. "It's so upsetting to us," Louis told me. "What could cause that?"

I was baffled myself. "Can you avoid that intersection?" I asked.

"No," Louis said. The crossing was along a route he and his wife regularly traveled, so it wouldn't be easy to stay away from it entirely.

I didn't have a ready answer, but I reminded him that parents often have to play the role of detective. I suggested that he keep his mind open to any possible connections.

Three days later Louis called again. "I think we figured it out," he said. He told me that when Julio had been much younger, the boy had experienced a dangerously high fever and become severely dehydrated. His parents had taken him to a medical clinic, where he had reacted with overwhelming fear and panic when staffers had to hold him down to insert an intravenous tube to replace his fluids.

Then Louis made the connection: at the intersection where Julio had experienced the screaming fits, there was a white stucco building that bore a resemblance to the clinic where Julio had been given the IV. Perhaps he had such powerful memories of that early experience that just seeing a similar building triggered the traumatic memory.

Just as Bernie had been transported back to the happy experience of learning to tie his shoes, Julio suddenly found himself recalling his moments of panic and sharp pain, as if he were experiencing a flashback. Seeing the white stucco building was enough to trigger a full-blown panic attack.

The Impact of Emotional Memory

These two stories—one of happy recollections, one of traumatic ones—demonstrate the powerful impact of *emotional memory* on people with autism. When we think about memory, we often think of facts—objective, neutral information about experiences we have had, people we have met or know about, or places. Beyond the facts, though, we have memories of our feelings about things. In our minds we subconsciously tag memories with certain emotions: happy, sad, painful, frustrating, joyous, stressful.

We all experience this to varying degrees. When I hear the song "Moon River," I become overwhelmed with melancholy. It was the favorite tune of my mother, who passed away when I was just twelve years old. I can hear her singing it to this day, more than fifty years later. A more common experience is attending a high school reunion and seeing a classmate whose name you can't recall, but you do recall strongly whether you liked or disliked him. Facts may be elusive, but the feelings associated with them remain powerfully embedded. We all function this way. If we have positive memories of people or places or activities, we're drawn to them. If we have negative, stress-filled memories, we avoid them, and just the thought of them can provoke uncomfortable feelings.

All of this is magnified in people with autism, for whom remembering is often a strength. Only a small proportion of people with autism possess the sorts of savant skills familiar from movies like *Rain Man*, but many parents and teachers marvel at their children's and students' remarkable feats of memory. Often these children have great memories for birthdays or geography or events in their own lives. What is less frequently discussed but important to understand in helping people with autism is the significant impact of *emotional* memories, both good and bad.

It's a perfect storm: a child has a powerful ability to remember the past, and because of neurological challenges, she also has accumulated more stressful experiences than typical peers because of the confusion, social misunderstandings, and sensory issues that come with autism. That's why a seemingly small association—seeing a white building or the face of an old teacher—can trigger what seems to be a disproportionately dramatic reaction.

How Memories Explain Behavior

When we find a person's behavior baffling or inexplicable, it's often because the person standing right in front of us is caught up in a memory so intense and vivid that it's as if the events are happening all over again. When Bernie delighted in our shared experience of tying shoes, he wasn't reminiscing about the distant past; the memories were so intense and overwhelming that it seemed as if he were there, in that place and time.

When a child has a sudden meltdown or goes into an extreme panic with no warning or apparent cause, one reason might be unrecognized negative emotional memories, like Julio's. Surely this little boy didn't *want* to be thrust back to those painful moments in the health clinic, but there he was: screaming with pain, beside himself, full of dread because of the sight of a white stucco house. There was likely no warning, no gradual increase in anxiety or fear so that a parent or teacher might step in and offer support before things boiled over. Emotional memory doesn't work that way. Julio couldn't perceive that his hospitalization was years earlier, under different circumstances, and that this was a different place and time. The visual image triggered the memory, and there was no easy way for him to turn it off.

The trigger can be something as simple as a name. Miguel was an eleven-year-old with autism who had only limited ability to communicate by speaking. But when his mother, Leslie, told him she was hiring a new aide named Jennifer to help him at school and at home, his reaction was quick and vocal: "No Jennifer!" he told her. "*No Jennifer*!"

He hadn't even met the woman, so his mother couldn't figure out why he was reacting so strongly. Sometime later Leslie realized what had triggered the outburst. When Miguel was a toddler, he'd had a babysitter named Jennifer. Leslie had been unhappy with her and eventually fired her. And Miguel later revealed that the sitter had been physically abusive; with great effort, he blurted out, "Jennifer hit Miguel!" Although the new Jennifer was a completely different person, that didn't matter. Miguel heard the name, it triggered an emotional memory, and he couldn't escape it.

In my work I routinely experience how a single word can prove traumatizing to a child with autism. When some children hear me referred to as "Dr. Barry," they become quite anxious—not because of anything I've done but rather because of the word *doctor*.

I once paid a home visit to Billy, an eight-year-old with autism. As I waited in the living room, his father called to him, "Dr. Barry is here!"

Instead of coming to greet me, the boy shouted in protest, "No needles! *No needles*! No Dr. Barry! No Dr. Barry!"

Billy hadn't met me before, but merely hearing the word *doctor* had triggered negative emotional memories of visits to his pediatrician's office. I tried to reassure him that everything would be okay, but he was so upset that he fled to a bathroom, locking the door behind him. Through the door we could hear him screaming, then whimpering, "I don't want a shot! I don't want a *shot*!"

His father tried to talk him down: "Honey, Dr. Barry isn't a needle doctor. He's a play doctor." It took about ten minutes for the boy to calm down enough to listen and take in the information. We could hear him repeat it to himself aloud: "Dr. Barry isn't a needle doctor! He's a *play* doctor!" Eventually he emerged from the bathroom and we spent a pleasant session together.

What if Billy had been a child who didn't speak—or if, instead of "No needles!," he had used words that had meaning to him but not to his father or me? His sudden, fearful response to my arrival would have been a mystery. Figuring it out would have taken more detective work.

The truth is that emotional memories don't require words at all. Naomi, a speech-language pathologist, could not get eight-year-old Max to come into her office at his school. She knew exactly why: for one of his early therapy sessions, she had gone to pick up Max from his classroom. It was a chilly winter day, and because the boy had certain sensory challenges, he had been in stocking feet. Together they made their way down the carpeted hallway—she walked, he shuffled—to the office, where she asked Max to open the door. When he reached for the knob—*zap!*—he was startled to receive a jolt of static electricity. Nothing dangerous, but still an unpleasant surprise.

For weeks after that, Max wouldn't come anywhere near her office. When he had to pass by in the hallway, he would press his body against the opposite wall. It was as if the doorknob had come alive and bitten him. It took her three months to help him overcome that negative emotional memory and come to her office for his therapy.

Why couldn't she reason with him? For children with autism, emotional memory responses are visceral and primal. Often the children lack the ability to reason through a situation, to remind themselves that just because something happened once doesn't mean it will happen again. Another child would probably be able to place the experience in context: *Oh, I got a shock. That's happened before, but it won't happen again, and even if it does it's not that bad.* He might even want to provoke the electric shock as part of exploring his world. But for a child with autism, a memory lodges itself in the mind and often can't be shaken.

That happened to Steven, who was making steady progress getting used to a new school one autumn until one unfortunate event: a fire drill happened at the very moment he was standing under the alarm bell. Steven had sensory challenges and was particularly sensitive to loud noises, so it took a number of weeks before he could enter the school building again without experiencing significant stress.

Anything Can Be a Trigger

As most parents of children with autism know, it's difficult to predict what might be a trigger. Often we say something with the best of intentions and unwittingly provoke an instinctive, powerful response. As part of a school visit to observe Scott, then seven, I watched him run laps in the gymnasium. At one point, as he ran past me, I instinctively smiled and said, "Good job, Scott!"

He paused in his tracks and glared at me, looking displeased. "No 'Good job'!" he said sternly. "Don't say 'Good job'!"

Was he just being defiant? Or asserting control in a distinctive way?

The next time he came around, I restrained myself and remained silent, but on the next lap I gave him a silent thumbs-up sign. Scott stopped in his tracks and glared at me again. "That means 'Good job'!" he said, then repeated: "No 'Good job'! No 'Good job'!"

Later I learned why Scott was disturbed by my innocent attempts to cheer him on. He had worked the previous year with a behavior therapist who relied on a traditional approach of sitting at a table for long periods and conducting teaching drills. She had rewarded successful efforts with praise and tangible rewards. "Good job!" had been her mantra, but he had come to detest those teaching sessions, understandably feeling controlled and manipulated. When I had said "Good job" in the gym, I meant it as a friendly gesture, but for Scott it sent him back to those difficult sessions and his unhappiness and discomfort. If I was going to be a "Good job!" person—or even a thumbs-up person—that was not going to work for him, and he wanted me to know that.

Children can't always make such clear efforts to communicate what's bothering them. Early in the school year, a second-grade teacher wondered why her student Alice habitually began crying and became despondent nearly every morning around eleven-thirty. Alice didn't speak, and no one could figure out what was causing her to be so upset. Thinking she might be hungry, the teacher offered her a snack. That didn't help. The teacher tried to adjust activities in the classroom, but still Alice got upset, every day. It was baffling.

Asked to intervene, I spoke to Alice's instructor from the previous year and described Alice's struggles. Almost immediately the teacher had an insight. "Last year, at eleven-thirty every day we took Alice outside to the playground and gave her time on the swing," she told me. It was a way to calm her down and help her feel more comfortable toward the end of the long mornings. If it was raining or snowing outside, someone would take her to a swing in the gym, but every day at eleven-thirty she had her swing time.

Mystery solved. Alice had no way to communicate it, but she had powerful positive emotional memories of that activity. Despite the interval of a summer vacation and the change to a new classroom and teacher, she associated that time of the school day with the positive, regulating sensation of being on the swing. Whether or not she was aware of the connection to the previous year's schedule, it showed the significant role that emotional memory can play.

I also witnessed that in Michael, the young son of a colleague, who often engaged in "self-talk"—speaking to himself in various ways. One afternoon I was driving Michael to the roller-skating rink, and there in the passenger seat he began a rather one-sided conversation with a particular doctor. "Dr. Boyer, good to see you!" he said to nobody in particular. "How are you, Dr. Boyer? What are we going to do today, Dr. Boyer?"

I happened to know that the doctor he was talking about was deceased. So I asked, "Michael, is Dr. Boyer here?"

"No, Dr. Barry," he said, smiling. "I'm *pretending* that I'm talking to him because Dr. Boyer is a very nice man."

It wasn't so different from the way anyone might recall a pleasant experience with a person who has passed away. Michael didn't have inhibitions or concerns about what another person might think, so he carried on the conversation aloud, and I had the privilege of witnessing his very positive associations.

The Lessons of PTSD

While we all experience emotional memory, for most of us it's rare for those memories to overwhelm us or significantly intrude on our lives and our ability to function. So when parents and teachers witness the extreme reactions their children and students have to negative emotional memories, they sometimes wonder whether the child might actually be experiencing some form of Posttraumatic Stress Disorder. PTSD is an extreme form of negative emotional memory and the unfortunate outcome when a person experiences severe trauma: witnessing or enduring a violent episode, suffering from physical or sexual abuse, or surviving a frightening car accident.

There are differences, but there is also overlap. PTSD is diagnosed when memories are persistently intrusive or incapacitating. Brain research shows that the brain processes emotional memories in the amygdala, part of the limbic system that is responsible for functions of memory and emotion. Situations that remind a person of traumatic events can trigger the release of stress hormones. This overactivates the amygdala, which sets off the release of still more of the hormones. The result: severe emotional distress in the form of racing thoughts, anger, and hypervigilance.

That's why a soldier returning from war can find himself thrust back to his most painful moments, feeling that he is reliving the events, not that he is remembering from afar. We might see the person at home, in his living room, but in his mind, he's back in Baghdad.

In children with autism, emotional memories rarely prove as debilitating or intrusive as PTSD can be. But they are often responsible for the sudden and dramatic changes in behavior that mystify parents and teachers. And research on PTSD has led to valuable lessons about how parents and professionals can help people with autism to cope with and overcome negative emotional memories. One significant insight: once you have a traumatic memory, you can't erase it; it lingers in the brain. To use a computer analogy, you can't delete it from the hard drive. And it can be triggered by an associated word, image, or smell.

Immediately after you experience a traumatic collision with a red Volvo, the sight of any red automobile approaching might trigger high anxiety. But after months of seeing red cars pass without incident, you begin feeling more secure and the panicky feeling abates. That doesn't mean the memory is gone; it's just been diminished and replaced by more positive or at least neutral memories. In the same way, a child's positive memories can override more painful and difficult ones.

Sometimes parents and others can help create the positive emotional memories. Anna was a preschooler who was terrified of the bathroom. Serious gastrointestinal issues had caused her great pain and discomfort. During her regimented toilet training at home, sitting on her potty seat at specified times, in discomfort, had made her miserable. Eventually dietary changes helped her overcome her GI issues, but not her fear of the lavatory. To help with that, her parents began playing her favorite music in the bathroom, sang songs with her there, and let Anna enjoy some of her favorite books. In time that strategy worked to override her painful memories with pleasant ones.

How Can You Tell Whether Emotional Memory Is the Issue?

How can you know when negative emotional memories are the root of a child's behavior? It's not always easy. As is often the case, getting to the root of what's underlying behavior takes some detective work. There are three significant clues:

- The child displays a strong behavioral reaction that does not seem related to something you can observe.
- The child consistently expresses fear or anxiety in relation to a particular person, place, or activity.
- The child engages in echolalia, repeating words or phrases linked to the person, place, or activity.

Coping with Emotional Memories: How to Help

The most important factor in helping a person with autism cope with negative emotional memories is to acknowledge and validate her experience and provide supports for emotional regulation. Often parents and teachers—with the best of intentions—have the opposite instinct. Some ignore the issue, hoping it will just go away. Others try to minimize the child's experience with reassuring statements: "Oh, don't worry about that."

However, those approaches aren't respectful of the person, they don't take the challenges seriously, and they do not teach the person strategies to stay emotionally well regulated. On a practical level they just don't work. Instead of feeling understood and supported, the person feels dismissed—and possibly even more anxious.

Once we understand the negative memories that are troubling the person, it's helpful to avoid the triggers, to steer clear of situations or people who cause the problem. It seems like a simple strategy, but it can be extremely helpful. If you know that noisy rooms cause anxiety in a child, be sensitive to that. If you've seen that the sound of a particular electronic toy provokes a little girl to cover her ears at the mere sight of it, then put it away. And let her know even before the issue comes up that the toy is not around.

Often the source of anxiety isn't avoidable. When that's the case, the best approach is to be respectful of the person and not to force things. George and Holly lived in an area with many theme parks. They had a daughter with autism, Amy, as well as three typical children. The other three children loved visiting the parks and went often, but Amy was afraid of visiting. She found most of the rides overwhelming and the sounds too much to tolerate. What could have been an enjoyable activity for the entire family instead divided them.

Instead of forcing Amy to go, the parents gave the girl control. They offered her the option to come along without going on any rides. They showed her pictures of the carousel and the food court, two things she typically liked. They brought the same noise-dampening headphones that her school used. When they saw her becoming anxious, her mother said, "Do you need your headphones? Do you need to leave, Amy? Are you finished?" If Amy said she was finished, they honored that request. When they next returned, they let her bring a favorite stuffed animal, and they bought her a favorite snack. The visits were on her terms.

They did this over five or six visits, never forcing Amy, always giving her a sense of control. When she understood that she was acting out of her own volition and not having anything forced on her, she relaxed and went willingly.

This gradual, empowering approach can apply to all kinds of experiences children might find overwhelming: crowded cafeterias, classrooms, bowling alleys—basically anywhere they've had difficult moments before. In my experience, forcing the issue only serves to create new fears and anxieties.

Creating Positive Emotional Memories

Another helpful approach is working strategically to turn a negative into a positive—to find ways to make places or activities associated with negative emotional memories more welcoming and comfortable. For people with autism, a dental visit, for example, is often rife with challenges: the unfamiliar noises of the drills and other equipment; the intense lights shining in their face; the lack of control over their own movements; the difficulty predicting what's going to happen next. And they might have experienced physical pain on a previous visit. A typical person can place the experience in context, understanding that despite those factors, the dentist is highly skilled and wouldn't intentionally hurt a patient, and dental care is an important part of staying healthy. We can reassure ourselves that we're safe, and we can cope by closing our eyes or tightly gripping the arms of the chair or sending our thoughts elsewhere.

When a person with autism becomes dysregulated, though, she can't instinctively calm herself in the same way. She may have a *fight* response or a *flight* response: either she struggles to protect herself, or she avoids the situation altogether or tries to flee.

Two different approaches to coping with dental visits offer lessons for helping people with autism cope with a variety of challenges.

Marquis was a fourteen-year-old with autism who generally spoke in one- to three-word utterances and mostly used pictures to communicate. His visits to the dentist always triggered such severe anxiety that his mother had a difficult time even getting him through the office door. But she knew exactly what to do to give her son the support he needed. She donated a rocking chair for the dentist's waiting room, so that Marquis—and others who shared his needs—could calm himself as he waited. She also brought music and headphones for him. And he brought along one of his favorite toys, a Shrek figure he could fidget with while he waited. Finally she met with the dentist to coach him on how to act, move slowly, and use positive language when telling Marquis what was coming next, so that things were more predictable. Marquis's mom knew that he couldn't avoid the dentist, but instead of merely forcing him to go, she helped transform the dentist's office into a safe place where he could feel regulated and calm.

Another mother of a child with autism took that approach a step farther. A dental hygienist, she combined forces with another mother, also a hygienist, and a dentist to open a practice specifically aimed at children with particular fears or sensitivities related to conditions such as autism or sensory-processing disorders. Their first strategy was to reduce uncertainty about visits by posting photos on a website showing the office, the people who worked there, and, with step-by-step photos, some of the procedures a patient might undergo. For one afternoon each week, instead of scheduling appointments they opened the office, put out toys, and welcomed patients and their families to come play and meet the dental staff. In short, they reduced uncertainty and created positive emotional memories in a place that could easily be a trigger for the opposite.

Therapists who work in schools often meet children who are resistant to engaging and seem overly anxious. Sometimes the problem is the space. The child might have worked in the same office or at the same desk with another therapist or teacher and found the encounters to be a source of stress rather than help. When it's time for a session, the child protests—"*No! No! No!*"—and drops to the floor.

The solution: create positive emotional memories. Before anything else, give the child a choice of two favorite toys. Spend the first five or ten minutes just having fun. Follow the child's lead and let her enjoy the time and the space so that she begins to associate more positive feelings with it. Make it a joyful experience, and only gradually add more challenging material.

An even simpler approach, especially for young children: don't call it "work." Too many therapists and teachers label their time with a child that way: *It's time to work. We can't play now—time for work.* Sometimes we're projecting our own concerns about how challenging the session will be for the child. The child hears *work* or senses our tone, and it triggers a flood of negative memories. Instead why not lighten the emotional tone and create a more positive, welcoming atmosphere?

Parents can take the same approach at home. One mother complained it had become a struggle to get her five-year-old, Judah, to join the family dinner each night. The problem: he so enjoyed being on his backyard swing that when she called him, he ignored her. I suggested she think about it from his perspective. When the child heard, "Judah! Time for dinner!," what he experienced was being taken from an activity he loved, that made him feel good (swinging), to one that was more challenging (sitting, listening, staying in one place).

"Is there anything he likes about dinner?" I asked.

His mother told me that Judah savored his Flintstones vitamins.

"Tomorrow," I said, "when you call him, hold up the bottle of vitamins."

The next week she reported that the visual cue had worked. When she simultaneously called Judah and held up the Flintstones vitamins, he ran right past her and into the house, repeating, "Time for dinner!," and sat in his place. Some might call that a bribe, but it wasn't. It was a visual cue that linked dinner with a positive association. And that began a series of positive memories, making the dinner table a more desired and welcoming place for Judah.

Of course that's the most helpful strategy of all: helping to create a life full of positive memories. As parents and professionals, we help to do that whenever we offer choices instead of exerting control; whenever we foster the child's interests and honor the child's strengths rather than redirecting; whenever we make learning, work, and life fun and joyful. When we do those things, our children, teens, and adults with autism will have far fewer negative emotional memories to cope with, making them more open to the joys and pleasures that life offers.

CHAPTER 6

Social Understanding

NEARLY every parent of a verbal child with autism has a version of this story: Philip's fifth-grade class was in the midst of studying the human body. He had worked hard to pay attention to the discussions on diet, exercise, and the many ways we can take care of our body. That same week his parents took him to the movies. They arrived at the theater only to discover a long line of people waiting for tickets. Excited, Philip took the opportunity to demonstrate his newfound knowledge. Pacing up and down the line, he pointed at each person and announced in a loud voice, "That's a fat man! There's a skinny man! That woman's very short! That man is obese and he might die soon!"

By the time Philip's parents shared this story, they recounted his obliviousness with amusement. But they weren't laughing when it happened.

Then there was Eli, a teenager who had just entered high school and was struggling to learn how to engage in conversations. Like many people with autism, he had a tendency to speak in detail about the topics he cared about, but he rarely bothered to ask others what they were interested in. I made some suggestions about asking questions and listening to clues about what the other person might want to discuss, but I could see from his facial expressions that he was feeling increasingly frustrated. "Other people can do that," Eli finally said, "but it's not easy for me."

"Why not?" I asked.

"Well," he said, "other people can read each other's minds."

That was how Eli made sense of the social world, where he was extremely aware that friends and strangers were interacting in all kinds of ways he could not comprehend. The only way he could explain how easy it seemed to them was to assume that neurotypical people must be imbued with telepathy, a power he lacked. What else could account for his struggles?

In a sense those two experiences—Philip in the movie line, Eli's assumption about mind reading—illustrate two extremes of how people with autism relate to the social world, with its hidden rules, unspoken expectations, and often nuanced use of language. Nearly every person with autism has some degree of difficulty navigating the social world. Some, like Philip, are so oblivious to social convention that they aren't aware of their own blunders and pay little attention to how others perceive their actions. Others, like Eli, struggle in a different way: they are all too cognizant that social rules and expectations exist, but since they don't intuitively understand them, they often feel anxious and their self-esteem suffers as they struggle to negotiate a world that seems to defy their grasp.

The Challenge of Learning Social Rules

For both groups—those who are blissfully unaware and those who worry excessively—the challenge is rooted in the same issues. Human beings are hardwired to be socially intuitive, but autism poses challenges to developing that intuition.

Consider the organic way we learn language. A mother doesn't sit her toddler down and explain the parts of speech or how to conjugate a verb. We learn by being exposed to language and immersed in it.

We listen and observe in order to construct our own knowledge of language. In the jargon of language-development research, we *induce* the rules of language, and as a result we learn the meanings of words and how to use them to express complex ideas.

The same is true of social rules. Typically people *induce* the often subtle, invisible conventions of social interaction. They learn by a process of immersion and osmosis, along with periodic coaching ("Please do not interrupt while Mommy's talking to Grandpa."). But for people with autism, the nature of their disability makes it very difficult to survey the social landscape and induce those rules. They can learn them, but it's like learning a second language as an adult, when it's much harder to achieve the same fluency and comfort as native speakers. What comes naturally and effortlessly to others always requires some degree of conscious effort, and one is constantly reminded of the struggle.

I first met Philip when I was doing a home consultation for his four-year-old son with autism. Philip was a successful investment banker in his forties and was diagnosed as an adult with Asperger's syndrome. He had graduated with honors from a prestigious MBA program, but he told me that was nothing compared to grappling with the social world. "Learning economics and finance was like breathing air to me," he said. "But to this day I have to read books to help me understand people—their facial expressions and social nuance and innuendo."

Imagine walking into an unfamiliar cafeteria for the first time. There are different types of cafeterias: in some, customers pay a cashier first, then pick up a tray and select food from various stations; in others you choose the foods you'll eat, put them on your tray, and then pay at the end of the line. Where does one pick up the cutlery, the condiments, the beverages? It's different at every cafeteria.

When you enter a cafeteria for the first time, how do you learn the rules? *You watch people.* You discover the unwritten rules of the cafeteria by observing how other customers make their way through the line, how they act, what they get where.

If you had autism, though, you probably wouldn't instinctively watch people in that situation. You might just head directly to get the food you want—possibly by cutting the line, as getting food is your goal, after all. As a person with autism, you might have some awareness that rules need to be followed, but because you don't know what they are, you might feel disoriented and lost, or you might look around for clues, bewildered. And it's unlikely that your impulse would be to learn by observing other people's behavior.

That's how the social world can feel to a person with autism: like an unfamiliar cafeteria, with rules that all the other diners apparently already know but that seem nearly impossible to learn.

Of course people with autism can learn the rules—with support. Another cafeteria analogy is helpful. On a visit to Denver I once dined in a salad-bar restaurant with its own unique arrangement. When customers entered, they were immediately directed to the salad bar, then they paid a cashier. Next came another area for soup, sandwiches, and desserts, all included in the fixed price. How was a newcomer to understand the proper sequence of steps? Someone had considered that question and developed visual supports to teach the rules, probably after bewildered customers were confused about how to proceed! The restaurant posted signs with visual diagrams breaking down the process for novices: start with the salad line, then pay, then help yourself to soup and dessert. It was as if every customer had autism, and the restaurant was accommodating us by providing a sequence of steps so we could understand.

In the real social world, people with autism are usually left to fend for themselves, navigating a reality that seems to make sense to everyone but themselves. It's no wonder Ros Blackburn is fond of offering a candid statement: "That's why I don't do social." Another young adult with autism, Justin Canha (see chapter 10), offered his own charmingly blunt assessment. Told by a friend—also on the autism spectrum—that he needed to practice his manners, Justin smiled and replied, "Manners suck."

Another social factor we consider, usually without deliberately thinking about it, is the cultural context in which we find ourselves. When I travel internationally I am reminded of how many of the rules governing social interactions are specific to our own society. On a trip to mainland China, I paid a visit to a large, crowded retail store in Guangzhou to get a feel for the local culture. I was waiting in line at the cashier when a woman behind me abruptly pushed me, apparently to join someone in front of me in line. As she passed, without warning she grabbed my shoulder and roughly shoved me aside, never pausing to excuse herself or apologize. If someone had done that to me in my local Target, it would have been grounds for confronting her. But I had learned that in China, where large crowds are common, such behavior is normal. I was able to put it in context and (shaken as I was!) react appropriately—which is to say, not at all.

Difficulty Reading Social Situations

When people with autism display behavior that appears to be abrupt or rude, or when they simply seem oblivious, it is often because their neurological wiring makes it difficult to weigh the many subliminal factors that help us read social situations. This lack of innate understanding manifests itself in all kinds of ways. Michael's family occasionally held Sunday barbeques for the twelve-year-old child's team, the professionals and teachers who worked with their son. In the midst of these gatherings, Michael would sometimes begin giggling to himself, sitting at the table but clearly occupied by his own thoughts. Even after one of his parents asked him to stop, he would continue. When it happened while I was visiting, I seized the opportunity to gain some insight into his behavior. "Michael," I said, "could you explain what's making you feel funny?"

He pointed at one of the therapists across the table. "It's *Susie*!" he said. "She has such a high, squeaky voice. It makes my body feel funny."

The young woman blushed, embarrassed. "Well, I guess I'm going to have to adjust my voice to a lower register during our sessions," she told him.

Michael was unaware that he had caused embarrassment. He was answering my question with an objective fact: she *did* have a high, squeaky voice. He didn't understand the social rule that it's best not to say anything about a person in public if it's not positive. How would any child learn that? A parent would likely provide some coaching for a younger child, but by age twelve most children would have had multiple experiences in surveying the social landscape, a process that leads to a fuller understanding of the unspoken rules of politeness.

Luke was another child whose social challenges showed up early, when his kindergarten teacher complained that he didn't know how to play with other children. Instead of playing the way other children played in his inclusive class, Luke would grab other kids and try to tackle them. Luke was a sweet child who had never been aggressive, and he was generally a happy youngster. In fact he flashed a broad smile while dragging kids to the ground, so it wasn't immediately clear why he was being so physical. When, in my capacity as consultant for his school district, I met with his parents and the team of educators who worked with Luke, his mother offered an explanation. Luke had two older brothers, and their play at home tended to be physical: lots of jumping on each other and tackling. So at four and a half Luke had taken that concept of play to school. He wasn't able to discern from the children's body language or facial expressions that they weren't enjoying his physical play. Nor did he intuitively understand that different rules applied at home and at school.

The Limitations of Teaching Social Rules

Schools are full of explicit rules, and children with autism often excel at following them, especially when a rule is explained and makes sense. In fact many children with autism become the rule keepers, pointing out when other children violate the tenets of acceptable behavior. It's the unspoken, subtle rules that are more challenging. Ned, a ten-year-old I worked with, always got excited when his teacher asked questions in class, especially about his favorite subjects. When he knew the answer, he would blurt it out. Why not demonstrate how interested and smart he was? He loved geography, so when the teacher displayed a map of Africa and asked the children to identify the countries, he shouted the name of one country after another without pausing: "Kenya! Tanzania! Tunisia!"

In his social skills group, the speech-language pathologist offered Ned instructions about the importance of raising his hand in class. "If you raise your hand," she explained, "it will make your teacher happy, and it will make your friends happy, because then everyone will have a chance to answer questions." The rule he was taught was this: If I raise my hand, the teacher will call on me.

The problem, of course, was that she didn't *always* call on him. Ned would raise his hand with great excitement and anticipation, struggling not to blurt out the answer, but the teacher sometimes seemed to ignore him. He had learned the rule but not the exceptions, so when he raised his hand and the teacher didn't call on him, Ned's mood quickly shifted, and he grew anxious and upset. In the next session of his social skills group, the therapist made sure Ned understood the rule more precisely from his perspective: If I raise my hand, *sometimes* the teacher will call on me, but sometimes she may call on my friends.

After he had practiced for a few weeks, I visited the classroom. I wasn't sure he was even aware I was there, until the teacher posed a question to the class. Ned immediately thrust his hand in the air to respond, then turned around and called out to me, "Dr. Barry! Just because I'm raising my hand it doesn't mean the teacher will call on me!"

To his credit, Ned was making great efforts to understand rules that made no logical sense to him: Why raise your hand at all? If you do, why doesn't the teacher call on you? And if she doesn't, why not state the rule aloud to explain why you are not being called on?

Ned's experience shows the limitations inherent in teaching the rules of the social world and the challenges we face when we try. We teach one rule, only to have the child encounter its exceptions. We teach the exceptions but forget to mention that generally *people don't talk about the rules, they just follow them.* The child wants so badly to get it right, but sometimes entering the world of social rules only brings more misunderstandings—sometimes comically.

Following Rules Can Be Confusing

Early in my career I worked with a student assistant to teach a boy named Michael the proper ways to address people. We were living in a small midwestern town in the early 1980s, and manners mattered. So we taught Michael to assess his relationship to the person quickly, and then use a corresponding term: "buddy" for a peer, "ma'am" for a woman, and "sir" for a man.

All of this was challenging for Michael because he wasn't just memorizing words. The process involved a central challenge: considering specific characteristics of people, such as gender and age, and where these individuals fit into his life. One afternoon my student working with him was delighted with how much progress Michael had made. Shown a picture of a woman, Michael would say "Ma'am"; shown a picture of another boy, he would say "Buddy," and so forth with perfect accuracy. So at the session's end he asked Michael to show off his new skills for me. Michael looked at me, smiled, and, overcome by confusion but with full enthusiasm, blurted out, "Hi Doctor buddy-ma'am-sir!"

Michael had learned the rules, but at the first opportunity to apply them, he was too excited and overwhelmed to do so. But what was even more evident was how hard he was trying, how challenging this was, and how much he truly wanted to connect with me. To this day I cherish that moniker, Doctor buddy-ma'am-sir.

Language can be a barrier to social understanding because people with autism tend to interpret language literally, and we often do not say what we mean. That's why they can find metaphors, sarcasm, and other nonliteral uses of language endlessly confounding.

Helen noticed that her son Zeke, who was nine, seemed particularly upset after school one day, so she asked him why.

"I don't want Mrs. Milstein to die!" he said.

Curious about what was ailing Zeke's fourth-grade teacher, Helen asked him to explain.

"I heard her tell Mrs. O'Connor, 'If it rains one more day this week, I'm going to kill myself.' "

Sandra went shopping with her daughter Lisa, who was seven, for a birthday present for Lisa's brother. Lisa chose a baseball. On their way home Sandra reminded Lisa that birthday presents are a secret until the big day: "You need to keep this under your hat." Later that day, when Lisa's father was in her bedroom, he noticed a beach hat on a bookshelf, out of its usual place. When he reached to move it, Lisa cried out, "No! Don't touch! It's a secret!"

Even simple exchanges can cause unexpected problems. A child answers the telephone, and when the caller asks, "Is your mother home?," the child says "Yes," and promptly hangs up. A child accidentally knocks over a can of paint, spilling it all over the floor. When the teacher responds sarcastically, "That's just wonderful!," the child thinks he's done well.

The Importance of Directness

To avoid such problems, parents and teachers should be as direct as possible in their communication with people with autism. It's also helpful to use "comprehension checks"—that is, to ask the person if he understands what is being said rather than assuming he does, and, if necessary, offer an explanation. And direct requests always work better than subtle hints. "Those cookies look good" might be the polite way to imply to a neurotypical person that you want one, but with a person on the spectrum, "Please give me a cookie" works much better.

For some people it may be necessary to explain the concept of nonliteral language and to teach the specific meanings of words and phrases (such as idioms) that aren't transparent or obvious. "That's a piece of cake" or "Break a leg" can be quite confusing, but such expressions can be taught directly, like words from another language translated into English. Many children keep lists of words or phrases that are confusing to them and review them with parents or teachers. It's important to remember that this issue varies greatly depending on a person's age, abilities in language, and social experiences.

We also need to be clear about the meanings of specific words we use. Nicholas's parents taught him to dial 911 when there is an emergency, which they described as when something very bad happens to you or someone else. The next day, when he asked for more dessert after dinner, and his mother said no, he called 911, telling the operator, "It's an emergency! My mom won't give me more dessert!" In this case it would have helped if his parents listed specific examples of emergencies: a fire, a car accident, or a bad injury.

When Honesty Isn't the Best Policy

The social world is infinitely complex, with no end of unwritten rules, exceptions, and variables. No matter how much effort parents and professionals put into preparing a child, we can never anticipate every possible misstep, even when we (or our children) have the best of intentions. Consider Ricky, a teenage boy with autism who was a talented pianist. Ricky once volunteered to entertain the residents of an assisted-living center. He had never visited such a facility, but his parents told him what a lovely, caring gesture it would be. They also informed him that some of the elderly people he would see had terminal illnesses and other challenges, so surely his music would help to lift their spirits. On the day of his performance, a few dozen residents gathered in a recreation room to listen. Before he sat down to play, Ricky introduced himself, said how happy he was to be there, and added this: "I'm very sorry that some of you are going to die soon."

Ricky had an appropriate sense of compassion for the elderly people he was meeting but couldn't yet discern that it might be considered insensitive to remind them so bluntly that they were at death's door!

We could also sum up Ricky's mistake another way: he was honest. As much as our culture purports to value truth and candor, interacting with people with autism can make us realize how truly deceptive and dishonest the social world requires us to be.

Donald, who was in his twenties, worked for a pharmacy chain stocking shelves and helping customers. "My manager tells me I'm a very valued employee," he told me when we met, "but my immediate supervisor doesn't like me very much. He calls me an asshole."

I asked why. He told me that an elderly woman had come to the store in search of a particular kind of battery. Within earshot of his supervisor, Donald suggested that even though the store stocked the battery, she would be better off buying it at the hardware store a block away, where the selection and prices were better.

Even as he recounted the story, he seemed not to grasp what had displeased his supervisor. "My manager tells us that our job as customer service employees is to be trustworthy so that customers think of this as their friendly neighborhood store," he said. "So why would my supervisor call me an asshole for doing just that?"

Why indeed? It's no wonder Eli assumed that other people could secretly read each other's minds. For people with autism, trying to comprehend the social world can mean living in an almost constant state of confusion, bewilderment, and frustration.

The Stress of Misunderstanding

I have met countless people with autism who misread social situations and behavior, and even after someone tries explaining what they hadn't grasped, they still don't understand. Enduring that experience again and again takes its toll. Knowing *I'm supposed to understand this, but no matter how hard I try, I can't* causes frustration, unhappiness, and anxiety. Many react by shutting down in the face of social encounters or simply avoiding them. Some turn inward and experience depression. Self-esteem suffers as they ask, "Why don't I understand this? What's wrong with me? Am I *stupid*?"

Social understanding is only one kind of being smart. You can be brilliant in many other ways and still struggle with grasping facial expressions and other subtle cues in social situations. Social understanding requires what Howard Gardner, famous for his theory of multiple intelligences, called interpersonal intelligence. A person with strengths in this area can assess the emotions, desires, and intentions of others across different social situations. Of course someone who struggles with interpersonal intelligence can demonstrate intelligence in, for example, music, math, or solving complex puzzles.

Aware of their difficulty, many children apologize for themselves, almost habitually—even without understanding what they're apologizing for. They may understand social rules in extremes of black and white. They're making every effort to get it right, and if they suspect they haven't said the right thing or acted the right way, their instinct is to blurt out "Sorry! Sorry!" No matter how many times parents or teachers reassure them, they come to expect that they will make mistakes, so they automatically apologize.

Living in a state of constant confusion about even ordinary social interactions can mean that when situations arise that are unanticipated or truly unfamiliar, it's likely the child will react in unexpected or extreme ways. To an observer the behavior can look rash, sudden, or inexplicable, but it's often the result of frustration and anxiety that has been building in the child for some time.

Benny, a thirteen-year-old, rarely initiated communication. He was struggling in his public middle school classes and often became irritable in the middle of the school day because of the stress and demands of his morning classes. He also had a difficult time when he was around people expressing negative emotions. When some people with autism encounter strong emotions in other people—happiness, sadness, excitement, nervousness—they become confused. It's as if they are absorbing the intensity of the emotions themselves, without understanding why they feel as they do.

A fire alarm at school rang at just the time of day when Benny typically became anxious and impatient. As he and his classmates filed out of their classroom and outside, Benny witnessed two boys roughhousing, ignoring the instructions of their teacher. When the principal spotted them, she stepped between Benny and the boys and gave them a harsh reprimand, wagging a finger in their faces and firmly ordering them to join their classmates immediately.

Benny's reaction was sudden and unexpected: he reached over to the principal and shoved her, knocking her to the ground. It didn't help that he was a fairly large boy and she was just over five feet tall. The principal got up and dusted herself off. Fortunately she was unhurt, though shaken. Later that day she suspended Benny from school.

Soon afterward I met with her in my role as consultant for the district. "Barry, I'll admit that I'm still learning about autism," she said, "but we can't have that kind of behavior in our school." She was concerned not only about herself but about how Benny's classmates might perceive his behavior.

I tried to explain my understanding of the incident as the result of a series of snowballing events invisible to everyone but Benny. Even before the alarm, he had already been feeling unusually anxious. The noise and surprise of the fire drill had thrown him off even more.

Then came the principal's harsh reprimand, which he found confusing and emotionally overwhelming. It upset him to see her so angry and to observe what he might have perceived as an aggressive act, so he reacted impulsively. The anxiety was building within him and the fire drill—and her confrontation with the boys—were simply the triggers that set him off.

There was no easy solution. It was impossible to anticipate every situation that might cause Benny anxiety. Middle school is full of situations that can be confusing and anxiety-inducing. What we could do was to make sure the school made every effort to help Benny communicate his anxiety, that staff were primed to notice the first hints of dysregulation, and that supports were in place so that when the unexpected happened—when Benny was pushed to his limit—someone could intervene. As part of his emotional-regulation plan, his team put an extra break in his schedule just at the time he typically became irritable and shifted an aide to his classroom to help Benny to cope and adjust.

Social Understanding and School

To her credit, Benny's principal made an effort to understand his behavior rather than merely dismissing his misconduct as naked aggression. Children with autism often act in ways that appear confusing and open to misinterpretation. When I work with various schools, it is common for me to hear teachers complain that a student is aggressive or noncompliant or manipulative, and then later discover the real issue: the teacher doesn't understand the student. Often that is because the child lacks a degree of social understanding, and the teacher misinterprets his behavior as intentional. ("He knows exactly what he's doing.")

Consider it this way: In most academic settings, most students feel innately motivated to please the teacher—to answer the question correctly, to earn an A on the exam, to succeed at the science fair, to behave in accordance with classroom and school rules. Many students also aim to make their parents proud. But a person with autism might lack those motivations. A boy might have so mastered an algebra unit that he can produce the correct answer to an assigned problem, but if the teacher asks him to describe the steps he went through to get to that answer, he might refuse. He's not being noncompliant; he just doesn't understand the social expectation of explaining his thinking. *I know how I did it, and I got the right answer*, he thinks. *Why should I have to tell you how I got it?*

Teachers are accustomed to pupils aiming to please, or at least understanding that they should. So if they lack proper training, they naturally find it confusing when they deal with students like Jason, a bright, verbal fifth-grader with autism with whom I worked. One day his art teacher asked each student to write down the names of two favorite animals. Jason wrote "horse" and "eagle."

"Now," the teacher said, "I'd like you to use your imagination and create a picture of an animal that combines the features of the two animals you selected."

From the back of the classroom, Jason responded immediately in a loud, stern voice, "I will not do that."

One of the classroom aides approached him and explained the assignment again.

"I will not do that!" Jason repeated.

"But Jason," the aide said, "that's our assignment today. Everyone in the class is doing it."

"I will not do that!"

Seeing that his anxiety was rising and hoping to prevent any further escalation, the aide asked if he needed a break. She took him for a walk outside, trying to help him calm himself and reiterating along the way that all the students were participating in the same project. When they returned to the classroom, the instructor asked Jason, who seemed calmer, if he was ready to create his picture.

"I will not do that!" he repeated, to her surprise.

It struck me that nobody had asked the most important question.

I approached him slowly. "Jason," I asked, "why don't you want to make the picture the teacher is asking you to make?"

"There's no such *thing* as an animal that's part eagle and part horse," he replied. "I will not do that."

Jason wasn't being intentionally defiant or disobedient. The assignment didn't make sense to him; it defied his sense of logic. It didn't matter to him that the unwritten social rule said he should do the assignment to please the teacher, that part of his job as a student was to go along with what was asked of him, whether or not he wanted to. That sense of social obligation wasn't part of his consciousness. And even if he knew that his teacher wanted him to cooperate—and that he should—in the heat of the moment, the challenge of dealing with subject matter that so violated his sense of the world triggered his instinctive refusal.

As in Jason's case, the way a child responds to a school assignment can provide unique insight into how the child processes information and understands the social world. Sherise was in third grade when, for Martin Luther King Jr. Day, her teacher assigned a worksheet about Dr. King. Like many children with autism, Sherise had an impressive capacity for memorizing dates and information and could reel off the dates of significant events in Dr. King's life better than anyone in the class. What she sometimes lacked was a sense of how to put all of the information in a social and cultural context.

One question on the sheet asked the student to list Dr. King's positive traits. Sherise wrote, "He likes dogs. He can read books." She continued in a similar vein:

Describe what you like best about Dr. King. "He helps me. He cleans my room."

Tell me one thing Dr. King has taught you. "He taught me how to write long and short vowel sounds."

Compare yourself to Dr. King. "Dr. King has a tie. I do not have a tie."

Explain why you think Dr. King is a good role model. "Because Martin Luther King Jr.'s birthday is a holiday."

Again, this was not a child who was being intentionally defiant. Sherise was a bright girl who astounded her teachers and others with her remarkable memory. But she couldn't grasp the intent of the assignment or the individual questions. Others might have intuited that the questions were about how Dr. King changed society and the way people live. But the assignment didn't explicitly state that. When the sheet asked for "positive traits," Sherise thought of *her own* positive traits. When it asked what Dr. King taught, she simply thought of something *she* had learned, albeit unrelated to the assignment. The assignment required deeper social understanding than Sherise had developed due to her social disability. It was almost like asking a child with a physical disability to compete successfully in the sixty-yard dash.

Teachers puzzling over responses like Sherise's might well slap their foreheads in frustration. Instead they should take heart and applaud the student's sincere efforts. Frustrating or baffling as the assignment might have been, Sherise didn't say, "I can't do it. I don't understand." She put in a full effort. And her lack of insight as a third-grader certainly didn't mean she would never grasp these social concepts. Social and emotional understanding, like so much else, develops over time. Different children move through various developmental stages at different rates, often only after considerable experience and with direct support. What was best for Sherise wasn't to be scolded for not cooperating but to be praised for her efforts and given extra support to understand the assignment.

Understanding Emotions

If it's difficult for children on the spectrum to comprehend the subtle, hidden rules of social interaction, it can be even more challenging to gain an understanding of emotions—their own and those of others. In 1989, the first time Oprah Winfrey interviewed Temple Grandin, Oprah asked, "What are your feelings like?" Grandin answered by describing how uncomfortable she was in "scratchy" wool sweaters. By "feelings," Winfrey meant emotions, the complex world of our inner lives. But Grandin assumed she was talking about sensory experiences—in particular, the sense of touch.

Or maybe she was avoiding the question. Emotions are abstract, intangible, and difficult to grasp, and people with autism often find it challenging to communicate about such matters, especially when doing so requires self-reflection. In the past some professionals and others have mistakenly believed that this difficulty and discomfort talking about feelings meant that people with autism somehow lacked emotion. Of course that's not true. They experience the same full range of human emotions we all do. If anything, theirs are magnified. Their challenge is understanding and expressing their own emotions and reading the emotion in others.

Alvin was ten, a very verbal child who struggled with anxiety and sensory issues. One day his special education teacher showed him a photograph of a baby crying and posed a number of questions: How does the baby feel? Why does the baby feel this way? Alvin was able to explain that the baby was crying because he felt sad. The teacher followed up with another question: "Alvin, what makes you feel sad?"

"What makes me feel *sad*?" he said. "What makes me feel ill? Yellow cheese." Somehow Alvin had transformed *sad* into *ill*, perhaps because it was a negative feeling that was more visceral, easier to grasp.

The teacher tried again: "What makes you feel *sad*?"

"What makes me feel *bad*? Diarrhea."

Alvin could easily identify an emotion in the baby, sadness, but couldn't yet relate it to his own internal experience. Surely he felt sad sometimes, but at age ten he couldn't verbally explain his own emotional experience. The exchange reveals how an individual might have the ability to identify emotions in another person but lack the capacity to express his own emotions—which requires reflecting on one's own feelings.

Another child, Eric, who was thirteen, struggled with a similar challenge. To help Eric and his class learn about emotions, his teacher had the children spin an "emotion wheel," a sort of roulette wheel with the names of various emotions (happy, confused, angry) placed around the wheel, and then answer questions about the particular emotion the pointer landed on. Eric's word was *jealous*. The discussion went like this:

Teacher: How are you feeling today, Eric?
Eric: I feel jealous.
Teacher: Can you tell us why?
Eric: 'Cause I'm so jealous.
Teacher: And why are you feeling jealous?
Eric: Because . . . Indiana will play LSU.
Teacher: Why does that make you feel jealous?
Eric: 'Cause feeling jealous makes me feel beautiful. (Eric looks away, confused)

The conversation continued, with Eric clearly not grasping the term.

Teacher: Do you understand what it is to be jealous?
Eric: What it is to be jealous?
Teacher: If Darrell has a brand new watch and I think it's the nicest watch I've ever seen, and I want it, then I'm jealous because Darrell has a better watch than I do.
Eric: Yeah.
Teacher: Okay, do you understand that?
Eric: 'Cause Darrell has a new watch.
Teacher: And I want it.
Eric: And you would want it. . . .
Teacher: So, do you feel jealous today?
Eric: Yes.
Teacher: Why?
Eric: 'Cause Darrell wants a new watch.

Teacher: No.
Eric: 'Cause you have a new watch.
Teacher: Why does Eric feel jealous?
Eric: 'Cause I have a watch at home.
Teacher: Would you please pick another feeling?
Eric: No. I picked jealous!

Eric was doing his best to get it right, and to his credit he wouldn't quit, even when his teacher suggested he do so. But he was clearly a concrete thinker struggling with an abstract notion.

How Not to Teach Emotions

Too often educators think they're teaching people with autism how to express their emotions when what they are actually teaching is how to label pictures of people expressing emotions. Using language to describe emotion is among the most abstract tasks a young child faces. It's one thing to recognize an apple or a table and identify it; conveying how you feel or how someone else might feel is far more complex. Emotions involve both cognitive and physiological reactions. We not only feel; we reflect on how we are feeling and why. We also experience emotions in our body.

Such reactions are dynamic and intangible. But some therapists recommend attempting to teach emotions to children with autism by having them identify facial expressions in diagrams: happy, sad, excited, angry, surprised, confused. Ros Blackburn pointed out to me the problem with this approach. "For years, people tried to teach me emotions by having me label happy and frowny faces," she said. "The only problem is that people do not look like that." These teachers aren't teaching emotion; they're teaching picture recognition. And they're certainly not teaching the child to express and understand why he is feeling a particular emotion.

A more effective approach is introducing a label—happy, silly, giddy, anxious—at the moment the person is experiencing that feeling. (For some people it's more appropriate to make the connection between a visual image such as a photograph and the person's feeling.) That way, he learns to express and communicate a cognitive-emotional experience, not just a facial expression. Once the person understands the emotion, he can learn categories of experiences he associates with that feeling.

Teaching Social: What's the Goal?

In the same way, adults often emphasize teaching what are called "social skills" over teaching *social understanding* and *social thinking*.* And they often teach the skills that are deemed important in a rote manner, with the goal of making a child appear "normal." This doesn't help a child to make good decisions when interacting with others, read social situations, or understand other people's perspective, emotional experience, or point of view.

Eye contact is a prime example. Many children with autism avoid looking other people in the eye, perhaps because they find it uncomfortable, perhaps because it takes focus and energy to do so, detracting from their ability to think clearly.

But since American culture values looking people in the eye, the late Ivar Lovaas, a psychologist at UCLA who was one of the first autism specialists, felt it was essential to train a child to make eye contact before moving on to other skills. For years a hallmark of his treatment approach was his claim—not supported by scientific evidence—that the ability to make eye contact on command was a prerequisite for learning other skills. He eventually retracted this position, but unfortunately many practitioners still engage in "eye contact training."

---

*Michelle Garcia Winner addresses this issue in detail in her book, *Why Teach Social Thinking?* (San Jose, CA: Think Social, 2014).

If you listen to people with autism, they send a clear message: looking at others in the eye can be extremely difficult. It makes them feel anxious. They're resistant to people who force them to do so. They're more comfortable, more regulated when they're *not* making eye contact. Neurotypical people develop the habit of looking directly at people from an early age, but gaze aversion serves a purpose as well. Conversations typically involve looking at the person you're talking to as well as moments of looking *away* from the person. That gives us a moment to gather our thoughts, to relax, to regulate ourselves.

I once taught a group of graduate students from Africa. During office hours I had a meeting with several of them. They were exceedingly polite, but I felt uneasy that none of them would look me in the eye while we spoke. Finally I raised the issue with them. "Is something wrong?" I asked. "I feel uncomfortable that you won't look at me."

"I'm sorry sir," one of them replied, "but in our culture, it is considered a sign of disrespect to look at a person of higher status when you're speaking to them, and you are our professor."

It was a reminder that many of the social traits and practices we consider important, even crucial, aren't inherent human behaviors but rather rules that can vary widely from one culture to another.

They also differ from person to person. When I was responsible for overseeing a department in a teaching hospital I noticed that one of my newly hired employees, a speech-language pathologist, spent her entire first department meeting doodling, almost never looking at me when I spoke. At the second meeting she did the same thing. I found it so disconcerting that I confronted her. "I don't understand why you aren't paying attention to me in our meetings," I told her.

She apologized for not disclosing it earlier, then explained that she had a learning disability that made it difficult to look at a person and simultaneously process what the person was saying. I had made inaccurate assumptions about my colleague's level of interest and attention in meetings based on the messages she was sending with her body and facial language.

Many people with autism say that it is often easier to focus on what a person is saying without the extra burden and stress of watching the person's face. Seasoned teachers know that certain students are listening and learning even though they may not be watching the instructor during a lesson.

Still, children can learn the unspoken obligation to let someone know you're listening. Taking a "social understanding" or "social thinking" approach, parents and teachers can help a child understand that he can indicate he's paying attention by looking at another person, even for brief moments during a conversation, or by saying "Uh-huh" and nodding. Some children find looking another person in the eye so difficult that it causes discomfort. In that case they can be taught to offer an explanation so the person they're with doesn't assume that they're bored or inattentive. ("Please understand that I'm paying attention, even when I may not be looking at you.") Doing so is similar to what neurotypicals do when they know they will have to exit a meeting or lecture early because of another commitment: it's polite to inform the speaker in advance in order to avoid having their behavior misconstrued and to show sensitivity to the speaker's feelings.

The Role of Unspoken Assumptions

We all make assumptions about each other's behavior that usually go unspoken but that nevertheless have great impact on our interactions. Often people with autism don't perceive the need to communicate what's bothering them—or sometimes they find unorthodox ways to do so.

An elementary school principal once showed me a collection of drawings a fourth-grader with Asperger's syndrome named Enrique had begun routinely leaving on her desk. Each depicted a devilish character with horns and a pointed tail. On each page the boy had written the principal's name, followed by her new title, "The Evil Principal."

"That's me," she said with a smile. "Whenever this child finds something he doesn't like in the school, he blames me." When Enrique was unhappy with the ketchup in the cafeteria, he would leave a devil picture. If he didn't think a rule was fair, he'd leave another. To her credit, the principal welcomed this unique form of expression, respected his attempt to express his feelings, and eventually helped Enrique find more conventional ways to come in and discuss his grievances.

Others don't have the instinct to communicate their displeasure. Bud, a bright thirteen-year-old with autism, was showing signs of severe depression. Instead of participating in his middle school classes, he would slump at his desk, face down, eyes closed, with his head resting in his arms. His teachers were baffled about how to deal with his melancholy, so they asked me to intervene.

At our first meeting Bud didn't hesitate to share. "I hate being in school," he told me, "because my teachers hate me."

His teachers hadn't expressed any negative feelings about Bud to me, only bewilderment about how to help him. I asked Bud why he thought his teachers didn't like him.

"Because," he said, "in all my classes, they try to teach me things I'm not interested in."

Bud made an assumption that his teachers, acting out of some kind of animus, had schemed to assign him exactly the material that would most annoy and bore him. What else would explain his difficulties?

"Do your teachers ever ask what you're interested in?" I asked.

"No, they *hate* me. Why would they ask that?" he replied.

I suggested to him that when I was his age, I too was required to take classes I didn't enjoy and that I was sure many of his classmates didn't like all of their classes all the time. What seemed like common knowledge to me seemed to be new information to Bud. A typically developing teenager would have understood that a student might not like every class and that part of being a student was learning to live with that. But to Bud the only explanation was that the teachers hated him.

After our conversation I suggested that Bud participate in a social skills group in which he could learn why people behave the way they do and say what they do, and all the possible ways to interpret their actions. There he learned things that other students understood more readily: sometimes you like your classes, sometimes you don't; if you are having difficulty, you can ask the teacher, who will be happy to help. Nobody had taken the time to explain these things to him because no one perceived how he misunderstood. The school also made an effort to integrate his interests—heavy metal music, video games—into his program. We didn't solve all of his problems, but asking him what was bothering him revealed that most of his unhappiness came from his own misunderstandings. All it took was asking him to explain, and then finding creative ways to integrate his interests.

PART TWO

Living with Autism

CHAPTER 7

What It Takes to "Get It"

I LEARN some of my most significant lessons just from watching, and I learned a lot from watching Paul.

Paul was a classroom aide who had been assigned to Denise, a sixteen-year-old with autism who had recently transferred to a new school. She had felt so frustrated at her previous school—and so frequently dysregulated—that she often attempted to hit teachers and had been identified as aggressive. In this new classroom setting, Denise often indulged in repetitive rituals. For instance, she would pull baggies full of compact discs from her backpack, then line them up in precise sequence across the desktop—a process that seemed to calm her. She rarely spoke, only occasionally uttering two or three words at low volume. Still, while she appeared cautious and edgy, Denise showed no obvious signs of aggression or anger.

When I observed her in familiar school routines as part of my work with the school, I immediately noticed how remarkably effective her classroom aide was. With his shaved head and large earring, Paul, who was in his twenties, reminded me of Mr. Clean, the face of the household-cleaning product. Paul would make sure Denise had the materials she needed for whatever work she was assigned and helped her get organized, but then he would back off and give her space.

He kept a close eye on her from across the room, and whenever she became agitated or distracted, Paul would draw closer to her. I noticed that each time he did so, she would calm down and relax. He was extraordinarily able to observe the most subtle sign that she was becoming dysregulated, and he knew the right thing to say or do to calm her down. Sometimes he did so from a few feet away, in barely noticeable ways, giving her a reassuring head nod, pointing, or saying a few words. It was as if they had a magical, silent, symbiotic connection. Whenever I suspected that Denise was becoming tense and anxious and might need assistance, he would help her stay calm and engaged.

I wondered how he had devised a method that worked so well to help this girl stay regulated, especially since she had struggled elsewhere. I wanted to learn from whatever strategy he was using. So I asked Paul to chat for a few minutes. I mentioned what I had noticed and told him how impressed I was that he was so readily able to read the girl's signals and intervene so appropriately. "Can you talk to me about what you were doing or what you were noticing?" I asked.

He shrugged his shoulders, seeming almost baffled by my question. His answer was brief: "I just pay attention."

I just pay attention. He made it sound so simple. But those four words said so much. Paul was effective in providing exactly the support this teenager needed not because he had mastered a particular kind of therapy, followed steps in a behavior plan, or dispensed the right "reinforcers." What enabled him to provide exactly the support Denise needed was that he had the instinct and ability to watch, to listen, and to be sensitive to her needs.

Where are the Pauls of the world? One of the most challenging aspects of raising a child with autism is finding the helpers—doctors, therapists, educators, and others—who are most effective, who best connect with the child, and who inspire the most progress. Particularly when parents are dealing with autism, or the possibility of autism, for the first time, it can be difficult to know whom to trust, whose advice is worthwhile, which teacher or therapist might be the best match for the child and the family.

My perspective on this question was forever changed when I met Dr. Jill Calder, a physician who is also the mother of a child with autism. Speaking in a packed lecture hall at the University of British Columbia in Vancouver, I asked the audience if they had ever encountered people like Paul, individuals who are naturals with their children not because of specific training but because of an innate ability.

About twenty rows back, Jill stood up. "In my family," she said, "we call it the 'It Factor.'" She explained that she had watched for years as various professionals interacted with her son. She noticed that when the school assigned a new aide to her son, the boy would often return home even more anxious and unhappy than before. But on other occasions the new person was able to make an immediate connection with the boy, and her son was noticeably calmer and happier.

What made the difference? Jill explained that some people are just naturals: within five or ten minutes they would know how to interact with her son and he would relax with them; there was a chemistry. "We say those people have 'got It,'" she said. No matter their title, no matter their training, they connect.

Next she described a second tier of people she called "It-like." These individuals may lack the natural, intuitive ability to connect with people with autism; they may even be nervous, hesitant, or uncomfortable. But they are eager to learn, and they seek support and advice from a parent or someone else who knows the child well. Jill explained that this included many professionals she met and that she was always happy to meet such people—people who are enthusiastic about working with children with autism, willing to learn and grow, and open to taking direction from the people who know a child best.

Jill also identified a third group: those who seem unable to connect and often are the source of dysregulation. These people are less open to learning from the child or family and come with their own preconceived (often inaccurate) notions. They lack the ability, either intuitive or learned, to get through to the child. In many cases they focus on discipline and consequences without asking the "why" question. Their goal is to be in total control, they're often insensitive to sensory issues and other autism-related challenges, and they impose their own goals.

"Oh," I chimed in, "you mean the 'It-less' people." Jill and the audience nodded knowingly.

She mentioned that on more than a few occasions, an adult had entered her son's life, only to cause him increased stress and anxiety. She paused, took a deep breath, gathered her emotions, and said, "And I will *never* allow that to happen again." That triggered a torrent of comments, as others in the audience described teachers who didn't understand their kids, therapists who were stuck on an approach that was insensitive to a child's emotional state, and doctors who saw the symptoms but not the child.

I'll never forget the father of an older teenager with autism who spoke up at the annual parent retreat I help facilitate. He kicked off a discussion session on the topic of parent-professional relationships with this bold statement: "I just want to tell all of you who are parents of young kids that you can't trust professionals as far as you can throw them."

Those kinds of strong feelings emerge from having too many encounters with "It-less" professionals, those who can't seem to connect with a child and who therefore lose (or never gain) the trust of the parents. Parents rarely begin the journey wary of professionals; they're usually eager for help, desperate to meet people with the experience and perspective to provide assistance. What makes them jaded and suspicious is repeatedly encountering people who are supposed to help but instead let them down.

So what are the ingredients that make a difference? What are the factors that enable a person really to "get It"? What should a parent look for in a professional or educator? What can you do to help a promising professional become more "It-like"?

Being a person who "gets It" is not about having a particular graduate degree or a certain number of years of training or experience in the field. I have met individuals with impressive résumés and stellar credentials who nevertheless lack the basic human qualities that enable others to connect with children with autism and their families. Many others, like Paul, lack advanced training but forge real human connections, intuitively sense the needs of children, and help support meaningful progress.

In my experience those who "get It" share a number of significant traits and instincts. Among the most important are these:

- **Empathy.** They try to understand how a person with autism comprehends and experiences the world. Rather than generalizing from their own experiences or from those of other people with autism or other disabilities, these people pay close attention to the individual, always reading and making sense of the person's behavior.

- **The human factor.** They perceive the person's behavior as *human* behavior, resisting the temptation to explain every behavior and reaction as stemming from autism. They ask "Why?" They don't simply label a child's resistance as "noncompliant" behavior, as if that explains why a child hesitates or refuses. It's easy to say a child is "stimming" and to call that "autistic behavior" without asking questions such as "Why at this time, and not at others?" A person who's "got It" will make the extra effort to explore what's underlying the behavior.

- **Sensitivity.** They're attuned to the person's emotional state, including the sometimes subtle signals indicating varying degrees of regulation and dysregulation. Like most human beings, people with autism often give outward signs of their inner feelings through the subtleties of body language and facial expression. A sensitive person who "gets It" recognizes that when a child averts her gaze in a certain way or when her body tenses, she is sending a signal that she is upset or is becoming overwhelmed; that when a child rocks his body it means he is feeling unsettled. The same person might notice that when a more verbal child becomes argumentative or refuses to participate in a conversation, it is likely a sign that she feels dysregulated.

- **Shared control.** They don't feel a need to exert control over the person with autism. Too many educators and therapists see their role as pushing a certain agenda or structure to keep the person with autism within certain bounds of behavior. Instead parents and professionals should *share control* with the person and provide guidance as needed. That approach is more respectful of the individual and his sense of autonomy and self. Just as important, giving the person with autism control in a variety of situations and settings ultimately leads to a greater sense of independence, self-sufficiency, and self-determination.

- **Humor.** They don't take things too seriously. Life can be rife with challenges for people with autism and their families, and sometimes professionals, educators, relatives, and others only make things worse by overly emphasizing the negative, seeming to view every difficult incident through a tragic lens. It's much more helpful for both the child and the family when those around them maintain a sense of humor (a respectful sense of humor, to be sure) and a healthy perspective about situations the child confronts or what the child says or does.

- **Trust.** They focus on forging a positive relationship and building trust. As in any relationship, the best way to build trust is to listen, to understand the other person and consider that person's needs and desires rather than imposing an external agenda. Professionals often forget the importance of building trust from the outset and spend the remainder of the relationship trying to make up for that. That's why it is essential to begin by listening and showing respect for the person with autism and by partnering with the family rather than arriving with preconceived notions.

- **Flexibility.** They adapt to the situation rather than stubbornly sticking to a fixed agenda or a prescribed program or plan that does not reflect the needs of the individual it is designed to help. Too often therapists pay more attention to the program they are given to follow than to the person they are supposed to be helping. Some approaches are so detailed in prescribing responses or consequences that they don't leave room for the professional (or even a parent) to try to feel what the person is feeling and to understand what's behind a behavior. When observing professionals at work, I often disagree with—or don't understand—a particular choice the professional has made. When I raise the matter, the response is "I agree with you, but I'm following the behavior plan." A plan needs to be flexible enough to be responsive to the person. It's important to recognize when Plan A isn't working and it's time to shift to Plan B. It's a mistake to impose a one-size-fits-all approach on a child when the approach isn't appropriate at all times with all children.

The "It Factor" in Action

Though I have been working in the autism field for four decades, I often learn the most from people with little formal training—people who just "get It."

Sometimes the simplest things can make a difference. Carlos, who was relatively new to his school, had had some significant outbursts in his seventh-grade class. Various teachers reported on how aggressive and unpredictable he could be, but one person had developed a relationship with him: the principal.

As an advisor to the school district, I paid a visit to the principal to ask how she had been able to connect with Carlos. She explained that after a particularly disruptive classroom episode, she had invited the boy to her office. Instead of reprimanding him or disciplining him, she tried something else: she shared an orange with him. He so enjoyed it that she told him if he could follow classroom rules and manage himself appropriately, she would invite him back.

That became a routine for the two of them. I asked her how it worked.

"It's very simple," she said. "We sit down together, we peel oranges, and we enjoy eating the oranges."

The principal understood that it wasn't going to help this particular boy for yet another adult to tell him that he was behaving poorly or that he needed to settle down. What he needed was to have a connection with a person, a trustworthy adult he could depend on in the school.

It's often small rituals like peeling oranges that are the basis of close bonds—and growth. People who have "got It" understand that: that the significant relationships people with autism develop often bear little resemblance to the relationships other people might have. Denise Melucci is a skilled artist who worked with Justin Canha, a talented artist with autism (see chapter 10), when he was young. Justin had displayed emerging talent as an artist, and when his parents asked Denise if she would tutor him, she was enthusiastic, though she lacked any formal training in autism and had never worked with a child with autism.

Justin was insistent on drawing cartoon characters—Mickey Mouse, Homer Simpson, Bambi—and resisted her suggestions that he move beyond that. Seeing his ability, she wanted to expand his repertoire and help him learn that he could enjoy and excel at creating other kinds of pictures. At first Justin stubbornly refused.

How did she coax him to expand beyond cartoons?

She meowed.

Denise knew that Justin's greatest passion besides animated characters was animals. He routinely visited zoos and enthusiastically greeted dogs and cats. In order to motivate him, she offered him a deal: every time Justin made an effort to draw something outside his repertoire of cartoon characters—a landscape, say, or a still life—Denise would meow like a cat. To her surprise, it worked. Not only did her novel strategy open Justin to exploring new areas of artistic expression, but it also helped inject fun into the experience and, most important, created the foundation for a trusting relationship between student and teacher.

Making a "meow" sound seems like a small thing, but what was significant was Denise's willingness to be flexible and creative in considering what might motivate her student. Another teacher might have resorted to making demands or simply given up, but she saw a challenge and met it with imagination.

Joshua, a sixth-grader, benefited from the same kind of creative thinking when his gym teacher devised a way to motivate him to participate in his class's exercise program. Joshua's passion was U.S. presidents. At an early age he had memorized the presidents in chronological order. Now he spent long hours on the Internet and with books, accumulating and memorizing facts about various residents of the White House.

The teacher's creative solution: she made connections between various exercises and presidents. She connected President Lincoln, known for his height, with stretching. She connected George Washington, associated with the story of chopping down a cherry tree as a youth, with arm swings. President Obama plays basketball, so she connected him with leaping as if the child were shooting a jump shot.

Instead of forcing the matter, the teacher found a way to motivate Joshua by following his lead and incorporating his interests. It wasn't just for Joshua; the entire class participated. And the teacher often let Joshua decide which exercises the class would do on a given day. With creativity and flexibility and by paying attention to what motivated Joshua, the teacher achieved multiple objectives: she motivated Joshua to get physical exercise, she engaged him by giving him a say in what he did in class, and she connected him socially to his classmates.

When teachers are resistant to such innovative strategies, it's not always because they lack creative impulses. Sometimes they fear that school administrators are not willing to support approaches that vary from the normal curriculum. In most schools the principal is the one to set the tone and determine priorities for the entire staff. When a principal "gets It," that can make all the difference for students with autism.

Nina was a pretty, petite first-grader whose mother liked to dress her in bright, flowery dresses. In preschool Nina was constantly in motion, spending much of the day rolling on the floor and crawling on tables. By first grade she had made great strides but still had difficulty with impulse control and awareness of her body. When her classmates would sit on the rug for their morning meeting and she wanted to join them, she would throw her body in the middle of the group instead of sitting as expected.

To help Nina control herself, one of her therapists provided her with a small, circular rubber pad—a colorful disc, about twelve inches in diameter—to help Nina know where to sit. When the children were seated on the rug for an activity, the teacher would designate a spot for Nina and place the pad there. It was a simple solution to help her control her impulses and understand where she should be.

Just as Joshua's classmates wanted to join in presidential calisthenics, all of Nina's classmates wanted colorful discs of their own. And the teacher complied, giving each child a circle with its own color and number. That helped to normalize what had been helpful to Nina. She wasn't the only one with a disc; she was just one of the kids.

The problem arose when the class moved to other parts of the school, in particular to the music room. The music teacher had her own methods of classroom management and wasn't open to change. When the therapist explained to her that Nina would be sitting on her colored disc in class, the music teacher rejected the idea, not wanting to offer any kind of special treatment. The girl needed to learn to sit, she said, despite her problems with body awareness and impulse control.

Of course Nina struggled to sit still in music class. When the children sat on the floor, she rolled about, awkwardly trying to move her body into the group, causing havoc.

The matter came up at a meeting of the various educators and therapists working to support Nina. Everyone agreed that the disc had been beneficial, providing the key to helping Nina to organize her body and understand where to sit. Finally the principal spoke up. "Are you convinced that this works?" he asked the group.

Everyone agreed that it did.

He pounded his fist on the table. "If this helps Nina, then *everyone* in the school will honor and respect that."

Some at the table doubted the music teacher would cooperate.

"It's not her decision," the principal responded. "This is a school decision. We support every student at the level they need to be supported to be successful."

That was a principal who "got It," who understood that it's essential to be creative, responsive, and flexible in supporting children of different abilities. When a principal takes such a stand, not only does it help individual children like Nina, but it also makes the teachers and therapists working with those children feel valued, supported, and validated. Knowing that they have that kind of support gives these educators the motivation and confidence to seek out the solutions that will best support their students, no matter how unorthodox they might seem.

Principals who "get It" see it as their responsibility to ensure that families of children with disabilities feel welcomed. They visibly interact with students and their families, and when problems or challenges arise, they see it as their role to help devise creative and appropriate solutions. Such principals create compassionate, caring communities.

In some school districts, particularly smaller districts, the special education director sets that tone, sometimes from the very beginning of a family's journey. Stacy, a special education director in Connecticut, made it her business to initiate contact with families in her district whose toddlers were in early-intervention programs and would likely be enrolling in her district's special education programs. She visited the families at home to listen to their concerns and inform them of the ways her schools could help.

Some of Stacy's colleagues from other districts questioned the wisdom of these personal visits, wondering whether a busy district administrator was overly burdening herself by calling on every new family. But Stacy knew that the transition to school for such families is fraught with anxiety for both students and parents. She also understood that one of her most significant roles was building trusting relationships with families. When parents feel nurtured from the beginning of a child's educational journey, that serves to enhance that relationship for years to come.

Linda, a special education director in another district where I consulted, learned of a family in her district with twin girls approaching three years of age, both with autism. Having learned from Stacy, I suggested we pay a visit to the twins and their parents. In their home, a cluttered trailer, Linda and I sat on the floor and played with the two girls while we answered questions from their parents. Over the course of ninety minutes, Linda helped ease the minds of these parents, who were relatively new to the challenges of autism and how the schools could help.

As the visit ended and we drove away together, I noticed Linda had a smile on her face. "That just felt so right," she said. "I am so proud of what we did." In that brief visit she had sent a message about her district's open and welcoming attitude toward families struggling with disabilities and planted the seeds of a trusting relationship with an anxious, overwhelmed pair of parents.

Teachers Who "Get It"

Teachers don't have to specialize in autism or special education to understand the challenges, strengths, and needs of children with autism. Visiting a school I consulted for in Virginia, I watched one elementary school music teacher show remarkable skill incorporating three students with autism seamlessly with their twenty typical classmates.

One of the children, an eight-year-old boy, sang a part from the opera *Aida* in Italian. The teacher explained later that the boy had perfect pitch and had demonstrated the ability to memorize nearly any piece of music. Another boy played piano, leading the rest of the class in a song. When the teacher used a SMART Board to display an animated musical staff as part of a lesson in reading music, the children with autism were just as engaged, motivated, and focused as any of their classmates.

When I asked the teacher later about his approach, he explained that he actively sought to find the strengths and talents within each student, including those with autism, and to put them on display. "These children have so many obvious challenges," he told me. "I'm not doing my job unless I make sure that all of the students participate and that all of the students see the abilities of their classmates."

Other educators stand out by creating innovative ways to engage and motivate students. At a middle school on Cape Cod, I once observed a speech-language pathologist leading a group of special education students as they shared the process of baking chocolate chip cookies. After the children had completed the work and distributed the cookies onto plates, the therapist eagerly announced, "Okay, now it's time for the rest of our activity!"

Together the children took to the halls of the school, each carrying a plate of cookies. Each took a turn knocking on a classroom door, the teacher's lounge, and various offices, then greeting the person who came to the door and engaging in a conversation.

"Welcome to our classroom! What kind of cookies did you bring today?"

"We made chocolate chip cookies."

"How many do you have?"

Clearly this had become part of the school's routine, a regular opportunity for the students to be active participants in the community of the school, to engage with teachers and other students, and to have a sense of giving back. (And who doesn't like cookies?)

Diane was an educator who worked with a number of middle school students on functional academics—that is, improving reading and mathematics skills in order to use them in practical, everyday ways. She also sought out ways to create opportunities for natural social interactions. Diane worked with her students to create a store in their school where they sold snacks and drinks to staff members and students.

It was a simple idea, but it magically drew other students into the room where the students with autism spent much of their time. Diane did not rely on programmed interactions based on a formal social skills curriculum; instead the store provided a space in which the children experienced natural interactions and learned in the process. Even the students with the greatest challenges had opportunities to contribute, and the school's typical kids didn't have to be coerced into artificial social connections with Diane's students; they came for the snacks and stayed for table games. Her creative approach offered opportunities and helped foster a sense of community for all.

Encountering It-less People

As much as an educator or therapist who "gets It" can make a positive difference for a student and a community, encountering someone in the "It-less" category can make a challenging situation even worse, whether the person is a teacher, a therapist, a neighbor, or the cashier at the local pharmacy. Unfortunately I have seen far too many school administrators, teachers, and therapists whose ignorance, stubbornness, and inflexibility create more problems than they solve.

They Have a "Deficit Checklist" Mentality

Some professionals view a child solely as the sum of his deficits, when it's more valuable and sensitive to take a developmental approach, understanding children's strengths and needs as they grow and evolve over time and through stages. When professionals merely deliver a checklist of what the child cannot do, they emphasize a comparison to other children or some standardized measure rather than giving a whole picture of the child standing in front of them.

In most cases parents know their child better than anyone. And because diagnosing autism is a collaborative process, it is essential that mothers and fathers be included. Professionals should communicate to parents that their observations are valid, respected, and important. Rather than simply delivering a verdict, the professional should look to the parents to validate the professional's observations and reach a consensus.

The most common mistake professionals make in diagnosing is providing a diagnostic label but nothing beyond that. That is both irresponsible and insensitive. Professionals should also seek to identify relative strengths, especially those that can play an important part in a child's future. That helps parents understand that diagnosis represents only one step in a long journey. Receiving a diagnosis is often helpful, especially when it helps parents move beyond uncertainty and confusion about their child. The crucial question isn't what the child's label is but rather Where do we go from here? What is the best array of services we can assemble to assure our child the best possible future?

Parents receiving a diagnosis usually have another question: What is the long-term prognosis? The answer: What's most important isn't where your child is now; it's the *trajectory of growth* the child demonstrates over time. In other words, the child's progress will tell us about her potential. Our job and obligation is to make sure that the right supports are in place, including the right people. Despite the fears some professionals instill, there is no limit on a person's potential. For all of us—including people with autism—development is a lifelong process.

They Pay More Attention to a Plan Than to the Child

The parents of a child I had known as a preschooler asked me years later to visit the private autism school where their son, then twelve, had just enrolled in middle school. Alex was a thin, gangly boy who did not speak due to a severe motor speech disorder; aware and intelligent, he was unable to coordinate and sequence the fine-motor movements to produce intelligible speech. He also had extreme sensory sensitivity and found certain noises torturous. Over time he had become self-injurious and had to wear a helmet for his protection.

At one point during my visit, an administrator told Alex it was time to go from his classroom to the gymnasium. I saw an expression of fear and anxiety flash across the child's face. The teacher mentioned that Alex often experienced difficulty with excessively noisy and busy rooms such as the gym, but the administrator, a strong, young man, was insistent.

"He doesn't have a choice," he said, then picked up Alex under his arms and dragged him up the stairs as I followed closely behind. It had been six years since I had seen Alex, but he looked at me, pleading with his eyes, and then reached out and grabbed my shirt, seeming to beg for support. The administrator dragged him all the way to the gym, where he threw him onto the mat, as if to show him who was in charge. "This is our intervention for noncompliance," he said. I was a visitor and guest, and it happened so suddenly, I felt powerless to do much to intervene, but my heart broke for him.

I later informed his parents and another administrator of the abuse I had observed. To this day I am haunted by situations such as this and it fuels my passion for change. It is difficult to understand how it served any purpose to force a child into a setting that would certainly cause him emotional and physical pain. Unfortunately this wasn't an isolated incident but rather an extreme result of an approach predicated on controlling the child. The educator was blind to the boy in front of him and of the damage he was doing.

They Focus on the Child's Reputation, Not the Child's Potential

When students transfer to new schools, teachers and therapists appropriately familiarize themselves with the child's history and learn what challenges caused difficulty previously. The problem arises when they make assumptions about the present based on past and, in some cases, inaccurate accounts of the person.

One girl I knew had a history of lunging at therapists when she was particularly agitated. I observed that even newer therapists tended to be on guard with her, treating her as if they *expected* her to be aggressive. The one aide who was able to help her the most ignored what he had heard, treated her with respect, paid close attention, and expected the best from her.

As David Luterman, one of my mentors, teaches, people conform to expectations. Children often come with baggage: a label, a history of a particular kind of behavior, a reputation. While being familiar with history may be helpful, it should not be an obstacle to creating a new, more positive course by being open to a child's potential growth and development.

They Try to Control Rather Than Support

When a student is assigned an aide or paraprofessional, the hope is that the individual will be well trained and sensitive to the child's needs, intervening when needed, providing support when it's called for, and keeping a distance when that is more appropriate. Although most paraprofessionals fulfill their duties well, sometimes the problem stems from an aide who lacks proper training. Allen had an aide who hovered within inches of his face and physically prompted him so frequently that her very proximity became a dysregulating factor. As time passed, Allen became more and more agitated—mostly because of the aide's behavior.

Some adults who work with children have the misguided concept that to be effective, it's best to be in the child's face, even to give positive support. But for a child with autism who has social anxiety and sensory challenges, that can be scary and intimidating. It can also impede progress. The child can't decipher the social intentions, so instead of perceiving a helpful, energetic person, the child sees only an adult hovering frighteningly close.

This aide also made the common mistake of forcing her agenda on the child. Instead of reading the child's signals, she put all of her energies into telling him what to do, no matter what. That approach is disrespectful and often provokes resistance and anxiety.

They Are Insensitive to Parents' Hopes and Dreams

The Individualized Education Program (IEP) meeting was coming up for a seventh-grader I had followed for several years. Though he was bright and communicative, the teachers and therapists who saw him regularly made it clear that he was falling behind academically and having significant challenges. He had been in an inclusive classroom alongside typical peers, and it was clear to everyone that it was time for him to focus on more functional academic skills rather than struggling to stay at grade level in his academic subjects. Still, I knew that for his mother, Gloria, academic achievement was important, so it would be difficult to hear his educators recommending that he be moved off the standard academic track.

When I met with the administrator who would be running the

IEP meeting, I raised this concern and suggested that she broach the topic first in a private meeting with Gloria, not the larger meeting. "She's at a fragile point and will take this as a symbol of failure," I said. But the administrator, who prided herself on running an efficient operation, assured me it would be fine.

When the day came, I watched around the long table as one member of the team after another reported on the boy's limited academic progress and suggested that his program be shifted to a more functional, life skills focus. With each report, Gloria's hopeful expression grew more and more despondent. By the time the fourth person spoke, the air in the room felt heavy, and Gloria burst into tears and bolted from the room.

The administrator had prioritized efficiency and standard operating procedure over sensitivity to the mother and what she needed to hear: that the team wasn't giving up on her son, just appropriately adjusting his program. As a result she not only caught Gloria off guard, but in doing so she lost her trust because she didn't take into account where Gloria was on her journey.

By the nature of their work, teachers and other autism professionals deal with many families at once. But they need to treat each child, and each family, as unique and important. Being sensitive to the needs, hopes, and dreams of each child and parent is essential to building trust, working collaboratively, and serving the best interests of all.

The Importance of Knowing Your Role

One of the key ingredients of "getting It" is humility. The first time I taught a university course on autism, in 1979, one of my guest speakers was Terry Shepherd, then a professor at Southern Illinois University, who is the father of a son with autism. He told my students that life with his son was like living on a carousel, with each year representing another rotation. "Please understand that you will be getting on the merry-go-round with different families," he said. "You might be on my family's merry-go-round for one or two years before you get off. But please understand: we *live* on this merry-go-round."

I have heard that sentiment echoed again and again when I ask parents of children with autism what are the most important qualities they seek in the people who work with their children. Perhaps the most eloquent answer came from the mother of a young man who was then in his twenties. "The people we valued most were the ones who never judged us," she said, "but joined us on the journey."

Nothing could better sum up what it means to "get It."

CHAPTER 8

Wisdom from the Circle

ONE weekend each year I sit in a circle of friends and acquaintances, old and new, and take in wisdom.

The ritual began more than two decades ago. My wife, Elaine, and I were on vacation, hiking in Olympic National Park, when we began discussing the value of what we were doing: getting away to enjoy nature and escape the stress of everyday life. We reflected on how rarely most parents raising children with autism had such chances to escape the constant demands of their daily routines. So we set about creating a way to offer that opportunity.

The result was a retreat, created in partnership with Community Autism Resources, a parent-run agency in New England that supports families of children with autism and related challenges. For one weekend each year, some sixty parents come together at a New England retreat center to step away from their pressures at home and connect with others who understand the experience of autism. Together they share their stories—joyful, humorous, frustrating, agonizing—in a place where they know compassionate moms and dads who share similar challenges will listen and understand.

Of all the places my career in autism has taken me—workshops in St. Croix and Singapore, classrooms across the country, living rooms and playgrounds and hospitals—this is where I have learned the most. In particular I am moved every year at the closing circle, where the participants—some newcomers, some veterans, some parents of preschoolers, others of adults in their thirties—gather to reflect on the past two days and the past year. There are no rules, except to be open and honest and to listen.

The circle is where I heard a father tell me that every night he watches his son with autism fall asleep and sees the face of God. The retreat is where a mother called her son, then in his twenties, "the best human being I know," and tearfully shared her frustration that employers wouldn't give him a fair chance. It's where I heard one father agonize over not finding an appropriate school for his child and another chuckle over his son's habit of telling every young woman with long blonde hair that she looks just like Britney Spears. It's where one mother shared that while others may see her family—a blind husband and two daughters, one blind and the other with autism—as strange, she knows that they are really "hip" and that all the parents who have children with autism should know that they, too, are hip, because they really are.

Parents raising a child with autism can gather information, advice, and fortitude from a variety of sources: therapists, doctors, educators, books, and websites. In my experience, however, the most valuable, useful, and empowering wisdom often comes from other parents, mothers and fathers who have already been down this path. Over the years these parents and their children have been my best teachers, and their messages continue to inform my work and my understanding of autism.

Parents Are the Experts

It's natural to feel overwhelmed, confused, and even fearful about finding the best ways to help a child on the spectrum. For many parents their instinct is to rely on the wisdom of others who seem better qualified and more knowledgeable. Here is the advice I have heard parents of older children and adults share: Those experts might know more about autism, but you're the expert on your own child.

Nobody has the perspective, the sensitivity, or the ability to perceive the nuances of a child's behavior that a parent possesses. No one knows what a subtle facial expression means or what a particular cry or moan or giggle means the way a mother or father does. A parent knows when a daughter needs a break, when a son might be open to connecting. One dad told me how much he cherishes reading stories to his son at bedtime, an hour when he can "get in deep." Mothers and fathers are the ones who notice breakthroughs and milestones that even so-called experts might miss because they're just not as attuned to the child.

Of course there are exceptions. All parents aim to be the best providers, the most understanding caregivers, and the greatest supports for their children. But often circumstances make that challenging. When parents struggle financially or have their own myriad difficulties, they face significant obstacles in raising children—even more so when the child has her own serious challenges.

When parents are present and able, though, it makes all the difference. Researchers studying child development have posed this question in various ways: Child-rearing practices vary so dramatically from one culture to another, how can parents in *all* of these cultures raise children who are emotionally healthy? In a developed country a stay-at-home parent might spend hours interacting with an infant or toddler, face-to-face, while in a developing country the mother might spend half the day in the fields with her child on a cradleboard on her back. What both mothers offer is responsive caregiving. Whether the mother is sitting on a playroom floor full of toys or in the field, when her child cries or fusses, she responds and calms the child. When the child is most alert and available, the parent seizes on the opportunity to teach and interact. The best predictor of emotionally healthy children is having highly responsive caregivers.

Autism can add a challenge to this scenario since it can be more difficult for a parent to attend to a child's needs when the child is difficult to read. But parents learn and adapt and are far better equipped to understand their child's communication and state of regulation than anyone else. Professionals can offer perspective, resources, experience, and insight, but that doesn't replace or trump an attentive parent's perceptions, whether the child is three or thirty and whether the parent is new to autism or has decades of experience.

Natalie was one such mother, with a keen sense of her son Keith's abilities and challenges. When I first met Keith, he was five years old and not speaking. In addition to autism, he suffered from a seizure disorder; he also had severe food allergies and gastrointestinal issues. Keith, with flushed skin and tense posture, often appeared to be in significant pain. As his medical issues were addressed with some success, he began speaking and he progressed socially, finding some degree of comfort and stability in his elementary school.

When Keith was in his last year at the school, his mother sought my help. It was many months before Keith was to move up to middle school, but Natalie confided that she was already so worried about the prospect of that transition that she was losing sleep. She and her husband felt that it would be best for him to stay in the elementary school for another year rather than moving on with his classmates. They believed that the familiarity and stability would benefit him, and they valued that his current teachers were well acquainted with Keith, were able to read his signals, and provided the support he needed. Natalie understood the district policy that students at a certain age progress to the next school, but her strong maternal instinct was that it would serve her son to wait. Because of the severity of his disability, he had made slow progress for many years, but important gains had accelerated in the past two years. Why take the risk of setting him back?

I trusted their hunch, and I agreed to advocate for their position in my role as a consultant for the district. It was extremely rare to hold students back, and Keith didn't meet all the criteria for doing so, but I suggested that in this case the educators should pay attention not to the policy but to the child and his parents. "These parents know their child," I said. "They're invested in him, and they know what's right."

In the end the special education director and principal agreed and gave Keith another year in his elementary school. After that year he made a successful transition to middle school. The district also won the trust and appreciation of a pair of parents, grateful that their instincts about their son were honored and respected.

Trust Your Gut, Follow Your Instinct

Almost weekly I have an exchange of this sort: A mother or father asks me advice about a particular activity, a therapy, or some approach involving their children. When I reassure the parent that her own hunch is probably correct, the inevitable reply is "That's what I thought, but my therapist (or doctor or teacher) disagreed."

Trust your gut.

David and Susan had two teenage boys, both on the autism spectrum. Though they lived in a beautiful part of New England, they hadn't been outdoor enthusiasts until after their boys were diagnosed. Spending time in a state park, they took a one-mile family hike and discovered that the boys not only enjoyed the activity but also found it calming and regulating. When the boys were in their early teens, David and Susan hatched a plan to tackle the rigorous nine-mile hike up Franconia Notch, the famous New Hampshire mountain pass.

When the boys' occupational therapist heard the plan, she warned against it, cautioning that the two lacked the physical conditioning and the stamina to make the hike. Besides that, the boys, like many children and teens with autism, had a tendency to wander off.

In the end, though, David and Susan ignored the advice of the therapist and made the trip. Not only did the boys handle the challenge of the trek; they thrived, enjoying the outdoors, the experience, and even the physical challenge.

As Susan explained, she heard so much about her sons' limitations that she rarely considered their potential. By following her own instinct instead she opened up a new world of possibilities for the boys and the entire family. For years Susan kept a photograph of Franconia Notch posted near her desk as a reminder of the rewards of her journey with her children. "It's my own visual reminder," she said, "that one fine day we accomplished a goal I'd always wanted not just in spite of autism but because of it."

Find Community

When parents discover that a child has autism, it's natural for them to feel alone and isolated. Their social circles shift. Neighbors, friends, even relatives sometimes distance themselves, in many cases because they don't know what to say or how to interact with the child. They're uncomfortable; they can't relate; their own children are on different paths, different trajectories, and they pull away. Even those who wish to help may not know how. Parents often describe this shift: people who had been in their lives previously don't know what to say or do about this new reality. Those changes can be painful and disorienting for parents who are already dealing with the difficulties that come with the child's diagnosis.

It's essential for such families to connect with others, to find a community where they are understood, accepted, and welcomed, where they can be comfortable and don't need to explain themselves. Community can take many forms: groups of relatives; school support groups; churches, synagogues, or mosques; informal circles of friends. I have learned the importance of connecting with other parents and families from the instant community that forms each year at our parent retreat. I experienced it again when I partnered with members of my temple and an extraordinary rabbi to create a special Sabbath service as an option for families of children with special needs. After all, shouldn't your place of worship be the place where you can find acceptance and nonjudgmental attitudes toward children who may look or behave differently?

When parents share time and stories with others who have experienced similar setbacks and breakthroughs, who have struggled to support their children in the same ways, they form an almost instant bond. What had been painful—a child's meltdown, an embarrassing public encounter—becomes the source of laughter and release. What had been isolating—disappointments with schools or friends or professionals—becomes the basis of connecting with others. Newcomers to our retreat often tell me that they hadn't even realized how much they had been missing this vital connection until they discovered it at the retreat. Fathers in particular gain from hearing other fathers express the same emotions that they feel but rarely share. Parents who have returned again and again to the retreat say they feel much more deeply connected to other retreat parents, whom they see just once a year, than to people they see routinely at home.

That said, it's important to find the right community. Sometimes other parents want to vent but not support. And it's important to remember that children with autism fall on a broad spectrum of ages and abilities, so one family's experience may not bear much resemblance to another's. When there is a good match, the best community is the one that offers companionship, understanding without judgment, and support without needless criticism.

See the Cup as Half Full

It is also essential to seek out those who pursue and find the positive along the way. As one father on our retreat put it, "We've learned to avoid the doom-and-gloom crowd." He recounted how, feeling the need for connection and understanding, he and his wife had joined a local support group for parents of children with autism spectrum disorders. "All we heard about at that first meeting was how stressed out everybody was, their conflicts with the schools, what their kids couldn't do and the therapy they needed," he said. They had gone in search of sustenance, but the session had left them with a dark, hopeless feeling.

A mother explained the issue this way: "We know the difficulties twenty-four/seven. We want to hear some of the positives. We want people to celebrate with us."

That doesn't mean being Pollyannaish or avoiding the truth. It means surrounding yourself with people who can see—and help you see—your child's beauty, wonder, and potential.

Parents face the same sorts of challenges in their encounters with professionals. Some physicians and therapists feel obligated to deliver diagnoses and opinions in the worst possible light, informing parents of the direst prognoses: what the child will never do or accomplish. Some teachers report only a child's struggles and problems, losing sight of the progress and breakthroughs, however seemingly insignificant. Not only can this cast a negative pall on the child; it can also affect parents' perceptions of their children. When I hear of the negative ways some practitioners present information, I'm reminded of the Paul Simon song "Tenderness": "No, you don't have to lie to me. Just give me some tenderness beneath your honesty."

Parents who are veterans of the autism journey have put it this way: Many factors about your child and your child's disability are out of your direct control. But you *can* control your choices: with whom you and your family spend time, which professionals you pursue, whose advice you listen to. Why not choose the people who give you tenderness with their honesty?

Have Faith

I once listened to Maria Teresa Canha, mother of Justin, the talented artist, tell her family's story to a rapt group of parents. Afterward the audience peppered her with practical questions: How had she found an art tutor for her son? How had Justin learned to care for himself? How had he learned the social skills required for job interviews? Then a mother in the front row raised her hand and asked how the Canhas could send their son from their home in New Jersey on public transportation to a job in New York City: "How do you deal with the fear?"

Maria Teresa did not hesitate to answer. "I have faith in God," she said, "and I have faith in Justin."

Parents frequently express the importance of maintaining those two kinds of faith: in your child and in something larger than yourself. Admittedly, as a young professional I held less stock in the role of faith, especially within organized religion, and placed more confidence in science and research, probably due to my own discomfort. But over time and in hundreds of encounters with families of all kinds, I have seen firsthand how important a strong sense of faith can be to families coping with autism.

At a school meeting about her five-year-old son, a mother marveled at the progress the boy had achieved. Before age four he had been unable to speak; then, after considerable work with therapists, he had begun communicating with the help of a keyboard and, later, an iPad with a text-to-speech app. Before long that led to the beginnings of actual speech. The mother was clearly delighted. She had questioned whether he would ever be able to develop speech to communicate, so she was overjoyed that this ability had emerged so quickly.

"Well," I told her, "your son has done a lot of hard work."

The mom smiled and praised the teachers and therapists who had been working with her son. Then she told me that every night, she prayed for her son. "I see this as a collaborative team effort," she said, "between God and the school staff."

Faith can take many forms. Parents struggle to have spiritual faith and faith in their children but also to have faith in doctors, in therapists, in teachers, and in school districts. Do they understand my daughter? Do they have my son's best interests in mind? Can they see how very special she is? That's not always easy, and for some that faith is routinely shaken. But the parents I know who cope the best are those who find a way to have faith and trust.

Many parents see themselves in partnership with a higher power in raising a child. This brings comfort, a sense of shared responsibility and trust, and decreases anxiety. For others what is important is developing faith in their own ability to know what's best for their children. When I see these issues raised in discussions with parents, I am always struck by that breadth of the continuum, from those who see a divine hand in the process to those who feel that they are on their own.

The common factor is hope. The poet Maya Angelou once said, "In order to survive, a human being needs to live in a place furnished with hope." Of course the hope should be tempered by realism. Raising false hopes or expectations about a child's prospccts serves neither the parents nor the child. Plenty of parents have come across quacks and charlatans who promise "cures" and "recovery," only to lose money, time, and ultimately some degree of faith. (See chapter 11.) For many professionals it is a tricky balance to convey the real potential for positive growth for the child without minimizing the significant potential challenges.

Hope can come from paying close attention to a child and celebrating progress, even in its most subtle forms. It also comes from meeting parents who are farther down the road on their journey and who can share their stories of unexpected progress. Research shows that when parents are more optimistic about their prospects, children are less likely to display problematic behaviors.

Accept and Express Your Feelings

Being the parent of a child with autism takes most mothers and fathers to uncharted emotional territory. Raising a child with challenges brings powerful feelings they may not have experienced previously in the same way: guilt, resentment, anxiety, anger. Fathers often describe feeling frustrated that they can't connect with their sons. A mother might share how her daughter's endless chatter about a particular topic drives her crazy. Then the parent often says, "I know I shouldn't feel this way."

Raising a child with autism doesn't mean you have to be a saint. We're all human. Our feelings are both natural and legitimate. Parents need not be hard on themselves. Nor should they try controlling what is beyond their control.

In some cases the troubling feelings aren't about the child but about other people close to the parents—relatives, close friends. An uncle might offer unsolicited advice about raising a child with autism, or the child's grandmother might criticize how the parents discipline their child—or don't. It's important to realize that autism can be disorienting and provoke anxiety in the extended family as well as in parents. Most often the comments and suggestions come from a place of caring, judgmental as they can sometimes sound.

"We pretty much have this autism thing down," one father said, "but our greatest challenges, by far, have to do with pushy, insensitive family members."

The parents who cope most successfully with such situations are those who are the most honest and direct. They express gratitude for the person's caring and interest, but then they draw the line: "We appreciate your concern. Please understand that we are doing things the way we feel is best for our family."

Be Appropriately Assertive, Not Aggressive (and Know the Difference)

Raising a child with autism means constantly acting as the child's advocate, working to secure the proper supports and services. Parents routinely find themselves making requests of school district administrators, teachers, therapists, insurance companies, and others. As one mother said, "I need to be the Warrior Mom."

Seeking and securing the best options for a child often feels like going to battle, but parents often tell me they experience a delicate balancing act: sometimes they're locked in conflict with the very people in whom they entrust the care of their child. The instinct is to push and push, but if you push too much, you may damage relationships with those you rely on.

Here's the essential thing: Keep the child front and center.

Many parents have described finding themselves in a clash of adults, a personal struggle between parents and educators. Those battles are unlikely to end well for anyone. Consider these encounters from the point of view of the teacher or other professional whose work entails serving multiple students and their families. If every meeting with a parent is a skirmish, if the parent makes contact only to complain and make demands, it hardly feels like teamwork. And to a professional who feels she is doing her best, it may cause confusion and dismay.

In some cases having a child with a disability comes with so much anger, resentment, and disappointment that a parent needs a way to channel these feelings. Autism is a passionate affair, full of strong emotion, and we need to somehow direct and resolve that energy. Some find the answer in the battle, hiring lawyers or professional advocates—or threatening to—and issuing demands of all kinds. Of course sometimes that's unavoidable, but more often, finding a positive way to channel the energy is more helpful to all. One important strategy for staying positive: Keep the focus on the child. Some parents make a practice of always coming to IEP meetings and other conferences with a photo of their child. They place it on the table in front of them so that if things become contentious or difficult, they gesture to the photograph—a reminder that, while things might get testy, "this is about what's best for our son."

When parents keep the focus on the child rather than blaming or berating administrators or teachers, it provides openings for the professionals to rise to the occasion. They see the parents as human beings, assure them that they are heard, and work in collaboration to serve the child's best interests.

It's also nice to ask how you can help: Chaperoning the class field trip? Sorting books in the school library? When teachers perceive parents as disengaged, showing up only when they have complaints or criticisms, that can undermine the trusting relationship that is so important to the child's well-being. When teachers know that a parent is present, engaged, and interested, they are generally more open to constructive criticism.

Pick Your Battles

When their child is young and newly diagnosed, parents can feel overwhelmed by the need to find schools, communicate with educators, and shuttle children to various therapies. They have diets to consider, alternative approaches to weigh, teachers and administrators to meet with. And all of that is in addition to the routine details of life: attending to their other children, the stresses of work, the demands of family life, and (for those in a relationship) care of the marriage or partnership. Some parents feel that it's their job to become superhuman, to take it all on and do it all well. Most often the child with autism dominates the agenda out of the parents' fear that the child will not progress, could regress, or that, at the very least, opportunities will be missed.

One of the most common bits of advice more experienced parents share with newer ones is this: Pick your battles.

That approach applies to dealings with schools. Parents might disagree with a teacher's assessment of a child or the way the child's schedule is arranged. They might feel strongly that a child needs one-to-one support throughout the school day, while the school staff believes the child has made so much progress that less support and more independence is appropriate. When parents participate in decisions as part of the child's team, reasonable compromise is part of the process. It's important not to make life one big battle but to decide what's important and what's not.

The same tactic can be helpful in dealing with patterns of behavior at home. Others might express the opinion that a particular pattern of behavior poses problems and ought to be dealt with. But parents might decide that it's not a significant priority at that moment. Sometimes these decisions relate to what else is occupying the child's and the family's time and energy. A developmental perspective says it's important to take on challenges when it's developmentally appropriate to do so, for both the child and family.

Often a parent will admit, "I know we have established a behavior plan that's laid out in detail, but my father has been in the hospital several times this month and I'm drained. I can't be consistent with that plan now."

These plans are created to serve the child and the family. There is no perfect plan, no boilerplate approach that works in every situation. And no one can decide what's important more accurately than mothers and fathers can.

Find the Humor

Bob smiled when he told the story of accompanying his son Nick to a fast-food restaurant. On his way to sit down, Nick approached a table of strangers, reached out, and grabbed a couple of French fries from a man's tray. "That's delicious!" Nick said.

Bob smiled, shrugged, sheepishly said "I'm sorry," and escorted his son away.

When their children act out in unexpected and surprising ways in public, many parents feel embarrassed and humiliated, struggling with how much they need to explain their children.

Sometimes it's healthier for all just to laugh.

Another family was shopping at Home Depot around the time the parents were working with their young son with autism on toilet training. He had been resistant, so they had worked on motivating the boy to spend more time in front of the toilet. In the middle of the Home Depot visit, the boy decided to test his newfound abilities—on a nonworking display toilet.

The parents glanced at each other, as if to say, "What do we do now?" Their quick decision: leave. They felt badly, but realized that their priority at the moment was to prevent him from having a meltdown, and to escape.

Looking back, they could have laughed or cried. They chose to laugh.

Both stories also serve as a reminder of the importance of connecting with other parents of children with autism. Such moments can feel embarrassing, difficult, and humiliating, but when we share similar stories with others who understand, they become the basis for laughter, comfort, and shared connections.

Finding humor is essential for professionals too. When I was a summer camp counselor, I was assigned to pay attention to Dennis, who was twelve, on an outing to a rodeo. As our group enjoyed the show, I suddenly heard a little girl behind us cry out, *"Daaady!"*

I turned to see Dennis happily chomping on a huge clump of pink cotton candy. When nobody was looking, he'd snatched it from the girl. Nervously I turned to apologize to her truck-driver-size dad, fearing the worst.

"Oh, let him enjoy it," he said, chuckling. "We'll get another one."

When visitors' day came, I shared the story with Dennis's parents. They both broke into broad smiles and laughed. "Welcome to our life!" they said in unison.

Insist on Respect

When I first met Teddy, he practically tore my office apart. He was an energetic six-year-old who stopped speaking around age three, at the time his seizures began. His parents, Jack and Karen, had already taken him to countless specialists before they found their way to the hospital where I was providing outpatient evaluation services. As I tried to evaluate him and hear about him from his parents, Teddy became so agitated that he was throwing books and files from my shelves.

At the end of the appointment his parents apologized, but I assured them that was unnecessary; I knew Teddy was extremely dysregulated, confused and upset, as I could see it in his eyes. Later they told me how much my response had comforted them. In earlier appointments they had met professionals who—perhaps not in words but in tone—seemed to question why they couldn't do a better job controlling their child.

I continued to see Teddy and his parents for decades. Years later Karen told me that when they encountered teachers or therapists who they felt were being judgmental, they would flee. "There's enough guilt that goes along with this role—we don't need those looks and comments," she said.

Early in the journey of raising a child with autism, parents often feel disempowered and disoriented. Perplexed and confused by the child's behavior, they don't know where to turn or whom to trust. That is when Jack and Karen's advice is particularly pertinent. Some parents, particularly those with less experience with the medical establishment or school district bureaucracies, assume that they don't have a choice, that dealing with professionals who are condescending or patronizing is a necessary part of raising such a child.

It's not. And both the parents and their children deserve better.

At our retreat's closing circle one year, a father echoed Karen's sentiment. "We're not asking a lot," he said. "When we deal with administrators and professionals and our relatives, all we want is to be respected as parents and for our children to be respected."

I can't remember a comment in that setting that so resonated. Looking around the circle, I saw nearly every head nodding.

The good news is that caring, respectful, and responsive professionals are out there, and they want to help. Sometimes the challenge is in finding them.

Channel Your Energy

Not long after my dear friend Elaine Hall adopted her son Neal at twenty-three months, his challenges became clear: the toddler had trouble sleeping, spun in circles, opened and closed cabinet doors, pulled pictures off walls, and could tantrum for hours. At three he was diagnosed with autism. Elaine surrounded her son with artists and actors, and Neal responded. With their creativity and energy, they were able to draw him out, and Elaine saw Neal connecting in ways she had never seen before.

Yet all around her Elaine saw other children with autism struggling, other parents perplexed, frustrated, and anxious about their children. So she created a program that would bring to others what had been so effective for Neal. In 2004 she launched the Miracle Project, a theater and arts program for children with autism. Within a few years the program had grown from its base in Los Angeles to a national organization with affiliates in several cities. It was featured in an award-winning HBO documentary, *Autism: The Musical*, and Elaine spoke at the United Nations on World Autism Awareness Day.

And it all began with one mom who was confused and perplexed.

Raising a child with autism can be draining, emotionally and physically. But again and again I have seen parents who not only rise to the task but actually change the course of their lives to help others facing the same challenges. It's easy to feel frustrated and angry, but instead of directing their anger at teachers or school administrators, these mothers and fathers have channeled their energies in creative directions or opted for new career paths based on their parenting experiences.

Many parents initially direct their energy in adversarial ways, battling with school administrators, sometimes on the advice of lawyers or professional advocates. But later they channel their efforts more positively as fundraisers, volunteers, and advocates for political change. Many pursue degrees in special education, counseling, or therapeutic fields.

A lawyer became an expert on government policy affecting people with autism. A father joined his local school board. The parents of three children on the spectrum were spending so much time focused on autism that they eventually decided to make it the focus of their careers: the mother earned a nutrition degree and opened a practice focused on children with disabilities, and the father created a non-profit organization offering activities for children with various disabilities. Another mother who had to learn to negotiate two different school district bureaucracies to secure the best setting for her son became a consultant for one of the districts, enlisted to help other parents in their own struggles. A father retiring from twenty years in a state corrections facility wants to be a classroom aide, so that he "can truly make a difference in people's lives."

None of these parents set out to change their careers. What they share is that they were open to seeing in their journey not just struggle but possibility. In the process each discovered the gratification and inspiration that comes from helping others.

CHAPTER 9

The Real Experts

In 1986 Temple Grandin forever altered public perceptions about autism when she published her first book, *Emergence: Labeled Autistic*. Here, for the first time, was an articulate, intelligent adult who could describe with insight and clarity the experience of living with autism. She detailed her thinking processes, explained her sensory sensitivities, spoke of the different learning styles within autism, and recounted the numerous and varied challenges she had faced growing up.

Before Temple began writing and speaking publicly, our understanding (and misunderstanding) of autism had largely been based on research and the accounts of parents and other observers, some ill-informed. Much of what she said confirmed long-held beliefs; some of her insights contradicted them. But one thing was clear: people with autism have intact minds and strong opinions, and some have tremendous insight into their own experience.

Decades later Temple remains the most famous person with autism, but many others have emerged as articulate spokespeople and astute chroniclers of their own experience. My work has offered me the privilege of getting to know many of these people, some of whom have become valued friends. The experiences of sharing time with them and their friends and families, listening to their accounts and presenting workshops with them, has deeply informed my understanding of autism, providing insights and perspectives I would otherwise lack.

Three in particular have truly enhanced my thinking and understanding, and their insights guide me almost every day in my work: Ros Blackburn, Michael John Carley, and Stephen Shore have each helped me and countless others to understand autism and how best to help people on the spectrum lead fulfilling and meaningful lives.

When I mention such people, some express doubt about (or silently wonder) how these articulate individuals can accurately represent the experience of individuals who cannot speak or are otherwise severely challenged. My response: If they can't, then who can? Who better to explain the experience of autism than those who live with it every day? I am eternally grateful to these three individuals because they explain things that no amount of research can reveal. I am happy to share some of what they have taught me.

Ros Blackburn: "I Don't Do Social"

I first met Ros Blackburn at an autism conference in Michigan, when my colleague Carol Gray, the well-known autism expert, beckoned me over to meet this young woman visiting from England who would be speaking about her experiences growing up with autism. We shook hands, and Ros, then in her midthirties, said something that sounded like "Wannameesteert?"

I had to ask her to repeat herself. It took a few repetitions before I heard clearly what she was asking: "Want to meet Stuart?"

I offered a blank face.

"Stuart," she said. "Stuart Little."

I nodded, and Ros—with an impish grin—pulled a hand from her coat pocket and revealed what she was holding: a tiny stuffed mouse, based on the character from the children's movie. "Barry, this is Stuart. Stuart, this is Barry," she said.

And that is Ros: playful, quirky, mischievous, unique—and full of surprises (not to mention passionate about the movies she loves).

Ros explains that this is her true self, her autistic self. She has also learned, over time, to present a different self to the world: restrained, polite, controlled.

That dichotomy originated in her childhood. She was diagnosed with autism as a child. Her parents clearly understood her challenges but taught her the social skills she would need to function in the world.

While they were compassionate, her mother and father were also demanding, never accepting autism as an excuse for inappropriate behavior. Their approach helped inform the advice she often shares: that parents should have high expectations of their children with autism, matched by equally high levels of support.

When she explains autism, Ros describes living with an almost constant feeling of anxiety and fear. She is fond of pointing out that people in the military, police officers, and firefighters are trained to be calm in the face of panic. Not so for people with autism: "We don't receive the same type of training, yet we experience this level of panic every day."

What most exacerbates that fear is being forced into social situations. She is comfortable and never experiences nervousness addressing large audiences, where she feels in control. But more informal social settings can terrify her because she cannot predict what others will say or do. "I don't do social," she likes to say.

I once met her in a hotel lobby where, nearby, a group of young children were chasing each other. One slid across a coffee table and nearly fell on her. A look of fright crossed her face. "See?" she said, a bit shaken. "That's why I don't like children!"

Despite her distaste for social situations, she doesn't experience embarrassment because she doesn't worry about what others are thinking of her. Ros often says that her greatest ability—expressing herself verbally—is also her greatest disability. What she means is that people observing her assume that because she is an articulate, intelligent, and capable speaker, she must be a confident, comfortable person inside as well.

The truth is that Ros finds the world overwhelming—a buzzing, confusing, out-of-control reality filled with unexpected events and baffling social rules. And when she has strong emotional reactions, it can interfere with her ability to communicate or even to tolerate being in social situations.

She has developed ways to cope with these challenges. Her favorite is jumping on a trampoline, an activity that brings release and even joy. When she travels, she always has a traveling companion, one of several young women she describes as "carers."

Once Ros attended a conference I helped organize, where I had the privilege of hosting the actress Sigourney Weaver. I welcomed Sigourney to spend time with Ros to prepare for her role in the movie *Snow Cake*, in which she plays a woman with autism. When the conference concluded, the two of them were to be among a group I was gathering for dinner at my home. But as our small group was discussing logistics, Ros abruptly interrupted. "Barry," she said, "I could really benefit from some trampolining right now."

Trampolining? It was early evening on a winter day in Rhode Island, with snow on the ground. I had no idea where to find a trampoline. Then Sue, a mom who was among our group, spoke up: "Barry, we have a trampoline in our backyard that my son uses. We just shoveled the snow off."

Ros smiled like a child hearing there's a second day of Christmas. "Can I go?"

Off they went, Ros and Sigourney Weaver, to bounce in their winter coats in a suburban backyard. Earlier Ros had given a two-hour presentation. All day she had put on her act. Now she needed time to be Ros. (Based on this experience, Sigourney suggested the trampoline scene that director Marc Evans added to *Snow Cake*.)

One of my favorite moments during their visit was when Ros was teaching Sigourney how to act "autistic."

Sigourney: Ros, I noticed that when you get very excited, you lift up your hands to the side of your head and rock back and forth while flapping your hands close to your ears. *(Sigourney then demonstrated the action.)*

Ros: No, actually, it is a bit more like this. *(Ros proceeded to lean her body to the right while performing the same action, correcting Sigourney's attempts. Sigourney imitated.)* Much better, you've got it!

Ros's other loves are figure skating and certain movies. After her first visit to Providence to speak at our conference, I invited her for a return visit, but she was hesitant. She could not understand why I would want to invite her back since she had already presented her story. Besides, travel makes her very anxious, and attending conferences forces her to be in social situations. (Ros's carers offer great support as they help her negotiate unfamiliar situations and places.) Finally she agreed to come when I offered to take her to New York City so she could skate at the Wollman Rink in Central Park, which she had seen in a favorite movie. During her visit, the same woman who had so dazzled audiences with her insights took girlish pleasure in gliding across the ice, Stuart Little in her pocket, and later posing Stuart for photos around Central Park.

On that same visit Ros and I went to a crowded Italian restaurant with four others. The host led us to a table in the middle of the room and was about to seat us when Ros started shaking her head anxiously. "Can't sit here," she said.

I couldn't see another option, but the seating host read Ros's signal and gestured toward another section of the restaurant he hadn't opened yet. Ros chose a table against the wall so she could sit with her back to the wall.

"I hate quadraphonic sound," she said, "and when there's too much movement in my peripheral visual field, I get very anxious." For all of her challenges, one of Ros's great strengths is a keen sense of her own needs and limits.

Ros is blissfully unaware of things most people deem important. When we saw each other a few years after the trampoline episode, I asked her if she had been in touch with Sigourney Weaver lately. "Yes," she said, "she came to London last year, and we got together."

When I asked for specifics, she explained that Sigourney had invited her to the opening of "some movie," where they had walked down a red carpet together. Connecting the dots, I realized what she was telling me: Ros had attended the premier of *Avatar*, the highest grossing movie of all time, with one of its stars.

"Wow, what an experience!" I said. "How was it?"

Ros answered bluntly, "Really, really noisy and crowded."

Another challenge: being dishonest. "Lying is hard for me," she says. "For instance, saying 'It's very nice to meet you' when I'd rather be trampolining is still hard for me."

Still, her playful side is unrestrained. Ros often travels with favorite toys, such as a box of fidgets, including rubber lizards she shares with her audiences. As a sort of practical joke, she carries mirrors with her on airplane trips. Why? She uses them to reflect sunlight into the eyes of fellow passengers, endlessly amusing herself by watching their annoyed reactions.

After one of Ros's talks, I asked a mother in the audience for her reaction. The woman told me that she simultaneously loved and hated Ros's presentation. She loved the window Ros offered into how the woman's son experienced the world, but hated how painful Ros's experience of life sounded.

I knew just what she meant. Perhaps more than anyone I have known, Ros has made me understand the challenges of individuals with autism who find the world overwhelming and anxiety-producing. When I look into the eyes of a three-year-old who can't communicate verbally and is being forced into a noisy, chaotic room, I think of Ros and realize this youngster is not being noncompliant or uncooperative. The child is terrified.

Ros is also clear about how parents and professionals can best help in those situations when a person with autism is panicked or anxious. "Don't put your hands all over me, and don't talk a lot to me," she says. "Support me in silence. Support me with your presence."

Michael John Carley: "We Need to Hear About What We Can Do"

When Michael John Carley was thirty-six years old, his four-year-old son was diagnosed with Asperger's syndrome. After delivering the diagnosis, the clinician turned to Michael. "Now," she said. "Let's talk about you."

Within a few days, Michael too had an Asperger's diagnosis.

His first response was shock. How had he lived three and a half decades without realizing he was on the autism spectrum? He was happily married and had maintained a successful career as a diplomat, traveling to such hotspots as Bosnia and Iraq. He was also an accomplished playwright, a star baseball pitcher, a talented guitarist, and a host on a local NPR station.

At first he hid his diagnosis. But the more he reflected on his life, the more it made sense to him. He had always felt that he did not connect with people. In his buttoned-down private high school, he was such a misfit that teachers perceived him as a kid with behavioral problems and suspected he might have serious psychological problems. Eventually he transferred to a charter school with a more flexible, alternative orientation. There he flourished.

Still, as he went through life, many experiences and encounters left him baffled. He didn't understand why people engaged in small talk and had never been able to fathom the hidden rules of flirting. When an acquaintance asked him his opinion on a subject—politics or something in the news—he would launch into a reply so detailed and lengthy that listeners were rolling their eyes. Friends would abruptly cut off relationships with him, often after Michael said things that offended them. Afterward he still didn't understand what he had done wrong.

The initial shock of diagnosis gave way to relief—and eventually pride. The diagnosis became not a burden but a revelation.

Always passionate about his work, Michael gradually reconfigured his life to direct his energy and focus into advocating for people with autism spectrum disorders. In 2003 he founded GRASP, the Global and Regional Asperger Syndrome Partnership, and as its executive director helped it become the nation's largest membership organization consisting of adults on the autism spectrum. He particularly focuses on adolescents and adults, populations he considers underserved and largely misunderstood. He published an important and acclaimed book, *Asperger's from the Inside Out*, part autobiography, part self-help guide for people on the autism spectrum. And he went on to found and direct the Asperger Syndrome Training and Employment Partnership, which works with large companies to help train managers either to better manage existing employees with autism or to increase their confidence in hiring new ones.

Michael was an outspoken critic when, in 2012, the American Psychiatric Association was considering eliminating Asperger's Disorder as an official diagnosis, a change it ultimately made. He was concerned that the change would make accurate diagnosis more difficult and diminish public understanding of people with an Asperger's profile. He also felt strongly that people on the spectrum should have a direct voice in developing policies that affect them.

When I first met Michael years ago at a symposium I invited him to address, I was struck immediately by how articulate, intensely energetic, and focused he was. You might not guess that he has an autism spectrum disorder until he begins speaking about something he is excited about. He speaks quickly. His handshakes are extraordinarily firm. He gives extremely tight hugs. In conversation he stands unusually close. When you are engaged with Michael, it is a riveting experience.

When I learned that he had once represented a veteran's organization, Veterans for Peace, at the United Nations, I was astounded that a person with Asperger's had found success as a diplomat. One would think it would take great social savvy and flexibility to conduct oneself properly—greeting dignitaries in proper fashion, standing in the right place, saying the appropriate thing. But Michael explained to me that diplomatic protocol is so laden with rigid rules that once he had mastered them all, it was actually much easier for him to conduct himself in that world than in less formal social settings, where things are less structured and less predictable.

His considerable professional success made it easier for him to cope with his son's diagnosis than it might have been for other parents. While others might pray for a bright future for their children, he has said, "I had the advantage of evidence-based conviction." That is, his own life was a testimony to both the struggles and the potential of a person with an autism diagnosis.

Serious and driven, he also has an enviable sense of humor about himself. I once spent time with him at his vacation cabin, where I spotted a guitar. Knowing of his talent, I asked him to play a bit. Michael picked up the guitar and began finger-picking a blues progression. "Okay, but you're about to listen to twelve straight minutes of blues," he said, smiling. "Remember, I have Asperger's and need to have a sense of completion—I don't stop in the middle of songs."

A committed father and husband, he has coached his two sons' baseball teams. He is especially determined to be a positive role model for his son with Asperger's and frequently speaks of the importance of exposing young people on the spectrum to adults with autism who have managed to build successful lives, families, and careers.

Among Michael's great insights is this: a teen or adult with autism is more a product of his life's experiences than of his autism. Michael is very concerned about many of the serious mental health issues some people with autism develop due to their misunderstandings of social situations and being misinterpreted by others. While others may be tempted to point to autism as the cause of every struggle or setback, he says that, with proper support, many people can build emotionally healthy, productive, and successful lives.

He is also a spokesman, able to explain with insight and intelligence the experience of having autism. His central focus is the importance of developing trusting relationships and the many factors that make doing so difficult for people on the spectrum. In particular Michael explains the many painful experiences people with autism endure that neurotypical people might not perceive as unpleasant or difficult. To a person with autism, for instance, being restrained can be the equivalent of being physically and psychologically pummeled. For someone very sensitive to certain sounds, a high-pitched noise or even a shout can induce pain. The constant barrage of such aversive experiences can lead to considerable challenges. Michael's other main commitment is to supporting the many people with autism who lack family support and whose lives are filled with anxiety, stress, and fear, leading many of them to alcoholism and drug addiction. GRASP runs support groups in many cities, in person and online, to connect people who share the same challenges and struggles.

He is determined to share with others on the spectrum the insight that so transformed his outlook when he received his own diagnosis: that many of the painful experiences they have endured in life have an explanation that is not rooted in their character but rather in their wiring and others' unhelpful reactions.

That is the message he brought to Capitol Hill in November 2012 when the U.S. House Committee on Oversight and Government Reform conducted historic hearings about the dramatic rise in autism diagnoses. One of only two people on the spectrum to testify (the other was Ari Ne'eman, president of the Autistic Self Advocacy Network), Michael offered moving testimony that there was "no medical basis" for treating autism like a disease to be cured. "As we all grow, whether we're on the spectrum or not, we need to hear about what we can do," he said, "not what we can't do."

Stephen Shore: "They Accepted Me"

Stephen Shore describes his early childhood in this way: His development was typical until he hit eighteen months. That, he says, is when the "autism bomb" hit. His capacity for functional communication vanished, and he stopped making eye contact with his mother and father, who watched, bewildered, as he repeatedly banged his head. He seemed detached and distant and constantly engaged in self-stimulatory behaviors: rocking, spinning, flapping.

In the early 1960s that combination of challenges was so rarely seen that it took a year for his parents even to figure out where to have him evaluated. When he was finally diagnosed with autism in 1964, the physician who diagnosed him deemed Stephen too "sick" for outpatient treatment. The doctor's only recommendation was to have the boy institutionalized.

Fortunately for Stephen, his parents ignored that advice. Instead, operating only on their own instincts, they began what Stephen says would now be labeled a home-based early-intervention program. At the time it was considered just unusually strong-willed parenting. His mother was determined to keep him engaged, dedicating her days to encouraging his participation in activities with music, movement, and sensory integration. At first his parents attempted to teach Stephen by trying to get him to imitate them. When that didn't work, they began imitating *him*. That drew Stephen's attention and offered the beginnings of his ability to connect in meaningful ways.

"The most important thing about my parents is that they accepted me for who I was," says Stephen, who didn't speak until he was four, "but at the same time recognized there were a lot of challenges to overcome."

As an adult Stephen has dedicated his life to helping people with autism and their parents conquer those obstacles and build fulfilling, productive lives for themselves. He holds a doctorate in special education, has authored books, advised governments on policy related to autism, teaches at Adelphi University, and has spoken at the United Nations. He spends much of his time traveling the world consulting and delivering speeches to educate parents and professionals. He teaches piano to children with autism, but not to neurotypical kids since he finds it difficult to understand how they think and learn.

It surprises many people who meet him that a person with autism would spend so much time speaking to large groups of people. But to Stephen a presentation feels like nothing more than a long monologue—just his kind of conversation. When it comes to their enthusiasms, he says, people on the spectrum can talk for days.

That dry wit is part of his appeal. Of the many people on the spectrum I have met, Stephen has the greatest sense of humor about living with autism. Once, when we presented a workshop together, he and I went on a stroll. Stephen spotted a stick on the ground, picked it up, and held it up to his eyes to examine it closely. "Hey, Barry, great stim toy!" he said, grinning.

His sense of irony comes out when he talks about his marriage. Stephen met his wife, then an exchange student from China, when they were both studying music and were assigned to check each other's homework. They went on to connect socially, and one day on the beach she held his hand, kissed him, and gave him a deep hug. He explains his reaction in terms of "social stories," the technique developed by my talented colleague Carol Gray that helps people with autism understand and navigate social situations: "I had a social story which says that if a woman kisses, hugs you, and holds you all at the same time, it probably means they want to be your girlfriend." He knew his response could be "yes, no, or further analysis indicated." He decided on yes, and they have been married since 1990.

Stephen's ability to make light of his own mind—and the many challenges he encounters—brings a refreshing sense of perspective, a relief from the belief that autism is predominantly a heavy burden that casts a pall on life.

His sense of humor might be connected to the other distinctive quality that distinguishes him: for a person with autism, Stephen stands out as unusually grounded and calm. Most people with autism describe their heightened anxiety, but Stephen's relaxed demeanor is a reminder of the differences that exist among individuals with autism. I have seen him in a variety of situations—before audiences, in smaller groups, one-on-one—and he always is even-tempered, thoughtful, relaxed, and easy to be with.

That is not to say that he doesn't struggle with the same kinds of dysregulation as others on the spectrum. He experiences maddening discomfort when he has to wear a suit and tie, often wears baseball caps to keep glare out of his eyes, and recalls childhood haircuts as torturous, especially since he was unable to express his discomfort to his parents. He struggles so much with remembering people's faces that when he teaches college courses, he often can't put names with faces, even long into the semester.

On the other hand, Stephen knows exactly what it takes to calm his nerves. One reason for his extensive travel schedule is that he loves the experience of traveling on an airplane. That too is unusual among people with autism, who often find air travel dysregulating. Children in particular often find the cabins of commercial airliners to be overly confining and find it challenging to be in such close proximity to so many people. But Stephen craves the feeling his body experiences during takeoff. So he keeps traveling.

He also continues to spread the messages that are most important for him to share. Each adult with autism I have met who feels compelled to use personal experience to educate others has particular messages. Temple Grandin emphasizes the potential to turn special interests into careers. Michael John Carley focuses on the need to help those without strong family support and to educate potential employers about autism. One of Stephen's core messages is the importance of disclosure, that is, of informing a child of his or her own diagnosis at the appropriate time and in the most thoughtful way.

His sensitivity about that issue may stem from his own parents' care and attention in addressing his challenges. More than almost any person with autism I know, Stephen has a sense of his own story and how sharing it can be of benefit to others.

Central to that narrative is the story of two parents who, despite being told that there was no hope for their son, ignored the professionals, followed their own instincts, and used creativity and love to raise their child. It seems fitting that the child went on to commit his life to helping other families with similar challenges and to showing parents that their children, despite their diagnoses, have unimaginable potential.

CHAPTER 10

The Long View

It's hard for parents raising a child with autism to have perspective. Mothers and fathers are often so caught up in the day-to-day demands of parenting that they can easily forget that whatever is happening now represents just a single moment in time. When a child seems stuck in a pattern of troubling or perplexing behavior, it can be difficult to imagine her ever progressing further. Particularly in the earliest years, parents worry that their child might never develop language or might never progress beyond echoing a few phrases. Parents wonder if a daughter will ever stop lining up her stuffed animals in precise order, if a son might ever display interest in other children. What causes so much stress for people with autism also induces stress for parents: uncertainty—in this case, about the future.

It's important to remember that people with autism progress through developmental stages just as we all do. "One does not grow out of autism," explains Dena Gassner, a mother who is herself on the spectrum. "One grows into it." And no two journeys are alike.

To offer perspective, wisdom, and insight, I share the experiences of four families whose sons I knew as preschoolers who have moved into adolescence and on to adulthood. I share the stories of these four not because they are exemplary or a representative sampling but rather because of what I have learned from these young men and from observing and knowing their families. I hope reading how they have progressed, faced challenges, thrived, and found perspective and love will provide valuable lessons for your own journey.

The Randall Family: "If He's Given a Chance, He Runs with It"

It was Andrew Randall's grandmother who first suggested that his parents have him evaluated, that something might be amiss.

Andy was three years old but had been struggling for some time. When he was twenty months old, his mother, Jan, noticed that the language he had acquired was slipping away. Andy had learned about fifteen words but then stopped using some of them and clearly wasn't adding new ones to his vocabulary. A pediatrician assured Jan that her son was fine. Soon after that, their daughter Allison, two and a half years older, was diagnosed with a seizure disorder, and Jan and her husband, Bob, naturally shifted their focus to managing that crisis.

Meanwhile Jan became increasingly puzzled by the differences she noticed in Andy. He rarely made eye contact with her and wouldn't point at objects or people. Jan's mother, a first-grade teacher, sensed that these were red flags, but when she suggested that to her daughter, Jan at first ignored her.

Then, watching TV in December 1988, Jan caught a segment on *Entertainment Tonight* about a new movie called *Rain Man*. "It was like someone punched me in the stomach," she recalls. "I knew right then and there: that's what was wrong with Andrew."

After a school psychologist evaluated Andy, Jan asked point-blank if her son had autism. No, the psychologist said, noting—incorrectly—that a child with autism wouldn't demonstrate the strong maternal attachment Andrew clearly displayed. Her diagnosis: severe speech delay.

Jan felt relieved for a time, but Andy kept slipping. By then he didn't speak at all, just pulled Jan or Bob to the refrigerator when he was hungry. His tantrums could last an hour or more as he jumped up and down with such intensity that the downstairs neighbors could feel their apartment rattle. Fortunately for Jan and Bob, the neighbor was a sympathetic friend. For nine months the boy slept so fitfully that Jan had to post herself on a couch outside his bedroom so she would be available to soothe him.

Andy was nearly five when Jan finally appealed to the school district's special education director for more help. The district referred her to a psychologist—not to help Andrew but to help her develop parenting skills. Hearing Jan's account, though, and meeting Andrew and looking over his evaluations, the psychologist put the pieces of the puzzle together: clearly, she said, he has autism.

By that point Jan welcomed the news. "It felt like I had been in a very dark room and somebody opened all the blinds," she remembers. "I felt like I was basking in sunshine."

Armed with the diagnosis, she felt newly empowered. She began reading everything available about autism. She sought out other parents. She joined autism advocacy groups. She enrolled Andrew in a full-day special education program.

It took her husband longer to realize how profound his son's disability was. When Jan once mentioned wistfully that their daughter Allison would likely never become an aunt, Bob didn't seem to understand what she meant. "We just were not in the same place," she says.

At the time, the early 1990s, autism was much less frequently diagnosed than today and rarely discussed in the media, so the couple spent a great deal of energy explaining autism to friends and relatives—and fending off criticism. Jan's own father, baffled at his grandson's condition, blamed Jan. She took an active role helping her son to negotiate the world, but other relatives questioned her parenting, saying her coddling was causing the meltdowns.

While the criticism stung, she found support from a handful of other parents of children with autism, who not only understood her plight but encouraged her to raise her expectations of Andrew. The sky's the limit, they told her. Don't put the brakes on yet.

Despite Andrew's challenges, his personality shone through. Around the house he liked to stand on his head on a recliner, laughing uproariously. His parents found it hard not to laugh along. And children were drawn to him. A girl who lived in their apartment building took a particular liking to him, and when Andrew sat alone at the park or playground, she would draw him into the action, pushing him on the swing set or enlisting his participation in games like Duck Duck Goose. He took part amiably, though the rules defied him.

As for Jan and Bob, they tried not to let Andrew's challenges prevent their family from doing anything they otherwise might have done. They made a point of exposing him to a variety of people and experiences from an early age, taking him to church and letting him go on frequent sleepovers at an aunt's house or a neighbor's. Bob took him swimming weekly at the local YMCA, and the couple brought him along to restaurants and social gatherings. Those opportunities helped Andrew learn to adapt to changes and to different people and environments.

Though he used little spontaneous speech, he often communicated with echolalic phrases. A favorite was "We fight all night," a sentence he picked up from a Dr. Seuss book and used when he felt upset or thought someone else was angry. He still relied a great deal on physically manipulating other people in order to communicate, moving them next to objects that he wanted or places that he wanted to go. His struggle to communicate made him so frustrated that he routinely had meltdowns in stores and restaurants. But that didn't stop the Randalls from taking part in the routines of family life.

When Andrew hit adolescence, things became more challenging. Only in retrospect did his parents realize just how much. The private school where he was enrolled specialized in autism, but he was miserable there. When he had outbursts, the staff used four-point restraints and even locked him in a padded closet. He developed tics, quick and jerky head and shoulder movements, which the school staff tried to eliminate with behavior therapy, to no avail. A therapist who saw them at home encouraged a tough love approach, urging Jan and Bob to "get in his face" and "let him know who the boss is." Due to all these challenges, he had no afterschool activities.

He was so dysregulated so much of the time that he lashed out at home as well. He punched and kicked holes in the walls of the house. He broke car windshields and windows. He was angry, confused, and overwhelmed.

For a time his parents maintained faith in the private school, which had a good reputation, but eventually Jan's instincts told her his being there was doing Andrew more harm than good. Then a special education consultant helped confirm her feelings, telling her, "Andrew doesn't want to be acting this way. It's terrifying for him, too."

That proved to be a turning point. "All those people who were telling me to be in his face and 'put the thumb on him' when he gets out of control," she says. "They were wrong, wrong, *wrong*. He was hurting. He was treated as less than a person. That's why he was losing it."

They pulled Andrew out of the school when he was twelve. Jan tearfully apologized to her son for what he had been through there, and, remarkably, he seemed to forgive her. "We wanted more for Andrew," she recalls. They found it at South Coast Educational Collaborative, a public special education collaborative in southeastern Massachusetts, where Andrew was greeted by a warm and supportive community, including understanding teachers who welcomed parents' advice. When Jan suggested a reading program she had heard about that was particularly effective for students with autism, the teacher didn't hesitate to try it. On the first day she used the program, Andrew read words for the first time—at age thirteen.

"They understood that Andrew wasn't just a problem—he had skills and potential," says Jan. "They treated him with respect. They valued him as a person. And they respected me as a true member of the team."

That's what made it so difficult when Andrew hit age twenty-two, making him ineligible to continue in the program. Andrew had always been a hard worker; he was happiest when he was busy: taking out the trash, doing laundry, vacuuming. Jan surveyed ten different state-sponsored programs for adults with disabilities. Finding none appealing, she nonetheless signed him up for one since he needed to be in a program.

It proved a disappointment, suffering from poor organization, and was ill-equipped to support Andrew's challenges. His behavior regressed, but Jan and Bob kept hoping for improvement. When it never came, they took him out of the program and arranged to have him back at home, where Jan managed his time and work. Now he has a life skills coach who helps him with appropriate workplace behavior and everyday tasks like shopping and using transportation. At age twenty-eight, he works part time at a supermarket fetching shopping carts.

Looking back, Bob admits that it took a while for him to come to terms with having a son with autism, to accept that his son wouldn't play Little League, wouldn't drive a car, probably wouldn't have a family. "Once I finally got over all that stuff," he says, "then you just take him for what he is, and I'm proud of the person he has become. If he's given a chance, he runs with it."

Andrew still speaks little, communicating mostly in gestures such as putting his forehead on his mother's, and with a few favored phrases. A few years ago he started calling his sister Allie "Alliecat," and now appends the suffix *-cat* to the names of many girls and women, a sign he feels comfortable with them. He calls snack mixes "crunch stars," a phrase he heard long ago in Lucky Charms commercials. And when he feels the need to apologize, he sometimes says "Never ouch Mom," a phrase Jan says originated from her response when he would lash out in his early adolescence.

He plays basketball several times weekly, watches Boston Bruins hockey games, goes to the driving range, and visits the zoo. He enjoys creating abstract paintings using sand and paint, artworks that adorn the family's apartment and that have been displayed in local art shows. He also has an endearing mischievous streak. Riding in the car of one of the mentors who spends time with him, he sometimes slips bottle caps into the car's vents to playfully test her reaction.

Jan remembers that earlier in life, she was the kind of person who would hear a child crying at the supermarket and wonder what was wrong with the parents. Not anymore. "Andrew's taught me to be patient," she says, "and that good things come in many different ways."

No matter how much autism colors the way Andrew experiences the world, she likes to point out that there's more to him than that. "He is not his autism," she says. "He's an amazing human being."

The Correia Family: "He Teaches Me How to Live"

When she first sensed that her son Matthew might have autism, Cathy Correia's initial reaction was fear.

Just after college, Cathy had supervised employees at a sheltered workshop where adults with autism and other developmental challenges sorted jewelry parts. Some of the workers had spent their lives in institutions, a fate she could hardly imagine for her son. "When they started using that word about my own son, I thought, 'What are they going to *do* to him?' " she recalls. "That was my emotional reaction."

That's not to say she hadn't suspected from early on that Matt, the younger of two sons, had his share of challenges. As a toddler Matt was quite verbal, easily expressing his needs, but he didn't react in conversation the way Cathy thought he should. Instead of speaking spontaneously, he would echo whatever he heard. He'd stand in front of the TV, seeming not to notice that his brother was trying to watch. When she raised these matters with a pediatrician, though, the doctor suggested that she not jump to conclusions until Matthew was in preschool and more routinely interacting with other children.

It took just a couple of months of preschool before his teachers noticed his difficulties. At a conference with Cathy and her husband, David, they described how Matt rarely engaged in play with the other children, occupying himself with solitary, repetitive activities and flapping his arms when anxious. Though they weren't surprised by the teachers' descriptions, autism hadn't entered their thoughts. One of their neighbors happened to have a son, a few years older, who had been diagnosed with autism, but that boy didn't speak at all. Matt, in contrast, was a chatterbox, frequently repeating what his parents said.

When a doctor diagnosed him with Pervasive Development Disorder (a term then used for Autism Spectrum Disorder), the parents reacted in different but complementary ways. David believed the assessment of his son was accurate but wanted to wait and see how Matt's development progressed. Cathy immediately reached out to other parents and autism groups in search of whatever information and support she could gather.

She found comfort in connecting with other mothers as she watched her son struggle. At times Matt became so frustrated at not being able to communicate that he resorted to scratching his parents and others. If it was time to leave the house and Matt wasn't ready, he could be defiant, flailing and swinging. At family gatherings he sometimes made his cousins the targets of his swinging arms and scratching nails. Fortunately most of the Correias' relatives responded with love and support.

So did Traci, Matt's teacher for first and second grade, then a new hire at his mainstream public school with a natural ability to draw out her students and find the best ways to engage them. In the initial days of first grade, Matt would cry all day, but Traci supported him by paying attention to what mattered to him. When he once complained about a frightening dream, at his request she let him lead his classmates in acting out the dream, a process that helped him move past the fear the dream induced.

Looking back, David remembers what he calls two different

Matts: the locked-in, frustrated boy before he met Traci, and the more expressive, happier boy who emerged. His experience as a father paralleled that development. "It was very hard for me when he was little," David says. "Once he got to the 'other side,' it was a totally different experience."

Another teacher introduced the Correias to the technique of using soft brushes to massage the child's body as a way to work on tactile and sensory challenges. That sometimes seemed to work with Matt.

In other ways Matt's education proved disappointing and endlessly challenging, especially after second grade. Rather than identifying and addressing his unique style of learning, teachers were content with a one-size-fits-all approach. Like many children on the spectrum, he could decode—read the words on the page by rote—at about grade level, but his comprehension always remained considerably lower.

Cathy became frustrated with teachers who emphasized her son's behavior issues and learning challenges rather than seeking his strengths. She wasn't pleased by the excessive use of behavior-modification strategies, rewarding or sanctioning her son—an approach she found induced stress in Matt more than it helped him.

Cathy's continual efforts to educate herself about autism paid off. At one autism conference, she watched a film about how seemingly minor and invisible frustrations could build within a child, eventually causing him to lash out or display problematic behaviors. Teachers in the movie responded in ways that caused the child even more stress and dysregulation. She immediately thought of the tic Matt had recently developed, repeatedly twisting locks of hair in his fingers so frequently that he pulled out clumps. "When I saw that presentation, I realized it wasn't all his fault," she recalls. "It was the situation."

Just a few days later Cathy arranged a meeting with the school psychologist and shared her insight. She suggested a series of changes in Matt's schedule and the school's approach to help alleviate stress and support his ability to regulate himself. To their credit, the psychologist and teachers were open to making the changes. High school proved considerably happier for Matt, who was enrolled in a special education collaborative agency, continuing for three additional years in a program designed to support the transition to adulthood.

Cathy expanded her understanding and knowledge of autism, constantly sifting through what she read and learned for whatever she felt would help Matt to communicate and learn to regulate himself. Meanwhile David took the opposite tack, assiduously avoiding lectures and literature on the topic. "I have never read a *paragraph* about autism, let alone a book," he says. That was not because he didn't want to learn but rather from a determination to focus on his son rather than his diagnosis. "From the get-go, I just wanted to interact with Matt and trust my gut."

The more he did that, the more he discovered a delightful young man: open, innocent, guileless, loving. He delighted friends and acquaintances with his enthusiasms: time, clocks, the calendar, and sports (especially those that were timed, such as football). The boy who was so uncomfortable and agitated in preschool became a teen and young adult who was calm, easygoing, and, within certain limits, able to function comfortably and independently. When Cathy accompanied him to a memorial service for one of his former school administrators, "He worked the crowd, shaking hands and enthusiastically greeting people and sharing memories with people," she recalls.

He has become self-sufficient in a number of ways. He can walk into a Subway restaurant, choose the ingredients of his sandwich, and pay. He knows the shelves of the local supermarket by heart—a great help on family shopping trips. At home he keeps his belongings organized and participates in planning meals, expressing strong preferences and letting Cathy know when she's purchased an item he doesn't approve of. He's skilled at using a computer and is the keeper of the family schedule.

He still has his challenges, though they are not as powerfully disabling as in the past. Seeing a sign advertising a blood drive, for instance, can make him anxious, and in conversation he still overly focuses on his interests. He also seems aware of his limitations, whether they are real or self-imposed; for example, he declines offers of driving lessons, despite his remarkable sense of direction and knowledge about cars. "He just knows what's for him and what's not for him," Cathy says. "We're not trying to limit him, but he seems to know what he can and can't do."

Whether he understands the impact of autism is another matter. In his last year of high school the Correias learned that Matt's teacher planned to hold a class discussion about autism. The couple debated how to handle that, then opted to ask that Matt be excused from the session. Cathy had felt a duty to explain to Matt why he had never taken the same school bus as his brother, why he struggles with things that come easily to others, but she had never told him "You have autism." Matt's teacher argued that understanding his diagnosis would be important to Matt in the future so he could advocate for himself in employment situations and elsewhere. To his parents that potential was outweighed by the thought that learning of his diagnosis might give their son the idea that there was something wrong with him. "The child isn't his diagnosis," David says. "You don't want to interact with your *ideas* about who he is. You want to interact with the person standing in front of you."

Cathy has had occasion to discuss the diagnosis with Matthew from time to time. She keeps things factual and objective, to help him understand why he sometimes needs extra help. Matthew always listens and then quickly changes the subject to something he'd rather talk about, like his part-time job at a garden center. There he stocks shelves and helps clean and has earned the admiration and respect of his coworkers.

As for the future, the Correias are in no rush to push Matt out, nor does he seem in a hurry to take on the world. They delight in having him around the house, and Matt enjoys socializing with their many family friends.

When she thinks back on her job working with people with developmental disabilities, Cathy remembers the strong feeling that the individuals who were functioning best were those who were living at home with their families. For now, she and David are happy to offer Matt that option for the rewards they get in return.

"Living with him, it's a two-way street," explains David, who says he has learned kindness, honesty, and enthusiasm from his son. "Every day he teaches me how to live."

The Domingue Family: "We Have to Follow Our Gut"

In one of Bob Domingue's most painful memories, his son Nick was four. He could speak but occasionally shut down in silence and at times struggled to communicate. A speech pathologist had advised Bob and his wife, Barbara, that it was critical to force Nick to use words whenever possible. One afternoon in the kitchen, Nick approached his father, took his hand, and led him to the refrigerator.

"What do you want, Nick?" Bob asked.

Silent, Nick pulled his father's hand to the refrigerator door.

"What do you *want*?" Bob repeated, following the therapist's advice.

Struggling, Nick said one word: "Door."

Bob understood exactly what his son wanted: a cup of juice. But he pushed further, insisting that Nick use words to tell him. Nick only grunted.

"You want *milk*?" the father asked, holding up a carton.

Grunt. Head shaking.

Bob held up a jar of pickles: "You want a *pickle*?"

Nick, obviously frustrated and downcast, frowned, trudged to the corner of the kitchen, sat down, and quietly began to cry.

Decades later that moment still upsets both Bob and Barbara. "He was *communicating.* Why was I putting him through that?" Bob says. "There was absolutely no need for that."

Barbara says the lesson was clear: that they should trust their own instincts about their son. "If we as parents feel that this is what we should be doing, then this is what we should be doing," she says. "We have to follow our gut."

That intuition has helped the family over a journey of three decades, one that has included its share of challenges, tragedy, and surprises.

The journey began when Nick, the second of the Domingues' three children, wasn't yet two and seemed to have hearing problems. He didn't respond to his name or even respond to sudden noises such as clapping or the clang of pots and pans. But if his mother called "Popsicle!" from the kitchen, he always came running.

He also made a habit of lining up toys. He flapped his arms and hands. He became upset easily, screaming without apparent reason and once biting his sister Bethany on her shoulder with such force that he drew blood.

Nick was two and a half when a psychologist diagnosed him with autism. The couple knew little about autism, but perhaps because Barbara grew up with a brother who was blind and one of Bob's sisters had developmental delays, they spent little time mourning. Barbara immediately got to work, reading whatever she could find on the topic and even badgering authors and experts by phone for advice. They found supportive professionals and connected with other parents of children with autism through a program I helped run at Bradley Children's Hospital in Providence.

As much as the support helped, Nick still had significant challenges. Unable to communicate with words consistently, he was deeply frustrated at times, routinely scratching his parents and once tearing the cornea from his father's right eye. He was also prone to running. On one occasion Barbara left the room where Nick was watching cartoons, then returned to find he was gone—and nowhere to be found in the house. She ran outside in a panic, worried that if he reached a nearby lake he could drown. Fortunately a stranger found him before he got to the water and, suspecting something was amiss, stayed with him until Barbara showed up.

Nick communicated mostly by using echolalia. Sometimes he would surprise his parents with an unexpectedly sophisticated sentence, and Bethany, his older sister, would put things in context, identifying the TV dialogue he was echoing.

From early on, Bob found that keeping a sense of humor and making things fun were keys to Nick's development. Noticing that physical activity was calming to Nick, Bob devised a game called Stop and Go, in which the children ran wildly around the room until he told them to freeze. Bob also found that when he played tickling games with Nick, his son would be more open to social interactions, so he took those opportunities to connect and teach new skills.

When it came time for school, the family relocated from Fall River to Swansea, Massachusetts, mostly because Barbara felt the town's school district would offer the best services. Both Barbara and Bob had attended Catholic schools and had always assumed their children would too. They enrolled Nick in a Catholic school where he was one of the few children with a disability. To help with his challenges, Nick's teacher created a small, curtained-off area within the classroom where, when Nick felt overstimulated, he could escape, listening to music through headphones.

Though he struggled at times, he also excelled in some academic subjects. He did so well at math that classmates came to him for help. In middle school he was the occasional victim of bullies and once landed in the principal's office for threatening another student in a lavatory, saying "Right in the kisser!" It turned out he was just repeating one of his echolalic phrases, and Bob had to set him straight. "*We* understand, Nick," he told his son, "but when you say that to somebody, they think you're going to hit them."

From an early age he was drawn to video games. As a second-grader he wrote about himself, "If I could I would like to be in video games. I'm happiest when playing Nintendo." When he was about eight, Barbara noticed his habit of holding his hands in front of his eyes, forming a crosshatch. When she asked why he did that, Nick said it helped him to design mazes, running imaginary characters he called "stim creatures" through them in his mind. "If we had eliminated that, we would have been eliminating a creative process," she says. "The behavior might have looked odd, but we asked why he did it, and he was able to tell us."

Nick was in eighth grade when, in an instant, the Domingue family's fate took a tragic turn. They were driving home from a birthday dinner for Nick's younger brother, Nathan, when a truck ran a red light and crashed into their white Corolla, leaving Bethany with a traumatic brain injury just two weeks before her sixteenth birthday. In the hospital and rehabilitation for nearly a year, she survived but was paralyzed, profoundly disabled, nearly unable to communicate.

Though the brothers escaped unscathed, Nick regressed while Bob and Barbara focused on Bethany's recovery. Struggling to come to grips with his sister's fate, Nick wrote a letter to God. "The one thing I want to thank you for most of all is for my sister," he wrote. "She has always been understanding and kind to me. If I could have only one person to be with in the world I would choose my sister, Bethany."

Later he found it difficult to shake the painful memory of the accident. Before the crash Bob had hoped his son might one day be able to earn a driver's license, but when Nick began driving, he experienced such severe panic attacks triggered by memories of the accident that the family put that prospect aside.

Still Nick pursued his own dreams of creating video games, working his way through three different college programs to earn a degree in computer game programming and design. For transportation he mastered the bus system, memorizing schedules and maps. On Nick's first outing, Bob drove the family car just behind the bus, monitoring closely to make sure Nick made the correct transfer.

When Bob and Barbara would check on their son in his bedroom, sometimes they would catch him fastidiously lining up objects or pacing in circles. If they suggested he should be doing his homework, Nick would insist that he was doing just that. "He was processing," Bob explains. "That behavior—the pacing and the lining up—wasn't something we had to get rid of. It was a tool he used to help him think."

By the time he finished his college studies, gaming technology had changed so greatly that much of what he had learned was obsolete. And since Nick wasn't fond of three-dimensional games, the latest trend in gaming, he lost interest.

Still living at home, Nick is soft-spoken, thoughtful, and low key. In contrast with his younger days, when he was kinetic and distractible, as an adult he is keenly aware of how those around him feel. He also works part time selling tickets and concessions at a movie theater, where his inflexible thinking sometimes pays off. Once Nick stopped a patron trying to enter an R-rated movie, stubbornly demanding to see identification. It turned out the customer was a top manager in disguise. He had high praise for Nick's work.

More recently Barbara has given him work as a part-time bookkeeper for Community Autism Resources (CAR), the nonprofit she directs. There too his thoroughness and adherence to rules has paid off, and he has shown interest in pursuing a certificate in bookkeeping.

Barbara remembers one of the first times she reached out to another parent raising a child with autism. Someone had given her the number of an autism advocacy group, and Barbara told the woman who answered the phone that her three-year-old had recently been diagnosed.

"My son is eight," the woman said. "You will be fine."

It's not so different from the advice Barbara and her parent-professional staff dispense these days at CAR, which provides assistance to parents across southern New England: One day at a time, one step in front of the other. Keep the future in mind, but don't be wedded to any one plan. If anyone knows that, it's the Domingues.

That doesn't keep Nick from thinking about the future. Not long ago he told Barbara that when she and Bob are elderly, he will care for his sister, as his sister used to care for him. Though attending to Bethany's medical needs may be too complex for Nick, Barbara was gratified that it's on his mind.

"I thought, 'Wow, we're not the only ones thinking about the future,'" she says. "One step at a time."

The Canha Family: "You Have to Be in the Trenches Making It Happen"

Maria Teresa and Briant Canha still sometimes watch the videotape that shows a family gathering when their son Justin was two. Holding a stick, Justin wanders about aimlessly, seemingly oblivious to his cousins and everyone else. Even when his parents call his name, Justin doesn't look up.

It's difficult to believe that remote, silent toddler grew to be the Justin of today: outgoing, ebullient, funny, an accomplished artist who delights in teaching children to draw and paint.

That transformation has much to do with his parents, who have embraced and encouraged Justin's quirky, singular personality—and, when necessary, pushed the people around their son to help Justin make the most of his life.

The younger of two sons, Justin had developed normally until around two, when he lost most of the language he had acquired and seemed to retreat from the world. "All of a sudden," Maria Teresa recalls, "we were back to zero."

A doctor told the Canhas their son didn't have autism; he had Pervasive Developmental Disorder. Looking back, Maria Teresa sees that diagnosis as a disservice: "It took me a year to figure out that it was the same thing."

Not long after that, they visited my office, then at Boston's Emerson College. I found that while he was not very responsive to people, Justin was curious, alert, and concentrated in his focus. I confirmed that he had autism, but I told his parents that his potential was unlimited, provided they worked to give him appropriate support and keep their expectations high—an approach Briant summarizes now as "high support, high demand."

They found little assistance, though, in Belgium, where they had relocated for Briant's work. Justin's international school offered little support, and Maria Teresa felt increasingly alone and despondent, wondering if her son would ever speak.

Searching for ways to get through to Justin, Briant employed his artistic talent, creating storyboards and videotaping them to teach basic skills such as toileting and avoiding danger. Justin immediately responded in ways they had not imagined. "I realized then that Justin was smart," Briant recalls. "If we could figure out how to shape the information and get it into his head, he immediately got it."

Still the Canhas knew they required considerable assistance to help Justin make the most of his life. Since they couldn't find it in Europe, they moved back to the United States, settling near family in Rhode Island. There they enrolled Justin in a public school inclusion program, which, after a few years, proved a disappointment. In their opinion the teachers didn't truly make Justin part of the class but rather taught him separately. And the aide assigned to him, whose qualifications for the job were impressive, failed to take a strong personal interest in Justin.

That disappointment brought with it a lesson: that the most effective professionals were those who were invested in Justin. "I don't care what education they have, what background," says Maria Teresa. "If they believe in Justin and they're enthusiastic about working with him, when they teach him according to his interests, it's contagious."

Frustrated in their attempts to find such people in Providence's public schools, the family relocated again, this time to Montclair, New Jersey, where they found a school strongly committed to including children with disabilities and providing an appropriate level of support. In that nurturing environment Justin's personality emerged: his goofy sense of humor, his strong work ethic and desire to please parents and teachers, his affection for his family. From an early age he loved giving and receiving hugs.

Even before he could speak, Justin drew, and over time it became clear to his parents that he had remarkable artistic talent. He spent endless hours drawing cartoon characters—his favorites were from Sesame Street, Disney, and Looney Tunes—and his early language was focused on talking about them. That budding ability might have become little more than a hobby if not for Maria Teresa, a tenacious and creative advocate who explored all avenues in search of whatever might benefit her son. "In terms of promoting myself, I'm shy," she says, "but for Justin—no shame."

That meant finding him an art tutor, Denise Melucci, who found ways to push Justin, then ten, beyond his comfort zone, successfully persuading him to expand from reproducing cartoon characters to the more ambitious realm of drawing figures and landscapes (see chapter 7). Maria Teresa also pursued dedicated and energetic social skills tutors, occupational therapists, and other professionals to maximize her son's potential.

"Parents send their kids to school and think, 'They're taking care of it,'" she says. "It doesn't work that way. You have to have a goal in mind, and you have to be in the trenches making it happen."

Throughout the secondary school years, Justin benefited from the support of an aide in his inclusive public school program. He took part in an innovative post–high school transition-to-adulthood program run through Montclair High School in which students who had been previously enrolled in special education learned to shop for food, use public transportation, and gain employment experience through internships. In social skills workshops, the students learned how to conduct themselves in a job interview and, later, among their coworkers.*

In the process Justin began focusing on a long-term goal: to support himself independently by selling his artwork and teaching art. By his early twenties he was well on his way, represented by New York's Ricco Maresca Gallery, which sold his paintings and charcoals and sponsored shows of his work. Justin also began to volunteer as

*Justin and the program were featured in the article "Autistic and Seeking a Place in an Adult World," *New York Times*, September 17, 2011.

an art teacher in various classrooms, with both typical children and children with autism. But the art market is notoriously unstable, and when Justin emerged at twenty-one from the transition program, he hadn't secured stable employment.

That didn't dampen his determination. Though he continued living at home into his early twenties, he made his way around the New York City area on public transportation, often turning down offers of rides because he was intent on being self-sufficient.

At first his parents focused on finding him jobs that required little social interaction since they knew Justin found that challenging. But when he worked at a series of bakeries, he seemed to seek out opportunities to interact with customers. And he truly shone in the classroom, developing his skills teaching art to elementary school students in Montclair and in a New York City school serving children with autism. He also began earning money decorating birthday cakes and working at children's birthday parties, taking drawing requests from the guests. He has begun to speak in front of large conference audiences, to the delight of those in attendance. If an audience member poses a question he doesn't like, Justin, always direct and honest, blurts out, "Next question!"

In those settings, say his parents, when most people meet Justin they are intrigued by his delightful personality. Ebullient and engaging, he likes singing Disney tunes to himself and is prone to inventive and descriptive language. When he finds someone annoying, he says the person "must be subtracted." When his mother asked about future relationships, Justin told her he didn't plan on marrying "because marriage is too complicated."

His father finds irony in his son's magnetic presence. "We came to realize that his real strength is his communication skill with other human beings," says Briant. "I'm still trying to get over that."

As much as they encourage him to push himself into the world, at home Justin's parents make it a priority to let him relax and to be himself. That includes spending time alone, playing on his computer, listening to music, and engaging in "self-talk," endlessly repeating scenes from movies and pieces of conversation floating in his head. It's not unusual for Maria Teresa to be in the kitchen and suddenly hear a loud, high-pitched voice from upstairs: Justin, playing out yet another scene in his head.

His parents understand that's part of having autism. Earlier, Briant admits, he expended more effort on helping Justin to fit in social situations, preferring environments where he could be around more neurotypical peers so he could learn from the model of their behavior. Over time that has seemed both less achievable and less important.

That particularly struck him when they traveled with Justin, then twenty-two, to Los Angeles, where he collaborated with Dani Bowman, a teenager with autism who ran her own small, independent animation company and eventually contracted with Justin to create storyboards for her. At first the Canhas expected to play an important role in helping Justin and Dani to communicate and relate. But they quickly observed that the two artists with autism had their own language, their own way of collaborating, and had no need for assistance.

To the parents it was both humbling and remarkable to see the son they once watched wander amid his cousins, aloof to the world, now fully engaged and fully himself.

"When you meet Justin, you immediately know he's different," says Briant. "And he's successful not in spite of that, but because of that."

CHAPTER 11

Energize the Spirit

SOMETIMES a question is a revelation. Not long ago I was at the parent retreat I facilitate when a mother seated beside me tapped on my arm to get my attention. It was Cynthia's first time attending the weekend. Her son, just two and a half, had recently been diagnosed, so most of what she was hearing was new to her. Over two days she had taken in the discussions among parents, many with years, even decades of experience with autism. She had listened as some parents recounted their children's enthusiasms and idiosyncrasies, and others discussed battles with school administrators. She had met one mom who expressed gratitude for discovering a suitable residential school for her nineteen-year-old and another who spoke openly about the challenges of balancing work with motherhood.

Then, just before the retreat's emotional closing circle, Cynthia turned to me. "Dr. Prizant," she whispered, "I have a question for you." She told me about a website she had come across that claimed its online program helped children with autism in such extraordinary ways that some had "recovered" from autism. She wanted my opinion.

She described the testimonials she had read from parents whose children had made remarkable strides in reducing the symptoms of autism within weeks or months merely by following the recommended activities. The cost? Nearly a thousand dollars. "What do you think, Dr. Prizant?"

Her question reminded me of the many times parents have approached me with a related query. "If money weren't an object," they ask, "if I weren't bound geographically by my career or family, where would you suggest that we relocate to get the best services for our child?" These parents harbor the belief that somewhere out there is a mecca of autism services. There's a school or a doctor or a therapist that just might be able to rid their child of all of the challenges associated with autism.

Where, they ask, should we go?

The answer: It's not out there. There is no one professional or clinic, no magical place, no treatment approach offering all the answers and the plan to render a child "normal" so that families can put autism behind them and move on with their lives.

Nobody would blame Cynthia, the mother of a young child, for pursuing all options in her quest to give her son the best possible life. Nor would anyone fault families for seeking out the best services available. They want what all parents want: for their children to be happy, to lead fulfilling lives, to make the most of their potential, and to be respected and valued members of their communities. In short, parents want what's best for their children. But when the challenges associated with autism enter the equation, it's easy to lose track of what's important.

The Question of Recovery

Some approaches to autism make "recovery" their explicit goal—the notion that a person can overcome autism the way one might conquer cancer or rebound from a heart attack. Whether that is possible, or desirable, remains an open question. While a 2013 study found that, over time, a very small percentage of children experienced such improvements in symptoms that they no longer fit the *DSM* autism diagnosis, the study found no way to predict which children would show such gains, or why.

This view of autism defines recovery as reducing the number of "autistic symptoms" below a certain threshold to such a degree that a person no longer meets the criteria for diagnosis. Yet many of the most successful people on the autism spectrum (Temple Grandin, Stephen Shore, and Michael John Carley, to name a few), who by all measures enjoy full lives, do not refer to themselves as having recovered. They have fulfilling careers, are active community members, and some have families with children. Others who were once considered to have recovered from autism later identify themselves as having Asperger's syndrome. And many other adults with autism, even some who say they are free of most obvious symptoms and are largely able to pass for "normal," resent the emphasis on recovery, some viewing autism as an inseparable, integral part of who they are.

A person can enjoy a good quality of life whether or not his behavior meets the criteria for autism. As one teenager told his parents when they first broached the topic of his diagnosis, "I *love* my autism."

Whether or not "recovery" is possible, pursuing it as a singular goal and viewing it as the principal marker of a successful outcome can be emotionally and financially exhausting for parents and stressful for children, particularly when the focus is on reducing "autistic behaviors." And when professionals present recovery as likely, despite research indicating it is rare, they violate ethics of professional practice, especially when they make such claims to promote their services.

Maintaining hope in the prospect of minimizing the challenges associated with autism and achieving good quality of life need not be inextricably linked to "recovery." (Some simply call it "making great progress" or "overcoming challenges.")

When families make recovery their preeminent goal, they can miss the beauty of the child's developmental breakthroughs, just as a driver focused only on the destination doesn't notice the scenery along the way.

In contrast, I have watched many parents derive great enjoyment from the small gains and daily progress their children make—precisely because they are focused on the journey. Often the incremental gains add up to large transformations that improve the quality of life for people with autism and their families.

Sheila described that distinction better than anyone I've met. Her son Pablo was a sweet ten-year-old who had high anxiety and sensory sensitivities. He could speak, but his dysregulation made it difficult to keep him consistently engaged. For years Sheila felt desperate to change him and rid him of his autism, trying a multitude of alternative diets and various other treatments. It was only when she came to the retreat, met parents just like her, and heard of their struggles and triumphs that she paused and saw her efforts in a new light.

With tears in her eyes, she shared with the group her epiphany: "I keep trying and trying to fix Pablo, and what I've learned is that he's whole and he's happy." Voice quivering, she added, "We do need to pursue whatever we can to make our children's lives more comfortable and happy, but they really are whole—and *they* can fix *us*."

Different Families, Different Dreams

Focusing on the journey looks different in every family, just as it does for parents raising any child. As part of my private practice, I once visited two different families for consultations in their homes within a few days. Each set of parents had a child under three recently diagnosed with autism. My role in each case was to confirm the diagnosis, and then to begin a conversation about what the future might hold and how the family might proceed.

After the initial discussion of the diagnosis, the first father asked me a question: "Do you think he'll ever go to college?" That was his top concern: Would his son succeed academically?

With the second family, our initial discussion was almost identical, but then the boy's mother asked me her own question: "We want to know, will our daughter be happy?" That question led to more: "Will she have friends and be around people who love her? Will she be a respected member of her community?"

Every family is different. Same diagnosis, same stage in the journey, very different priorities.

My friend Barbara Domingue (see chapter 10) once gave me a framed print I hung in my office. It's a surrealistic picture of a man on a tightrope walking toward a distant, sun-like light. Only one end of the rope is secured—the end behind him. The segment of the rope extending in front of where he stands he's holding in his hands, so his next step is into thin air. In Barbara's interpretation, the man represents a family just after receiving an autism diagnosis: the parents realize they are beginning a long journey, but it's one they will have to invent with every step.

In fact every part of the journey can feel that way. Even when things are stable, even when parents feel like they're walking on solid ground, at any moment things can change—a beloved therapist moves away, a school program is a bad fit, a child reaches adolescence—and the parents become tightrope walkers again.

To extend the metaphor, there is a complicating factor: as you improvise your way, trying to keep your balance, all kinds of people offer advice and direction, too often resulting in distraction and even guilt.

"Make a right turn here!"

"Take a left turn there!"

"Now, do a double flip!"

Parents can feel chronic stress as they constantly second-guess whether they are making the best choices for their children. At many junctures there is no clear answer, no certain choice. A professional might insist that the child needs forty hours of therapy per week. A parent might swear that a particular treatment did wonders for her child, and surely will for yours too. One swears by inclusion; another insists on a private autism school; a third asserts that a gluten-free diet is a must. Parents can feel that one misstep, one wrong choice (or failure to make a choice) will cause irreparable harm.

All of that can make it difficult to look toward the future, for parents to consider *What is it that I'm walking toward, anyway? What is my light? What are our hopes and dreams for our child? How should we make the right choices to fulfill them?*

Every parent answers differently. Every family has a unique set of priorities.

Small Steps, Shifting Perspective

It's natural to have anxiety about the future. The mother of a five-year-old boy told me recently that she sometimes wakes up in the middle of the night, filled with worry about what her son will be like when he's fifteen. Other parents say they don't allow themselves to get caught up in worry about the future. Parents often express concern that if a child hasn't reached a certain developmental milestone by age three or five or seven, it's too late. Somewhere they have heard that if a child doesn't speak a certain number of words by age five, hope is lost. Or that a young child's IQ or academic achievement can predict the child's future. (Not true.)

When the challenges seem greatest, hope can be in short supply. I have met many parents whose children have not developed speech at a young age. They've heard that if a child doesn't speak by age five, she will likely never speak. That's not true; development continues throughout life. Still these parents feel desperate to see the child develop speech as quickly as possible. When that doesn't happen, they feel discouraged. They feel burnt out. Their hope dissipates. Overly focused on a particular goal, they see everything through that prism, and it becomes difficult for them to perceive the strengths, the breakthroughs, or even to see the child.

What helps in those situations is reframing. Even when a child is not speaking, there are often signs of engagement: he might be intentionally looking at his mother or father; she has started pointing or waving. These are initial indications of social interest, a stepping stone to communication. Often parents are so singularly focused on getting the child to speak that they don't notice such promising indicators. When a child takes her mother by the hand to bring her to the refrigerator, she is not merely "using a person as a tool," as some dismiss such actions; it is intentional communication, a starting point from which to build. As much as we dream about major leaps, often it's these small steps that indicate progress and offer hope.

It's also helpful to get to know families that have been down the same road. At our parent retreat, the mother of a three-year-old might meet the father of a teen or young adult who had the same challenges. The young adult might not speak but uses a tablet computer to communicate. Her parents maintain a positive attitude, they surround her with love and affection, and it's clear she leads a happy and fulfilled life.

Amir is a young man with minimal speech who runs a business baking cookies that are sold in local shops. His parents admit that when he was a teenager, they could not have imagined him doing such a thing. He has a good quality of life. He has a purpose. He is involved with his community. He takes pride in his work. He feels good about himself. And his parents say they cannot imagine life without having their adult son living at home.

It's a reminder that human development is a lifelong process—and that priorities shift. What seems critically important at one stage might feel less so in a few years.

Happiness and Sense of Self, or Academic Success?

Parents want to know what a child's school program should focus on to guarantee the greatest success when he becomes an adult. What abilities and qualities are important for a person to have to help assure the best quality of life? Here are my top priorities: building self-expression and self-esteem, instilling happiness, creating positive experiences, and emphasizing healthy relationships. It's also important to increase self-awareness and the ability to emotionally self-regulate.

When you have positive emotional experiences, it motivates you to learn and explore, connect with other people, and seek out more varied experiences. In other words, it enhances your quality of life. Being happy also makes you a more desirable person to be with. It makes people seek you out. This becomes obvious when you watch children interact in groups. When a child is anxious and edgy or sullen and dour, others avoid her. But if the same children encounter a child who is cheerful, smiling, and playful, they are drawn to him. Happiness is a natural connector.

Yet many parents, educators, and therapists prioritize academic achievement over instilling happiness, even if it greatly increases stress. In fact I have heard proponents of some approaches take issue with the idea of emphasizing happiness, arguing that for children with autism, it is far more important to develop skills than to be happy. In other words, instead of measuring happiness, we should be measuring skills.

Not only is this way of thinking misguided, but it misses the point. Children—and all human beings—learn more readily when they are happy. They retain information more effectively when they feel positive emotion. When we try to learn under persistently stressful situations, we retain less, and it's more difficult for us to access what we learned. But when we're feeling a positive emotion, we're more primed for a learning experience, and our learning is deeper and far more effective.

Again and again I have encountered educators who push students too hard, stressing academics instead of considering the big picture. Often educators are under pressure from administrators following policies that measure success only in terms of academic performance. In extreme cases the result is that the child refuses to go to school.

Other children simply shut down. At the very least the pressure creates stresses and negative emotional memories that can be difficult to overcome. Instead of narrowly focusing on academics or letting the standard curriculum be the guide, it's essential to consider the development of the whole person and to make the necessary accommodations and choices that foster happiness and availability for learning and engaging. *That* results in the best quality of life.

The Importance of Self-Determination

I was once invited to present a workshop in Christchurch, a picturesque city that is among the largest in New Zealand. I learned it was customary for representatives of the local indigenous people, the Maori, to open such events with a brief prayer service. When I arrived at the crowded conference hall, an organizer introduced me to the Maori elder, a tall, broad gentleman holding a carved wooden staff. I felt touched and honored when the elder invited me to take part in the brief ceremony. It opened with the participants greeting one another, each pressing his nose and forehead against the other's, proceeding down a line. The exchange, called a *Hongi*, symbolizes a sort of sharing of spirits.

Then, seconds before I was to begin my presentation, the elder approached me, leaned over, and with his lips practically touching my ear, whispered a short sentence: "I trust that you will convey the message that in order to advance the mind, we must first energize the spirit."

As I took in the words, I felt a vibration shoot through my body. For in that sentence he had summed up much of what I believe about the lives of people with autism: that the best way to help these individuals progress toward fulfilling, meaningful lives is to find ways to engage them, to build a sense of self, and to foster joyful experiences.

We must energize the spirit. Each year I meet dozens of people with autism. When I think about these encounters, it's often in terms of spirit: *He's got a great spirit. She's a spirited child. They're such free spirits.* These are the kinds of people who draw people to them, who can fill a room with joy. Others seem lethargic, passive, disengaged. About those people we might say, *His spirit has been broken*, or *We need to lift her spirits*.

The difference is sometimes innate, but more often the more spirited individuals are those who have been given choices in life, who have been given a say in their own situation. That doesn't mean they can function with full independence; for some that's possible, and for others it's not an immediate goal. What they have is *self-determination*—a sense of who they are, what they want, and some degree of say over their own lives. Their lives aren't orchestrated by someone else. Their days don't consist of responding to prompts.

Some parents begin thinking about self-determination only when their children with autism are entering adulthood and weighing the (sometimes limited) options. But the conversation should start earlier—as early as preschool. In raising, teaching, and supporting young people with autism, we ought to ask constantly "What can we do that will ultimately help this child to lead the most self-determined, fulfilled life possible?" That's why it is essential to offer choices whenever possible instead of forcing a particular expectation on a child. The goal shouldn't be to fix the child or make the child "normal" but rather to help the child develop the ability to make his own decisions, to exert control over his own life.

When Jesse, who had once been deeply dysregulated, got the opportunity to deliver mail and organize recycling, contributing to his school as a middle schooler, he was taking steps toward self-determination.

When Ned, who had been so annoyed by his previous therapist, forbade me from using the term "Good job," he was preparing for self-determination.

When Simon, who was afraid to ride the ferry, was given the chance to opt out but instead decided he would be brave, he was learning about being self-determined.

When Ros wouldn't come to dinner until she'd had her chance to jump on a trampoline, she was demonstrating what it means to be an adult with autism with full self-understanding and control of her own life.

When parents and teachers and members of extended communities offer choices and empower individuals with autism, we not only help to advance their minds; we also energize their spirits.

CHAPTER 12

The Big Questions

Not long ago I traveled to the emirate of Dubai to present a workshop on autism. Parents and professionals had flown in from all over the Middle East and as far away as Nigeria. In appearance the audience hardly resembled the kinds of groups I'm accustomed to addressing in the United States, Europe, or Australia. Many of the women were dressed in burkas, and some wore the traditional head coverings known as niqabs. But their questions were practically identical to those I have heard from parents, educators, and therapists in places as varied as mainland China, New Zealand, and Israel: Why does my child spin and rock? Should I let my son have so much time with the iPad? Will my daughter ever speak? What can I do about a girl in my class who won't engage with other children? How can I get my student to stop biting his hand? Parents the world over want the best for their children, educators want answers, all kinds of professionals want the best information available. To help, here are some responses to some of the many questions I most frequently receive.

How can you tell if a person has high-functioning autism or low-functioning autism? What about Asperger's syndrome?

At just two and a half Eric can assemble puzzles too complex for most four-year-olds. But he can't speak yet, and he communicates mostly through gestures. Is Eric high-functioning or low-functioning?

Eight-year-old Amanda is able to function at grade level in her fourth-grade class. But if she doesn't have the assistance of an aide, she can become so anxious that she bolts from the classroom, or even out the door of the school. Is Amanda high-functioning or low-functioning?

Dominic, who is fifteen, doesn't speak, communicating instead with a speech-generating device. He spends half of his school day in a special education classroom. His classmates and teachers love and appreciate him, and he enjoys greeting his many friends on the playground. Is Dominic high-functioning or low-functioning?

Though these terms have become commonplace, I choose not to use them. I have long been a student of child and human development, and I am keenly aware of how simplistic these characterizations are. People are infinitely complex, and development is multidimensional and cannot be reduced to such a simple dichotomy.

Besides that, the terms are so imprecise as to lack meaning. "High-functioning" and "low-functioning," along with "severely autistic" and "mildly autistic," have become pseudo-diagnostic categories without commonly accepted definitions or any corresponding diagnostic criteria. The most recent edition of the *Diagnostic and Statistical Manual of Mental Disorders*, the *DSM-5*, provoked controversy when it abandoned all subcategories of Autism Spectrum Disorder, so that Asperger's syndrome was no longer a distinct diagnosis. Long before that there was debate about whether Asperger's and high-functioning autism were the same or different since no clearly defined diagnostic boundaries existed.

I have often observed how terribly inaccurate and misleading the terms *low-functioning* and *high-functioning* autism are when applied to children and adults I have known well, and using them seems disrespectful. When mothers and fathers hear the term *low-functioning* applied to their children, they are hearing a limited, piecemeal view of their child's abilities and potential, ignoring the whole child. Even when a child is described as "high-functioning," parents often point out that he continues to experience major challenges that educators and others too often minimize or ignore.

When professionals apply these sorts of labels early in a child's development, it can have the effect of unfairly predetermining a child's potential: if "low," don't expect much; if "high," she'll do fine and doesn't need support. The label often becomes a self-fulfilling prophecy. Yet children who appear more challenged (and therefore need more support) early in their lives often make wonderful developmental progress over time. Some kids are later bloomers, and all development is lifelong. Instead of focusing on vague and imprecise labels, it's better to focus on the child's relative strengths and challenges and to identify the most beneficial supports.

I've heard that the window of opportunity for helping a child with autism closes after age five. After that is it too late?

In short, no. Many parents hear from another parent or from a therapist or they've read on a website that it's important to do as much early intervention as possible because at some point the opportunity for improvement vanishes. Some parents hear that if a child isn't exposed to a particular form of therapy by age five, the opportunity for progress has been missed. This makes parents feel guilty that they are letting down their children if they fail to provide the recommended level of intensive therapies.

The truth: There is no evidence that a window of opportunity closes at age five. Research does indicate that one of the predictors of better outcomes for children with autism is earlier intervention, but it simply doesn't follow that if you don't start early, the child has no hope, or little hope. Many parents notice significant growth and progress between eight and thirteen years and far beyond. It's also true that there are critical periods in human development; for example, if you're not exposed to a language early in life, it becomes much more difficult to master it later. In many other areas, however, development is truly a lifelong process of increasing competence and gaining skills—for all of us, including people with autism.

I strongly encourage starting early with a well-coordinated, comprehensive intervention plan that is a good fit for a family's lifestyle and culture. Yet many parents tell me that advice they received caused them such worry about missing the "critical window" that they poured money and energy into therapies that were not appropriate choices for their children. Many parents follow a prescribed plan, no matter how stressful or disruptive, out of anxiety and fear. That's not necessary, and it can cause stress on parents and children alike. At one of our parent retreats, a mother described how she surfed the Internet until 3 a.m. every night in search of the next breakthrough for her four-year-old son, not realizing her habit was having a debilitating impact on her family and marriage.

As a guideline, research indicates that twenty-five hours per week of active engagement, focused on social communication and learning, is the optimum level for most young children. These hours can be *a planned part of everyday activities and routines*, as simple as brushing teeth or making popcorn, not just therapies provided by professionals. Piling on additional hours of one-to-one therapy does not necessarily add value.

Some people with autism seem hyperactive, but others appear lethargic. What explains that?

Autism is called a *spectrum disorder* because the abilities and challenges of people with autism fall along a continuum, and no two people manifest autism in the same way. One child seems so revved up all the time he can't settle down, while his classmate with autism often seems sluggish and spacey.

This phenomenon is known as *arousal bias*. All humans navigate through various states of physiological arousal on a daily basis. The pediatrician T. Berry Brazelton described these "biobehavioral" states in infants that are relevant for all humans. The states range from the low end (deep sleep or drowsy) up to the high end (agitated, anxious, even giddy or elated).

We all have a bias in one direction or the other. The challenge for many people with autism is that they are either too "low bias" or too "high bias"; that is, they tend to be either underaroused (too low) or overaroused (too high). When the task or setting calls for a quiet state, the child is agitated. When the situation requires being active, the child is drowsy or unfocused. To complicate matters, children sometimes shift rapidly from being too high arousal to too low arousal, sometimes within a few hours.

People with autism often have difficulty navigating between different arousal states. A kindergartner's high-arousal state works well on the playground, but then she can't come down to a quiet alert state when it's time to sit for circle time. The goal is to find the right supports to help a person maximize his time in a state that is appropriate for the specific activity.

In working or living with someone with autism, it's important to be mindful of that person's arousal bias, which manifests itself in multiple sensory channels: tactile, auditory, visual, olfactory. A low-arousal, hyporeactive child might experience sound as so indistinct that it's difficult to get her attention. A high-arousal, hyperreactive person might be so sensitive to sound that even noises at normal intensity can be overwhelming and the pain from a small scratch can be excruciating.

How can a parent or teacher help kids who are too high or low energy or too under- or overreactive? Often what a child needs is a complement to his natural bias. If the child is lethargic, be energetic; if the child is anxious and hyperkinetic, be a calming presence. As always, the best approach isn't to try changing the person but to change our approach to be the most supportive and effective. (When natural supports are not effective for individuals with extreme high activity and anxiety, medication prescribed and monitored by a physician may play a supportive role as part of a comprehensive plan.)

What is the single most important thing I can do to help a child with autism?

In my experience, the best thing parents and educators can do for a child with autism is to get the child out in the world—with the appropriate supports. Of course that's true of all children, not just those with autism: the children who progress the most, who develop to their fullest potential, are those who are exposed to a wide variety of experiences.

Parents of young adults and older teens with autism who are successful in handling everyday challenges invariably agree about what made the most significant positive difference in their child's life: that they always made an effort to get the child out, to avoid sheltering the child—to make the child part of the mainstream of life. In doing so they exposed the child to challenges and offered opportunities to learn coping skills to stay well-regulated. Nobody wants to experience an embarrassing meltdown amid the crowds and noise at an amusement park or be stuck on an airplane with a child who can't sit still. But when you shelter a child from all the bumps of life, you're preventing him from opportunities for social and emotional growth.

A child might feel anxious and frightened about going into a noisy restaurant or experiencing a particular amusement park ride. But if she tries, and receives appropriate support, it can be a learning experience. Next time, the parent can say, "Remember last time? You were anxious about it, but it turned out you were fine." If the child never gets the opportunity to try, how can she progress? And if a child tries a new experience and finds it challenging, that's okay. There's always next time.

Can a child who is loving and cuddly still have autism?

People with autism display a wide range of responses to physical contact and affection. Many children experience sensory challenges that make physical contact so overwhelming that they avoid it, appearing to shun all social contact. Others have a strong desire to be physically close, seeking out hugs and cuddling, especially from their parents. In fact many of these children must learn not to hug strangers or, say, the UPS man. Others enjoy holding hands and other forms of closeness and affection.

For some, the key issue is control. While a child might enjoy a hug when he is the one initiating, if the hug is unexpected and is imposed by someone else—even someone with whom the child feels emotionally connected—it can provoke anxiety (however kind the hugger's intentions). It is important to be mindful of the person's particular sensory sensitivities, state of regulation, feelings, and preferences. Most important, the choice to reject a hug should not be mistaken for a lack of desire for emotional closeness or social connection.

It's incredibly stressful to endure the glares of strangers when a child displays odd behavior in public. What to do?

Nearly every parent and sibling of a child with autism faces this reality at one time or another; even professionals and caregivers experience it in a different way. A child has a meltdown at the supermarket, comments openly about a neighbor's haircut, brusquely collides with a stranger without apologizing, or bolts around the auditorium during a school assembly. The parents wonder: Should I explain? What should I say? Do I have an obligation to share my child's diagnosis? Or might that actually be wrong? In the moment, a parent might feel a surge of emotions: embarrassment, confusion, defiance, anger, sadness. Some parents move quite naturally into explaining and educating, while others are far more private and reticent or don't see the value of sharing such information.

One energetic and creative mother told me she had developed a four-tiered system for such situations, offering explanations that varied depending on the individual's relationship with her child and the family, and the likelihood that they will encounter the person regularly:

Level 4: strangers who react negatively. Sometimes the reaction is obvious—a comment or glare—but sometimes it's more restrained or even hidden. It's safe to assume that the reaction is more a reflection on the other person than on anything about the parent or child, so there's no need to respond.

Level 3: a familiar person, perhaps a neighbor. With such a person, whom you are likely to encounter again, it's sometimes best to offer a simple, neutral explanation: "My child has autism. That's why he does that."

Level 2: friends and acquaintances who aren't in your inner circle. If the person is open to it, it's often worthwhile to explain what underlies the child's behavior and how the person might react most supportively.

Level 1: grandparents, other close relatives, and teachers who will certainly be close to the child. It's worth deciding how much energy it is appropriate to allot to making such people comfortable with the child and able to be most supportive.

One school for children with autism supplies its teachers and staff with business cards to carry with them on field trips, community visits, and other occasions when the students are likely to be in public. When a child's behavior draws attention, a teacher hands onlookers a card with the school's contact information and, on the flip side, a paragraph explaining that the recipient of the card has just encountered a person with autism and that the accompanying staff is trained in providing appropriate support and intervention. Many schools and agencies now use similar strategies.

Another creative approach many families use in place of explaining is wearing T-shirts and other clothing with logos and names of autism organizations. If strangers are observant enough to notice those, they'll ask fewer questions and may learn something about autism just from watching the family members interact.

When is the best time to tell a child he has autism?

It's helpful to think of disclosure not as a verdict but as a process, one that varies for each family and each individual—not an instantaneous revelation but a discussion that transpires over weeks, months, or even years. As some children with autism gain social awareness, they begin to feel different from their peers and struggle to understand why they find some situations and encounters so challenging. Others, before knowing of their diagnosis, question their own intelligence and abilities, assuming there must be something wrong. "Am I crazy?" one boy repeatedly asked his mother. In still other cases, the person lacks the self-awareness even to notice or be mindful of these differences.

Many parents are hesitant to share the diagnosis with their child, or even strongly oppose doing so, fearing that placing a label on the child is somehow limiting or feeling (correctly) that the child is far more complex than one word can capture.

I have never met a person with autism who felt that being told of the diagnosis—or becoming aware of it over time—was a negative or damaging experience. To be sure, the responses fall on a continuum. Some recall the moment of suddenly understanding their difficulties, feeling relief that their struggles were not of their own making but rather a result of their internal wiring. Others describe how the disclosure immediately changed their lives for the better, marking a new beginning: "I finally understand myself."

When is the best time to raise the issue? Certainly when a child begins to express that he feels different from his peers, or questions why she has such difficulty with things that seem to come easily to others, there is a need to talk about it. When a child or teen makes self-deprecating remarks and his self-esteem suffers, it's important to discuss the diagnosis. If a child becomes a victim of teasing or bullying, disclosure can help her understand the social dynamic. Some children encounter a peer with autism; this is an opportunity to explain challenges or differences the child and peer might share.

What's the best way to talk to your child about autism? Stephen Shore (see chapter 9) recommends a four-step process that unfolds over time:

Step 1: Make the child aware of his distinctive personal strengths.

Step 2: Develop a list of the child's strengths and challenges.

Step 3: Without judging, compare the child's strengths with those of potential role models, friends, and loved ones.

Step 4: Introduce the label *autism* (or *Asperger's syndrome*) to summarize the child's experience and disability.

With that kind of thoughtful approach, disclosing the diagnosis is an essential step toward self-awareness, leading to a happier and more promising life.

Is it a mistake to let a child with autism "stim"?

I avoid using the terms *stim* and *stimming* (short for *self-stimulatory behavior*) because people often use them imprecisely and with a negative connotation. That said, we all have specific strategies to stay well regulated emotionally and physiologically. Many children engage in certain behaviors that give them comfort or help them be more alert: staring at objects, shaking their hands, spinning, fluttering their fingers, flapping their arms, repeatedly playing certain video games or lining up toys. There's nothing inherently wrong with any of these.

When a person needs to engage in such behavior excessively or if the behavior is potentially harmful or particularly stigmatizing, that may be problematic. If a child sits alone, flicking his fingers in front of his eyes for hours at a time, unwilling to engage socially, he needs assistance developing other ways to stay regulated, or we need to modify or change the activity. Changes to the environment, such as lessening noise and visual clutter, can also help. But when the behavior patterns are more limited—occurring during a break or at the end of a long day—there is less need for concern (unless the behavior is harmful or destructive).

Often the parent's concern is that such behavior attracts glares or makes others avoid the child. In that case it's sometimes best to help the child learn other ways to self-regulate that don't draw negative attention or to encourage the child to find a time to self-stimulate that is less problematic. For children and teens with more social understanding, it's sometimes worth explaining that, while there's nothing wrong with their behavior, *other* people may not understand it. Perhaps the child might want to replace finger flicking with doodling or squeezing a ball to stay calm or to request a movement break when she feels unable to focus. It's also worth using a "time and place" strategy, helping the child to understand that it's fine to indulge in such behavior at the time and place that's least disruptive.

Is it better for a child with autism to learn in a mainstream classroom, a self-contained special education classroom, or a private school?

No two children with autism are alike, so there's no such thing as a one-size-fits-all program. Children learn as much from watching and engaging with their classmates as they do from the formal classroom learning experiences. The more sophisticated their peers' social and language modeling, the better—as long as it is not too far beyond a child's abilities. That doesn't mean it's always better to be surrounded by typical classmates than by students who also receive special education services.

In many cases the choice isn't only between self-contained

special education classrooms and inclusive classrooms. Some schools offer a continuum of inclusive experiences, from all-day special education classes, to spending only part of the day in a smaller group and part in more socially typical environments, to inclusion much of the day with the support of an aide. Some communities have public agencies or private schools that are self-contained, serving only children or adults with developmental disabilities.

Should a very bright student with an Asperger's profile always be in an inclusive classroom with typical peers? Not necessarily. Often such students find themselves completely misunderstood, or even overwhelmed, in inclusive environments. Teachers without appropriate training or support may misconstrue their behavior as stubborn, oppositional, or withholding.

In some successful programs, a class of six to eight students serves as a home base, providing extra academic or emotional support and fostering a sense of community. There individuals who share a diagnosis can be open to sharing their feelings and experience, growing together and learning from the challenges and victories each child experiences. In stark contrast, some students with autism who have succeeded in typical school settings say they have no desire to be around others with autism or other challenges.

What's most important is looking at the child's larger environment and considering the various kinds of models she encounters throughout the day and week rather than viewing the classroom as the whole picture. A child with many siblings can benefit from the social experiences of day-to-day domestic life. A child who is involved in a theater program, a church or synagogue or mosque program, or a sports program with typical peers may have less need for an inclusive school environment, particularly if it presents its own challenges.

Is there such a thing as too much therapy?

More time in therapy does not automatically mean better quality therapy.

Parents often hear from professionals that in order to benefit from a particular kind of approach, the child will need at least thirty or forty hours of weekly, individualized therapy. The underlying message is that the more hours spent in therapy the better, and that a child who doesn't meet a certain time threshold will miss out on its potential benefits. But the number of hours alone does not determine a program's intensity or effectiveness. What's most important is the quality of the intervention, how well it is coordinated across settings and people, and how relevant the goals and objectives are to a child's life.

Intensive, individualized therapy can be an important part of a larger plan for very young and highly challenged individuals. The danger is losing sight of the big picture, the many different parts of a child's life. A kindergartner who receives intensive outside therapies might be too exhausted to participate in classroom activities. The parents might be shuttling the child daily after school to speech therapy or occupational therapy, or bringing a behavior therapist into the home, but after a while it's all just too much for the child and the family.

Sometimes a therapist will push for more hours of therapy, but the child is resistant. The professional might acknowledge the resistance but suggest that it's important to fight through it. Once again it's essential for parents to trust their instincts. When a child experiences overload and displays stress, exhaustion, and resistance to participating, it's important for a parent to ask, "Why are we doing this? And why are we doing so much of it?"

Often the problem isn't the quantity of time devoted to a particular therapy but rather that the therapy is disconnected from the child's life. The key is looking at the big picture and choosing therapies that are in line with the overall goals, objectives, and strategies that are appropriate for the child. The time allotted to any one therapy is far less important than taking a team approach and keeping the big picture in mind.

How can I deal with a teacher or therapist who seems ill equipped—or unwilling—to teach a child with autism?

Some teachers are open to the idea of including a child with autism in their class but feel they lack the necessary support of administrators, aides, or others. Another, more challenging problem is when teachers are highly resistant to teaching children with autism, perhaps feeling that they do not have the training or that it is simply not part of their job.

In either case, the crucial factor often is not the teacher but the school's leadership. A principal who is committed to leading a school that is inclusive and that supports every student will make every effort to support the classroom teacher and the student. When such a principal comes across a teacher resistant to including a student with autism, she will make it clear that, like it or not, the teacher is part of a team and needs to support the student. However, the school must help such teachers by providing training and support.

It's also essential for parents to understand that they play an indispensable part in the child's success in school. If a well-meaning teacher doesn't feel properly supported, the parents can make sure they have done all they can do to help. They can share their perspective on what best helps their child to learn and stay engaged, and they can lobby for more support.

Instead of pressuring teachers, parents should acknowledge that a child can be challenging at times and that if the child has a difficult day, the teacher isn't to blame. In short, parents should send the message that they are partners—active, interested, and involved partners—with school professionals. They should also make it clear that they expect teachers to be partners as well.

Sometimes the match between student and teacher just doesn't work. Then, rather than blaming the teacher or the school, parents should take an active role in solving the problem and seeking the best possible placement for the child.

Many children who have trouble speaking learn to communicate instead with iPads, other devices, or low-tech options such as picture-symbol systems or sign language. Doesn't that prevent them from learning to speak?

It would seem logical that teaching a child alternative ways to communicate would inhibit the child's speech development. The option to use sign language, picture communication systems, photographs, and speech-generating devices would presumably take away a child's incentive to speak. In my experience, though, using these methods to aid social communication actually *supports* speech development—a finding supported by many studies. The reason is simple: the motivation to learn to speak comes from success in communicating. The more a child is successful in relating to and connecting with others, even if it isn't through speech, the more desire the child has to communicate in the way that most people do: through speech.

Additionally research indicates that successful social communication helps a child to stay better regulated emotionally. In turn the child has less need to use problematic means to have social control. When a child becomes a competent and confident communicator, regardless of how he is communicating, he is more available for learning and engaging, which also includes learning how to pay attention to people speaking, and therefore learning how to speak.

What role should siblings play in the life of a child with autism?

Brothers and sisters can play a very important role in understanding and supporting a child with autism, but research shows it can vary greatly. Asking a sibling to do too much—and essentially act like another parent—may not be developmentally appropriate and often leads the sibling to feel resentment. At the other extreme, parents generally shouldn't tell siblings that they need not be involved or concerned at all. In general, siblings who adapt best are those who are given some age-appropriate responsibility and a degree of choice in how to be helpful.

Siblings go through their own developmental phases in how they relate to a brother or sister with autism. I knew a young girl who enjoyed helping, and even teaching, her older brother with autism. As she approached the early teen years, however, she avoided spending time with him, especially in public. Two years after that she became more involved again, and even more caring. Just as with typical children, sibling relationships are complicated. It is always helpful to have open communication and let brothers and sisters know that parents respect their feelings and will listen.

Does autism cause divorce?

A perennial myth is that three out of four marriages that produce a child with autism end in divorce. There is no reliable research to back up that claim. In any case, about half of *all* marriages in the United States end in divorce. Is the rate higher when autism is a factor? Nobody knows for sure.

What we do know is that stresses in a relationship cause divorce. Raising a child with a disability can be stressful. If there are already cracks in the foundation of a marriage, then having a child with autism adds additional pressure, and that could lead to divorce. But it's never the lone factor. In some cases, of course, separation or divorce is not a bad thing if it results in a more stable and peaceful home environment, which ultimately is of great benefit for most children. In the short term, however, separation or divorce can certainly be confusing—even overwhelming—to a child.

Surprisingly some parents feel that having a child with autism strengthens their marriage and the entire family. Faced with the need to solve problems, make tough decisions, and find the best help and opportunities for a child, couples can learn to negotiate and communicate more effectively. Parents frequently say making such difficult decisions makes them feel more confident in their ability to face other challenges. And when things are going well, families join in celebrating successes.

Still, it is common for parents to have contrasting perceptions about a child with autism, particularly early in the journey. Frequently one parent perceives that something isn't right with the child, and the other parent is dismissive, telling his partner not to be alarmist. One parent might be concerned about the child's future, while the other takes a wait-and-see approach.

These differences don't end in the early years. One parent might feel embarrassed by a child's behavior in public, while the other is immune to such feelings. One might be drawn to a particular approach, while the other favors a different one. Teachers and other professionals frequently find themselves drawn into a couple's marital differences when mothers and fathers ask for marital advice in the guise of asking about a child. Parents need not agree all the time but should seek to find ways to face the challenges that come with autism and use them to strengthen the marriage rather than letting them cause greater rifts. The parents I have known who have successfully done so have put their families on positive journeys of growth and fulfillment, improving the lives of every family member.

A GUIDE TO RESOURCES

So many autism publications and online resources have emerged in recent years that it can be difficult to know which are worthwhile or trustworthy. This selective list includes some of the most helpful books, websites and organizations for and about people with autism, their families and the professionals who work with them. While the resources are grouped by audience and category, many have relevance to multiple categories.

Resources for Professionals

Published Work

Alderson, Jonathan. *Challenging the Myths of Autism: Unlock New Possibilities and Hope*. Toronto: HarperCollins Canada, 2011.

Baker, Jed. *No More Meltdowns: Positive Strategies for Managing and Preventing Out-of-control Behavior*. Arlington, TX: Future Horizons, 2008.

Blanc, Marge. *Natural Language Acquisition on the Autism Spectrum: The Journey from Echolalia to Self-Generated Language*. Madison, WI: Communication Development Center, 2013.

Goldstein, Sam, and Jack Naglieri. *Intervention for Autism Spectrum Disorders*. New York: Springer Science Publishers, 2013.

Gray, Carol. *The New Social Story Book*. Arlington, TX: Future Horizons, 2010.

Greenspan, Stanley I., and Serena Wieder. *Engaging Autism: Using the Floortime Approach to Help Children Relate, Communicate, and Think*. Cambridge, MA: Da Capo Lifelong, 2006.

Hall, Elaine and Diane Isaacs. *Seven Keys to Unlock Autism*. New York: Jossey-Bass, 2012.

Hodgdon, Linda A. *Visual Strategies for Improving Communication*. Troy, MI: QuirkRoberts, 1996.

Kluth, Paula. *You're Going to Love This Kid*. Baltimore: Brookes, 2010.

Luterman, David. *Counseling Persons with Communication Disorders and Their Families 5th Edition*. Austin, TX: Pro-Ed, Inc., 2008.

Marquette, Jacquelyn Altman, and Ann Turnbull. *Becoming Remarkably Able: Walking the Path to Talents, Interests, and Personal Growth for Individuals with Autism Spectrum Disorders*. Shawnee Mission, KS: Autism Asperger, 2007.

Mirenda, Pat, and Teresa Iacono. *Autism Spectrum Disorders and AAC*. Baltimore: Paul H. Brookes, 2009.

Myles, Brenda Smith, Melissa Trautman, and Ronda L. Schelvan. *The Hidden Curriculum: Practical Solutions for Understanding Unstated Rules in Social Situations*. Shawnee Mission, KS: Autism Asperger, 2004.

Prizant, Barry M., Amy Wetherby, Emily Rubin, Amy Laurent, and Patrick Rydell. *The SCERTS Model: A Comprehensive Educational Approach for Children with Autism Spectrum Disorders*. Baltimore: Paul H. Brookes, 2006.

Rogers, Sally, and Geraldine Dawson. *Early Start Denver Model for Young Children with Autism: Promoting Language, Learning, and Engagement*. New York: Guilford, 2010.

Winner, Michelle Garcia. *Thinking about You, Thinking about Me*. San Jose, CA: Think Social, 2007.

Winner, Michelle Garcia. *Why Teach Social Thinking? Questioning Our Assumptions about What It Means to Learn Social Skills*. San Jose, CA: Social Thinking, 2013.

Wolfberg, P. J. *Peer Play and the Autism Spectrum: The Art of Guiding Children's Socialization and Imagination* (IPG Field Manual). Shawnee Mission, KS: Autism Asperger Publishing Company, 2003.

Wolfberg, P. J. *Play and Imagination in Children with Autism* (2nd Edition) New York: Teachers College Press, Columbia University, 2009.

Websites

Autism Institute on Peer Socialization and Play: www.autisminstitute.com

First Words Projects, Florida State University: firstwords.fsu.edu

Amy Laurent: www.Amy-Laurent.com

PrAACtical AAC (Augmented and Alternative Communication): http://praacticalaac.org/

Dr. Barry Prizant: www.barryprizant.com

Emily Rubin: www.commxroads.com

SCERTS Model: www.scerts.com

Social Thinking: www.socialthinking.com

Resources for Parents and Family Members

Published Work

Dalgliesh, Carolyn. *The Sensory Child Gets Organized: Proven Systems for Rigid, Anxious, and Distracted Kids.* New York: Simon & Schuster, 2013.

Kerstein, Lauren H. *My Sensory Book: Working Together to Explore Sensory Issues and the Big Feelings They Can Cause: A Workbook for Parents, Professionals, and Children*. Shawnee Mission, KS: Autism Asperger, 2008.

Kranowitz, Carol Stock. *The Out-of-sync Child: Recognizing and Coping with Sensory Processing Disorder*. New York: Skylight Books/A Perigee Book, 2005.

Robinson, Ricki G. *Autism Solutions: How to Create a Healthy and Meaningful Life for Your Child.* Don Mills, Canada: Harlequin, 2011.

Sussman, Fern. *TalkAbility: People Skills for Verbal Children on the Autism Spectrum. A Guide for Parents*. Toronto: Hanen Program, 2006.

Sussman, Fern, and Robin Baird Lewis. *More than Words: A Parent's Guide to Building Interaction and Language Skills for Children with Autism Spectrum Disorder or Social Communication Difficulties*. Toronto: Hanen Program, 2012.

Twachtman-Cullen, Diane, and Jennifer Twachtman-Bassett. *The IEP from A to Z: How to Create Meaningful and Measurable Goals and Objectives.* San Francisco: Jossey-Bass, 2011.

Wiseman, Nancy D., and Robert L. Rich. *The First Year: Autism Spectrum Disorders: An Essential Guide for the Newly Diagnosed Child: A Parent-expert Walks You through Everything You Need to Learn and Do*. Cambridge, MA: Da Capo, 2009.

Websites

Autism Asperger's Digest: www.autismdigest.com

Autism Neighborhood: www.autismneighborhood.org

Autism Speaks: www.autismspeaks.org

Denise Melucci (artist who works with people with disabilities): www.denisemelucci.com

First Signs (national organization educating parents about early signs of autism): www.firstsigns.org

The Hanen Center: www.hanen.org

SCERTS Model: www.scerts.com

WrightsLaw (Special education law and advocacy) www.wrightslaw.com

Resources by People with Autism

Published Work

Carley, Michael John. *Asperger's from the Inside Out: A Supportive and Practical Guide for Anyone with Asperger's Syndrome*. New York: Perigee, 2008.

Fleischmann, Arthur, and Carly Fleischmann. *Carly's Voice: Breaking through Autism*. New York: Touchstone/Simon & Schuster, 2012.

Grandin, Temple, and Richard Panek. *The Autistic Brain: Thinking across the Spectrum*. Arlington, TX: Future Horizons, 2013.

Higashida, Naoki, David Mitchell, and Keiko Yoshida. *The Reason I Jump: One Boy's Voice from the Silence of Autism*. New York: Random House, 2013.

Mukhopadhyay, Tito Rajarshi. *How Can I Talk If My Lips Don't Move? Inside My Autistic Mind*. New York: Arcade, 2008.

Newport, Jerry. *Your Life Is Not a Label: A Guide to Living Fully with Autism and Asperger's Syndrome for Parents, Professionals, and You!* Arlington, TX: Future Horizons, 2001.

Perner, Lars. *Scholars with Autism: Achieving Dreams.* Sedona, AZ: Auricle Books, 2012.

Shore, Stephen M., and Ruth Elaine Joyner Hane. *Ask and Tell: Self-advocacy and Disclosure for People on the Autism Spectrum.* Shawnee Mission, KS: Asperger Autism, 2004.

Shore, Stephen M., and Linda G. Rastelli. *Understanding Autism for Dummies.* Hoboken, NJ: Wiley, 2006.

Tammet, Daniel. *Born on a Blue Day: Inside the Extraordinary Mind of an Autistic Savant: A Memoir.* New York: Free Press, 2007.

Willey, Liane Holliday. *Pretending to Be Normal: Living with Asperger's Syndrome.* London: Jessica Kingsley, 1999.

Websites

Michael John Carley: www.michaeljohncarley.com

Temple Grandin: www.TempleGrandin.com

Stephen Shore: www.autismasperger.net

Books Written by Parents

Colson, Emily, and Charles W. Colson. *Dancing with Max: A Mother and Son Who Broke Free.* Grand Rapids, MI: Zondervan, 2010.

Fields-Meyer, Tom. *Following Ezra: What One Father Learned about Gumby, Otters, Autism, and Love from His Extraordinary Son.* New York: New American Library, 2011.

Gilman, Priscilla. *The Anti-romantic Child: A Memoir of Unexpected Joy.* New York: Harper Perennial, 2012.

Hall, Elaine, with Elizabeth Kaye. *Now I See the Moon: A Mother, a Son, a Miracle.* New York: HarperStudio, 2010.

Naseef, Robert A. *Autism in the Family: Caring and Coping Together.* Baltimore: Brookes, 2014.

Park, Clara Claiborne. *Exiting Nirvana: A Daughter's Life with Autism*. Boston: Little, Brown, 2001.

Peete, Rodney, and Danelle Morton. *Not My Boy! A Father, a Son, and One Family's Journey with Autism*. New York: Hyperion, 2010.

Senator, Susan. *Making Peace with Autism: One Family's Story of Struggle, Discovery, and Unexpected Gifts*. Boston: Trumpeter, 2005.

Suskind, Ron. *Life, Animated: A Story of Sidekicks, Heroes, and Autism*. New York: Kingswell, 2014.

National Organizations Providing Information and Support

Autism National Committee: www.autcom.org

Autism Research Institute: www.autism.com

Autism Self-Advocacy Network: www.autisticadvocacy.org

Autism Society of America: www.autism-society.org

Autism Speaks: www.autismspeaks.org

Global and Regional Asperger's Syndrome Partnership: www.GRASP.org

The Miracle Project: www.themiracleproject.org

National Autism Association: www.nationalautismassociation.org

National Autism Network: www.nationalautismnetwork.com

ABOUT THE SCERTS MODEL

Many of the ideas and explanations in *Uniquely Human* are based on the SCERTS® Model, an approach to autism Dr. Prizant developed with colleagues Dr. Amy Wetherby, Emily Rubin, and Amy Laurent. SCERTS (which stands for Social Communication, Emotional Regulation, and Transactional Support) is an evidence-based, comprehensive intervention model for children and older individuals with Autism Spectrum Disorder and their families. SCERTS provides specific guidelines for helping an individual become a competent and confident social communicator and an active learner, while preventing problem behaviors that interfere with learning and the development of relationships. It is designed to help families, educators, and therapists to work as a team in a carefully coordinated manner to maximize meaningful progress. School districts across the United States and in more than a dozen countries have implemented the SCERTS Model. For information, visit www.scerts.com.

ACKNOWLEDGMENTS

THIS book has been a long time in coming, and it could not have been written without the assistance and support of many people. I wish to express my deepest gratitude to the following people.

My collaborator, Tom Fields-Meyer, for his friendship, support, and great literary talents in helping to bring to life the stories that capture all I have learned over the past four decades. A special thanks to Rabbi Shawn Fields-Meyer, Ezra, Ami, and Noam for sharing Tom with me over the past year.

My wife, Dr. Elaine Meyer, who always loved my stories and learned from those I shared all these years. Her love and enthusiastic support kept the dream of *Uniquely Human* alive. Her innovative and compassionate work with families in hospitals and at our parent retreat weekend has been an unending source of inspiration.

My son, Noah, for his love and his deep interest in *Uniquely Human*. We are so proud of the caring young man he has become. As he embarks on his journey out of the nest, I pray he can find the same degree of fulfillment in his life's work that I have been blessed to find in mine.

My sister Debbie, for her love and support, and my father, Sam, of blessed memory, who always trusted in me to make the right choices and whose pride always buoyed my spirits.

My dear friend Wally Zembo, who has helped me keep my life in balance and in rhythm over the past thirty years.

My readers, Michael John Carley, Dr. Elaine Meyer, Eliza Beringhause, Rabbi Shawn Fields-Meyer, and Mary Hanlon, for their hard work, thoughtful input, and encouragement, which helped produce a much refined manuscript.

The Canha, Correia, Domingue, and Randall families, who were so generous in allowing me to bring their personal journeys to light so that other families could learn from their wisdom.

Our fantastic literary agent, Betsy Amster, for believing in this project from the outset, for her valuable contributions and expertise, and for cheering us on every step of the way.

Our wonderful editor at Simon & Schuster, Trish Todd, for embracing this book and shepherding it through the editing process with skill, care, and great enthusiasm.

My SCERTS Model collaborators and dear friends, Dr. Amy Wetherby, Emily Rubin, and Amy Laurent. So many of the values expressed in *Uniquely Human* reflect the ideals and practices we have infused in the SCERTS Model. I am so proud of what we have accomplished.

My career mentors, Drs. Judy Duchan, David Yoder, John Muma, and David Luterman, who believed in me and provided the support, values, and skills to pursue a most meaningful career. Special thanks to David L., who persistently encouraged me to write "your [expletive] book."

My former colleague and dear friend Dr. Adriana Loes Schuler, of blessed memory, truly one of the most gifted and unique humans I have ever known. Our initial common interest in echolalia blossomed into a deep and enduring friendship that I will always cherish.

Barbara and Bob Domingue, our valued friends and retreat partners extraordinaire, and all parents who have attended our weekend retreat over the past twenty years and make it the remarkable experience it has become. I am so grateful to have the privilege of witnessing, learning, and being inspired by their incredible stories, their love for their children, their great sense of humor, and their generosity in helping other parents.

The professionals, paraprofessionals, parents, and school and agency administrators across the United States and abroad who have chosen to devote their lives to helping children and families. I so appreciate their trust and the opportunity to work with and learn from them. Special thanks to my closest colleagues who serve children and families "in the front lines" every day: Elaine Hall of The Miracle Project; Eve Mullen, Tony Maida, and the staff of Cooperative Educational Services; and Diane Twachtman-Cullen of *Autism Spectrum Quarterly*.

All the individuals with autism and their families who have been such a vital part of my life. Many have become valued friends and mentors and have provided me with the great privilege of a deep and meaningful lifelong career. To them my gratitude is truly boundless.

—B.P.

I am grateful to Dr. Barry Prizant for giving me the opportunity to collaborate in bringing his life's work to these pages. As the parent of a child—now a young man—with autism, I have always sought professionals with compassion, wisdom, and love, the same qualities I value as a writer. Barry has all of those in depth and abundance, and it has been a privilege to learn from him and create with him. Thanks also to his wife, Elaine, and son, Noah, for their warm hospitality and friendship during my visits.

I am fortunate to have a stellar literary agent in Betsy Amster, who has become a trusted advisor and friend and whose counsel is always pitch perfect. The talented Trish Todd at Simon & Schuster could not have been more supportive, positive, or helpful. Thanks to my friend Shep Rosenman for generously sharing his legal wisdom.

I am indebted to my friend Elaine Hall, who has done much for people with autism and their families, including ours. It was Elaine who suggested that Barry and I meet, unwittingly setting in motion this project, which I hope will spread even more benefit and understanding.

I am grateful to my parents, Lora and Jim Meyer, for their thorough proofreading and helpful editorial suggestions. Along with my in-laws, Sandey and Del Fields, they are constant sources of support and love, and I feel blessed every day to have them.

I thank my sons, Ami, Ezra, and Noam, for their love and support, their music, and for making me laugh. Most of all I am grateful to—and for—my wonderful wife, Shawn Fields-Meyer, who encouraged my involvement with this project from the outset, who listened to every idea in this book with patience and insight, and who supports me with a smile in everything I do.

—T.F.-M.

INDEX

ABOUT THE AUTHORS

Barry M. Prizant, PhD, CCC-SLP, is one of the world's leading authorities on autism. He has given hundreds of seminars and keynote addresses, speaking in forty-nine states and more than twenty countries. An adjunct professor at Brown University, he has served on its medical school faculty and held tenured positions at two universities. He was founding director of Bradley Hospital's communication disorders department and served on two State of the Science in Autism committees for the National Institutes of Health.

Since 1998, Dr. Prizant has directed Childhood Communication Services, a private practice, and he has consulted for more than 100 school districts across the United States and abroad. He has advised thousands of parents as well as leading educators, policy-makers, and government officials. Since 1995 he has co-led an annual retreat that has drawn hundreds of parents of children with autism and hosted an annual two-day autism symposium in Rhode Island with internationally renowned experts.

Dr. Prizant is the lead author of the SCERTS (Social Communication, Emotional Regulation, and Transactional Support) Model, a comprehensive approach to addressing autism's core challenges. The author of numerous scholarly articles and chapters, Dr. Prizant has received the Honors of the American Speech-Language-Hearing Association, the Princeton University–Eden Foundation Career Award in Autism, and the Divine Neurotypical Award of the Global and Regional Asperger Syndrome Partnership. He lives in Cranston, Rhode Island, with his wife, Dr. Elaine Meyer, and their teenage son.

Tom Fields-Meyer is author of the memoir *Following Ezra: What One Father Learned About Gumby, Otters, Autism, and Love from His Extraordinary Son*, a finalist for the National Jewish Book Award. A former senior writer for *People*, he has coauthored many books, and his articles and essays have appeared in *The New York Times Magazine*, *The Wall Street Journal*, and the *Los Angeles Times*. He lives with his wife, Shawn Fields-Meyer, and their sons in Los Angeles, where he teaches in the UCLA Extension Writers' Program.